AMERICAN SMART CINEMA

Traditions in World Cinema

General Editors
Linda Badley (Middle Tennessee State
  University)
R. Barton Palmer (Clemson University)

Founding Editor
Steven Jay Schneider (New York
  University)

Titles in the series include:
Traditions in World Cinema
by Linda Badley, R. Barton Palmer and
  Steven Jay Schneider (eds)
978 0 7486 1862 0 (hardback)
978 0 7486 1863 7 (paperback)

Japanese Horror Cinema
by Jay McRoy (ed.)
978 0 7486 1994 8 (hardback)
978 0 7486 1995 5 (paperback)

New Punk Cinema
by Nicholas Rombes (ed.)
978 0 7486 2034 0 (hardback)
978 0 7486 2035 7 (paperback)

*African Filmmaking: North and South of
  the Sahara*
by Roy Armes
978 0 7486 2123 1 (hardback)
978 0 7486 2124 8 (paperback)

*Palestinian Cinema: Landscape, Trauma
  and Memory*
by Nurith Gertz
978 0 7486 3407 1 (hardback)
978 0 7486 3408 8 (paperback)

Chinese Martial Arts Cinema: The Wuxia
  Tradition
by Stephen Teo
978 0 7486 3285 5 (hardback)
978 0 7486 3286 2 (paperback)

*Czech and Slovak Cinema: Theme and
  Tradition*
by Peter Hames
978 0 7486 2081 4 (hardback)
978 0 7486 2082 1 (paperback)

The New Neapolitan Cinema
by Alex Marlow-Mann
978 0 7486 4066 9 (hardback)

The International Film Musical
by Corey K. Creekmur and Linda Y.
  Mokdad (eds)
978 0 7486 3476 7 (hardback)

American Smart Cinema
by Claire Perkins
978 0 7486 4074 4 (hardback)

Italian Neorealist Cinema
by Torunn Haaland
978 0 7486 3611 2 (hardback)

Forthcoming titles include:
The Spanish Horror Film
by Antonio Lázaro-Reboll
978 0 7486 3638 9 (hardback)

*American Independent-Commercial
  Cinema*
by Linda Badley and R. Barton Palmer
978 0 7486 2459 1 (hardback)

The Italian Sword-and-Sandal Film
by Frank Burke
978 0 7486 1983 2 (hardback)

New Nordic Cinema
by Mette Hjort, Andrew Nestigen and
  Anna Stenport
978 0 7486 3631 0 (hardback)

Italian Post-neorealist Cinema
by Luca Barattoni
978 0 7486 4054 6 (hardback)

*Magic Realist Cinema in East Central
  Europe*
by Aga Skrodzka-Bates
978 0 7486 3916 8 (hardback)

*Cinemas of the North Africa Diaspora of
  France*
by Will Higbee
978 0 7486 4004 1 (hardback)

New Romanian Cinema
by Christina Stojanova and Dana Duma
978 0 7486 4264 9 (hardback)

*Contemporary Latin American Cinema:
  New Transnationalisms*
by Dolores Tierney
978 0 7486 4573 2 (hardback)

Visit the Traditions in World Cinema
website at www.euppublishing.com/series/
TIWC

AMERICAN
SMART CINEMA

Claire Perkins

EDINBURGH
University Press

For Mum

© Claire Perkins, 2012, 2013

Edinburgh University Press Ltd
22 George Square, Edinburgh EH8 9LF

First published in hardback by Edinburgh University Press 2012

www.euppublishing.com

Typeset in 10/12.5 pt Sabon
by Servis Filmsetting Ltd, Stockport, Cheshire, and
Printed and bound in Great Britain by CPI Group (UK) Ltd,
Croydon, CR0 4YY

A CIP record for this book is available from the British Library

ISBN 978 0 7486 4074 4 (hardback)
ISBN 978 0 7486 7908 9 (paperback)
ISBN 978 0 7486 4654 8 (webready PDF)
ISBN 978 0 7486 5425 3 (epub)
ISBN 978 0 7486 5424 6 (Amazon ebook)

CONTENTS

ACKNOWLEDGEMENTS

This book was completed during a sad and difficult period of my life, and I was lucky to receive support and insight from a number of people. I would like to thank my friends and colleagues in Film and Television Studies at Monash University, especially Con Verevis for his help at every stage of the project, and for his feel for the smart film. I am also grateful for the advice I received from Alison Ross, and for the assistance and understanding of my editors, R. Barton Palmer and Linda Badley. Thank you to the School of English, Communications and Performance Studies at Monash University for providing images for the book. On a personal note, I have greatly appreciated the emotional and practical support of Alistair Perkins, Peter Perkins, Jennie Bremner, Orli Schwartz and Mary Harvey. My heartfelt thanks go to Liam Nolan for his love, generosity and perspective. Finally, I thank my mother, Jo Perkins, who was such a factor in this and everything else. This book is dedicated to her.

LIST OF ILLUSTRATIONS

TRADITIONS IN WORLD CINEMA

General editors: **Linda Badley and R. Barton Palmer**
Founding editor: **Steven Jay Schneider**

Traditions in World Cinema is a series of textbooks and monographs devoted to the analysis of currently popular and previously underexamined or under-valued film movements from around the globe. Also intended for general interest readers, the textbooks in this series offer undergraduate- and graduate-level film students accessible and comprehensive introductions to diverse traditions in world cinema. The monographs open up for advanced academic study more specialised groups of films, including those that require theoretically-oriented approaches. Both textbooks and monographs provide thorough examinations of the industrial, cultural, and socio-historical conditions of production and reception.

The flagship textbook for the series includes chapters by noted scholars on traditions of acknowledged importance (the French New Wave, German Expressionism), recent and emergent traditions (New Iranian, post-Cinema Novo), and those whose rightful claim to recognition has yet to be established (the Israeli persecution film, global found footage cinema). Other volumes concentrate on individual national, regional or global cinema traditions. As the introductory chapter to each volume makes clear, the films under discussion form a coherent group on the basis of substantive and relatively transparent, if not always obvious, commonalities. These commonalities may be formal, sty-listic or thematic, and the groupings may, although they need not, be popularly identified as genres, cycles or movements (Japanese horror, Chinese martial arts cinema, Italian Neorealism). Indeed, in cases in which a group of films is not already commonly identified as a tradition, one purpose of the volume is to establish its claim to importance and make it visible (East Central European Magical Realist cinema, Palestinian cinema).

Textbooks and monographs include:

- An introduction that clarifies the rationale for the grouping of films under examination
- A concise history of the regional, national, or transnational cinema in question
- A summary of previous published work on the tradition
- Contextual analysis of industrial, cultural and socio-historical conditions of production and reception
- Textual analysis of specific and notable films, with clear and judicious application of relevant film theoretical approaches
- Bibliograph(ies)/filmograph(ies).

Monographs may additionally include:

- Discussion of the dynamics of cross-cultural exchange in light of current research and thinking about cultural imperialism and globalisation, as well as issues of regional/national cinema or political/aesthetic movements (such as new waves, postmodernism, or identity politics)
- Interview(s) with key filmmakers working within the tradition.

INTRODUCTION

In 1999, screenwriter and film producer James Schamus delivered the keynote address at the Independent Spirit Awards in California, an event honouring achievement in the West Coast independent film scene. Subsequently reprinted with the title 'A Rant' in the collection, *The End of Cinema as We Know It: American Film in the Nineties*, Schamus' address traced some of the consequences of what he saw as the gradual absorption of the independent filmmaking sector into the commercial system. Citing the exponential increase in the total box office monies earned by independent films over the previous thirteen years, and, further, the massive increase in the percentage of these returns that ultimately went back to the major studios, Schamus was at once applauding and lamenting the fact that films recognised at events like the Spirit Awards had overwhelmingly succeeded in breaking into the major system of commercial exploitation and finance. While positively attributing the increased production and visibility of films with 'something to say' to the enormous growth in the major media empires, Schamus also voiced a common concern that these empires would ultimately threaten the existence of such films. Schamus was here arguing for the preservation of what he saw as a tangible 'civic space' where 'freedom of speech [was] the exercise of a fundamental right and not a privilege purchased with the promise of profit' (2001: 256).

In the years since Schamus' address, critical interest in the effect that he described has steadily developed into a range of differing contextualisations of contemporary American 'commercial/independent' filmmaking. Peter Biskind's *Down and Dirty Pictures: Miramax, Sundance and the Rise of Independent*

Film (2004), Sharon Waxman's *Rebels on the Backlot: Six Maverick Directors and How They Conquered the Hollywood Studio System* (2006) and James Mottram's *The Sundance Kids: How the Mavericks Took Back Hollywood* (2006) all take a specific interest in the simultaneously critical and popular success of directors including Quentin Tarantino, Steven Soderbergh, Paul Thomas Anderson, Spike Jonze, Sofia Coppola, Wes Anderson, Alexander Payne and David O. Russell. It is clear even from the titles of these works that the authors foreground the appearance of the hybrid field as a triumphant *event*. The cycle can be understood in more emergent terms by looking at the varying ways in which it is 'named' and described in other works: in Xavier Mendik and Steven Jay Schneider's *Underground USA: Filmmaking Beyond the Hollywood Canon* (2002), Geoff King's *American Independent Cinema* (2005), Chris Holmlund and Justin Wyatt's *Contemporary American Independent Film: From the Margins to the Mainstream* (2005), Jesse Fox Mayshark's *Post-Pop Cinema: The Search for Meaning in New American Film* (2007) and King's *Indiewood USA* (2009).

All of these books signal the late twentieth century and early twenty-first as a site of cultural transition in American cinema. In Schamus' evaluation, independent film is characterised as being in decline: the structural forces of media conglomeration mean the only transition being witnessed is from properly 'independent' film to properly 'commercial' film. For other commentators, this historical period is a site of genuine transition: the pure quality of certain systems may wane, but only to give way to new and different possibilities. Where the upshot of Schamus' purist argument tends to be a critical search for 'true' independence based upon economic and/or thematic criteria, other positions frame commercial/independent cinema in terms of the dialogue that these films set up between their two terms.

This book approaches the field by way of the notion of 'smart' cinema, as a tendency that acknowledges the porosity of this dialogue. Coined by Jeffrey Sconce as a 'sensibility' at work in a disparate but ideologically sympathetic group of films that 'are almost invariably placed by marketers, critics and audiences in symbolic opposition to the imaginary mass-cult monster of mainstream, commercial, Hollywood cinema', the 'smart' quality exists 'at the symbolic and material intersection of "Hollywood", the "indie" scene and the vestiges of what cinephiles used to call "art" films' (2002: 351). Basing his analysis of smart cinema on the premise that these films mostly eschew the formal experimentation that typifies previous forms of 'indie' and 'art' cinema, Sconce's take on the commercial/independent field consciously excludes the 'underground' work of directors such as Harmony Korine and John Waters. Delineating the smart sensibility as a nineties trend, Sconce instead focuses on a polished group of films that experiment by way of *tone*. Drawing on the comments of some LA film critics that lamented the release of *Happiness* (Todd

Figure 1   Philip Seymour Hoffman and Lara Flynn Boyle in *Happiness* (Todd Solondz, 1998). Courtesy October Films / The Kobal Collection.

Solondz, 1998), *Your Friends and Neighbors* (Neil LaBute, 1998) and *Very Bad Things* (Peter Berg, 1998) as evidence of a 'pointlessly and simplistically grim' trend in American filmmaking, the smart sensibility is broadly character-ised in terms of a predilection for irony, black humour, fatalism and relativism that has many variations:

> the arch emotional nihilism of Solondz in *Storytelling* (2001), *Happiness* and *Welcome to the Dollhouse* (1995), and of LaBute in *Your Friends and Neighbors* and *In the Company of Men* (1997); Alexander Payne's 'blank' political satires *Election* (1999) and *Citizen Ruth* (1996); Hal Hartley's postmodern screwball comedies *The Unbelievable Truth* (1990), *Trust* (1991) and *Henry Fool* (1998); post-*Pulp Fiction* black comedies of violence such as *Very Bad Things*, *Go* (Doug Liman, 1999) and *2 Days in the Valley* (John Herzfeld, 1996); Wes Anderson's bittersweet *Bottle Rocket* (1994), *Rushmore* (1998) and *The Royal Tenenbaums* (2001); P.T. Anderson's operatic odes to the San Fernando valley *Magnolia* (1998) and *Boogie Nights* (1997); the 'cold' melodramas of *The Ice Storm* (Ang Lee, 1997), *The Sweet Hereafter* (Atom Egoyan, Canada, 1997) and *Safe* (Todd Haynes, 1995); and the 'matter-of-fact' surrealism of *Being John Malkovich* (Spike Jonze, 1999) and *Donnie Darko* (Richard Kelly, 2001). (350)

This study aims to take the tendency named by Sconce and describe its function as a critical sensibility within contemporary American commercial/independent cinema. In seeking to make these films and the cycle itself intelligible in new ways, it aims to mobilise the sense of ineffability implied in Sconce's use of the term 'sensibility' and illuminate how the smart film performs the contradictions at the heart of the notions of genre and genrification. In distinction to the dominant characterisation of the commercial/independent field as an industrial phenomenon, this book takes up the notion of the smart sensibility as a way of addressing some of these films at the level of their critical aesthetics. In line with a conceptualisation of smart cinema's connection to both historical and international intertexts, this approach aims to demonstrate the idea not as a fixed type but as an affective force.

THE SMART TENDENCY

When set against the larger group of films and directors attended to across all the studies mentioned, Sconce's group of films immediately indicates how the notion of smart cinema performs issues relating to genre. For Rick Altman, one hypothesis regarding the genrification process is that a genre remains a 'cycle' until it is consecrated by industry-wide recognition (1999: 82). It could be argued that the commercial/independent cycle as a whole is in the process of being consecrated in this way by the types of works cited here. Within this process, the smart film is perhaps best understood as a nebulous *tendency*. As something like 'pre-genres', both 'cycle' and 'tendency' prove Altman's proposition that genre 'is not permanently located in any single place, but may depend at different times on radically differing criteria' (86). These films can be linked on the basis of characteristics pertaining to industry and production, textual properties and audience reception. As will be discussed further in Chapter 2, the works by Biskind, Waxman and Mottram favour an industrial approach that is broadly concerned with the studio system's accommodation of innovative new American filmmaking via the establishment of 'mini-major' arms such as (Disney's) Miramax, (Universal's) Focus Features and (Fox Filmed Entertainment's) Fox Searchlight (Mottram 2006: xxix).[1] By contrast, and under the broader rubric of 'American independent cinema', an approach such as Geoff King's skews textual, linking *Magnolia* and *Short Cuts* (Robert Altman, 1993) by way of their multi-strand narrative design, *Bottle Rocket* and *Lost Highway* (David Lynch, 1997) on account of the (varyingly) 'quirky' effects created by the use of a wide-angle lens, *Happiness* and *Trust* for their incongruous mixing of comic and non-comic modalities, and *Safe* and *Spanking the Monkey* (David O. Russell, 1994) in terms of their metaphorical 'sense of queering' (2005: 238–9).[2]

An approach that favours issues of audience reception in its constitution of the commercial/independent cycle is best articulated in the article from which the term itself is derived: R. Barton Palmer's 1988 piece '*Blood Simple*: Defining the Commercial/Independent Text'. Here, Palmer suggests that the term 'independent' has, throughout the history of the American cinema, been used to characterise two forms of film practice: that which is unwillingly marginalised by market forces, and that which deliberately seeks the ground of creative freedom (1988: 5). Palmer classifies the first type of 'independents' as those who struggle to make and distribute commercial films outside of the established procedures of 'doing business', and the second as those who exploit their marginal position to create texts that resolutely avoid being converted into objects of exchange. Palmer draws on the Coen brothers' first feature *Blood Simple* (1985) to describe how independent filmmakers will often negotiate between these two notions of independence to create 'a text that appeals, complexly and simultaneously, to both' (6). By attending to a number of reviewers' reactions to *Blood Simple*, Palmer delineates the commercial/ independent text 'not only as a semiotic structure, but as a special form of cultural production/ consumption'. In an effect partly attributable to its textual appropriation of *film noir* as both a conventional Hollywood film type and an important element in discourse *about* Hollywood films, Palmer suggests that *Blood Simple* 'issues a successful, multi-levelled call to be read' by advertising both the cinematic sophistication and commercial knowledgeability of its makers (8).

Sconce evokes this reception-based model of commercial/independence by noting the typical exhibition forum for the smart films he identifies, admitting that they may 'have little more in common than their shared target market of younger, more educated, "bohemian" audiences who frequent the artplexes now central to every European and North American city' (2002: 351). Further, he uses the deliberately vague term 'sensibility' to indicate his reliance upon the ideas of 'tone' in narrative poetics and 'structure of feeling' in cultural theory. Both these notions are determined by a certain ineffability that means their objects cannot be reduced to finite stylistic or sociological terms but, rather, are 'only fully realised within a narrow historical moment' (352). Naming smart cinema as a 'sensibility' thus opens the way for Sconce to consider both 'the sociocultural formation informing the circulation of these films (a "smart" set) and a shared set of stylistic and thematic practices (a "smart" aesthetic)'.

Central to this analysis of smart cinema is the idea that these practices are informed by a strategy of ironic disengagement. Smart cinema is an example of a type of ironic art that is the result of 'a coalition of cultural producers and consumers who find this to be the most compelling voice through which to intervene in the contemporary cultural, artistic or political terrain' (353). Naming the tendency as 'drama born of ironic distance', Sconce finds this sociocultural position expressed in a shared set of stylistic, narrative and thematic elements that are employed in differing configurations by individual films:

> 1) the cultivation of 'blank' style and incongruous narration; 2) a fascination with 'synchronicity' as a principle of narrative organization; 3) a related thematic interest in random fate; 4) a focus on the white middle-class family as a crucible of miscommunication and emotional dysfunction; 5) a recurring interest in the politics of taste, consumerism and identity. (358)

While for the most part indicating the smart film's reliance on classical narrative strategies, these elements also express a common tone that is mobilised as a means of critiquing bourgeois taste and culture. The move can be contextualised historically, politically and generationally. As Sconce characterises it, 'American smart cinema has displaced the more activist emphasis on the "social politics" of power, institutions, representations and subjectivity so central to 1960s and 1970s art cinema (especially in its "political" wing), and replaced it by concentrating, often with ironic disdain, on the "personal politics" of power, communication, emotional dysfunction and identity in white middle-class culture' (352).

Generation X

As the cultural category of youth that Sconce notes many of the directors at the heart of the smart cinema debates were born into, this displacement from 'social' to 'personal' accords with a number of the central tenets of Generation X. For cultural theorist Tara Brabazon, this generation is the first 'post youth' culture, where the 1980s represents a fundamental break in the narrative of 'revolutionary potential' advanced by the events and ideas of the 1950s, 1960s and 1970s (2005: 11). In the popular imagination, the story of Generation X relies on the idea that the youth of the 1980s and 90s made no political or cultural statement comparable to the Jazz of the 1920s, the Beats of the 1950s, or the 'Protest' generation of the 1960s. Against these 'active' and 'authentic' moments, Generation X is located as an atomised, introspective culture, aiming for the political outcome of 'consciousness – not class struggle' (11). In early interpretations, the attitude is cast in overtly negative terms, with Generation X described as apathetic consumers whose contribution as twenty-somethings was to sneer at or quote from that which preceded and surrounded them. As Jonathon Oake has noted, such coverage sought to define the *character* of Generation X in a 'quasi-anthropological approach' (2004: 84). Focused largely within the pages of American news magazines, observations that this youth culture had 'few heroes, no anthems, no style to call their own' (Scott 1990: 56) became the prevailing evaluation of a generation perceived to be over-educated, under-employed, and over-invested in popular culture.

In other, later commentaries, the orientation toward 'consciousness' and 'revelation' is presented in more rounded terms through attention to the social, cultural and economic factors impacting upon the youth of the 1980s and 90s. Demographer Tamara Erickson gives a good summary of these aspects in her career-oriented book *What's Next, Generation X?* – tracing a cycle of events including economic stagnation, adult unemployment, the *Challenger* disaster, the rise of Microsoft and MTV, the birth of the first test-tube baby, advances in women's and gay rights, and a spike in divorce and abortion rates (2010: 3–20). With a pragmatic agenda, Erickson draws out what she sees as the positive consequences of these experiences, making a case for the resourceful, self-reliant, divergent and tolerant character of Generation X. In this analysis, the popular charge of apathy is cast as an attitude of scepticism that is skilful in its ability to see through political and institutional rhetoric that channels traditional values concerning power, morality and success.

Historically focused media analyses of Generation X foreground this constructively sceptical attitude as an element central to the representation of its youth. In *The Cinema of Generation X*, Peter Hanson observes how the forces of social change that characterised the period in which Generation X grew up, especially the 'anticlimactic' conclusion and aftermath of the Vietnam War, occurred such that 'even the youngest Gen Xers were born too late to participate in the historical social unrest that reaches its twilight in the mid-1970s, so all Gen Xers grew up in the aftermath of a beautiful but unrealized dream' (2002: 9). With this observation, Hanson contests the simplification of the Generation X mentality as one of negativity and indifference, demonstrating how the disenfranchised 'slacker' stereotype is rooted not in (pseudo) existentialism but in cynicism, frustration, uncertainty and paralysis. He demonstrates his point in analyses of several of the best-known Generation X films, showing in one interpretation how Richard Linklater's treatment of the Jesse character in *Before Sunrise* (1995) – played by Ethan Hawke whose performance in *Reality Bites* (Ben Stiller, 1994) made him the popular face of Gen X apathy – elevates slackerdom to poetry: 'the combination of the brevity of Jesse's affair with Céline, their over-intellectualized discourse, and the hesitancy that they both exhibit about becoming grown-ups brands the characters as youths on the verge of joining a society they don't understand' (67).

In these historical approaches to Generation X, the logic of a 'post youth' culture with no insurgent agenda is found in the drifting characters of films that resonate closely with smart cinema: *Slacker* (Richard Linklater, 1991), *sex, lies and videotape* (Steven Soderbergh, 1989), *Clerks* (Kevin Smith, 1994), *Kids* (Larry Clark, 1995), *My Own Private Idaho* (Gus van Sant, 1991) and *Natural*

Born Killers (Oliver Stone, 1994). Such films are approached as portraits of alienated, exploitative lives which – in the face of a disappointing youth economy – are leading nowhere (Erickson 2010: 13). The pervasive force of media as a dimension that has surrounded this generation its entire life is interpreted as one factor contributing to a conversant, sceptical outlook. In film and cultural studies approaches, the place and function of media is considered differently. For theorists such as Brabazon, media literacy is not a characteristic of Generation X identity; Generation X is itself a constructed and *mediated* category. The force of media means that popular culture creates the sensibility, rather than offering a 'statement' of the 'authentic baby buster *mentalitae*' (2005: 19). Oake extends the point when he says that 'the term *Generation X* designates not an authentic subculture that pre-exists its media representations but an identity that is always already performed within mediated space' (2004: 85). In this way, he argues, 'cinema was singularly influential in the production and dissemination of the idea of Generation X'.

POST YOUTH

It is in line with this perspective that smart cinema accords historically with a generational position. The films that will be discussed in the chapters that follow are not obviously 'portraits' of a disaffected youth culture, but their common situations and character types inform – and are informed by – the mediated sensibility of Generation X as a category conceptualised in terms of social changes of the 1970s, 80s and 90s. In many smart films, the resonance with the ideas popularised by the take-up of films such as those listed above is strong. The diverse examinations of identity and dysfunction foreground characters whose atomised existence within their home, work and social environments give rise to an overwhelmingly sceptical outlook. The recurrent interest in morally provocative issues around sexuality and violence can be read in terms of what Hanson calls the 'fuzzy parameters of the new morality' that Generation X were born into after Vietnam, Watergate and the civil-rights conflicts of the 1960s and 70s (2002: 9). The highly intertextual nature of the films demonstrates a comprehensive ease and familiarity with both 'high' and 'low' culture as points of reference. And – perhaps most persuasively – the signature blankness of the smart film is a compelling illustration of a generation with 'nothing' to say.

As Sconce's observation on smart cinema's fundamental shift from social to personal politics makes clear, though, the broader accordance that this mode of filmmaking demonstrates with generational politics lies in its concentration on the emotional problems of white, middle-class society. Central to this focus is the smart film's articulation of situations and conflicts stemming from the rapid reconceptualisation of ageing and life cycles in Western culture in the years in which Generation X was born and grew up. As the 'baby buster' label proves, the perspective that this generation holds on the passage of life is fundamentally different to that of its parents and predecessors. For Brabazon, this distinction is the key outcome of other aspects of social and economic change that impacted upon young people in the 1980s and 90s. As she writes, 'this group first confronted post-Fordism, underemployment and media(ted) identity. The desire to impose 1960s life paths and trajectories – of birth, school, marriage, family, death – over all of society was becoming inadequate, inappropriate and politically misguided' (2005: 20). 'Post youth' is here understood as a term that can describe Generation X not only in their departure from traditional youth activity such as protest, but in their transcendence of the categories of a traditional life cycle that proceeds smoothly from youth to adulthood. In the face of rising unemployment and divorce rates, and falling birth rates, the markers of adulthood were transforming as this generation grew up. The 'drifting' character of Generation X is thus cast as a particularly unclassifiable quality: 'without steady employment, a mortgage and family responsibilities (post)youth never made it into adulthood as defined by the standards of preceding decades' (Brabazon 2005: 11).

Many commentaries on media representations of Generation X find that these changing conceptions of adulthood are illustrated in film and television images of eternal adolescents with 'families' of friends – in the sitcoms *thirtysomething* (1987–91) and *Friends* (1994–2004), and in *Reality Bites, singles* (Cameron Crowe, 1992) and *Trainspotting* (Danny Boyle, 1996). Other critics look beyond such representations to identify images that signal the transformation of youth and ageing more broadly. Oake, for instance, suggests that the 'first inklings' of Generation X on-screen came with the changing representations of children in the 1980s and 1990s, where films like *Back to the Future* (Robert Zemeckis, 1985), *Home Alone* (Chris Columbus, 1990) and *Ferris Bueller's Day Off* (John Hughes, 1986) pit savvy kids against dim-witted authority figures who are metonymically associated with the world of 'grown-ups'. As Oake observes, 'it is implicit here that youth is not understood as a primarily developmental or biological concept but as a social formation that stands in resistance toward grown-up society' (2004: 85).

Smart cinema takes an overwhelming interest in this concept of youth as a socially inscribed category. While many of the most enduring images of the cycle as elaborated in this study do depict Generation X-age characters in search of their place in the world – the three adult Tenenbaum children in *The Royal Tenenbaums*, the naïve Barry Egan (Adam Sandler) in *Punch Drunk Love* (Paul Thomas Anderson, 2002), the young graduates of *The Last Days of Disco* (Whit Stillman, 1998), the brothers in pursuit of their father in *Simple Men* (Hal Hartley, 1993) – the films as a group are all more broadly interested in the passage of life as lived in a culture where 'adulthood' is not automatically achieved with age. As will be discussed in Chapter 3, this is represented in varying ways across the cycle: in the squabbling adult siblings of Wes Anderson and Noah Baumbach's family dramas, the disillusioned professionals of *Magnolia* (Paul Thomas Anderson, 1999) and *The Safety of Objects* (Rose Troche, 2001), and the uncannily mature attitudes and desires of the teenagers in *Rushmore*, *Election* and *Palindromes* (Todd Solondz, 2004). The strongest sense of this generational shift in smart cinema, though, lies in its overall impression of damaged individuals, whose dysfunction is rooted in a general lack of 'adult' perspective. Within the cycle's central concern with the context of the family, this state is – in turn – implicitly linked to a host of forces traditionally associated with childhood and youth: namely to those family relationships, experiences and patterns of behaviour that impact on personal development. In this way, smart cinema is a post youth cinema insofar as it accords with Brabazon's observation that 'youth is not a halfway house between childhood and adulthood . . . adults do not cannibalize their past, nor do they arrive at the age of twenty five as an ideological clean skin' (2005: 13).

THERAPY CULTURE

Situating smart cinema in this way emphasises how the cycle can be historically contextualised in terms of another key cultural development that was occurring as this generation of directors grew up. The smart film's focus on the psychological state of middle-class America resonates closely with the tendency in contemporary culture to make sense of the world through the prism of emotion. Conceptualising this tendency as a 'therapeutic turn' traceable to the period of the late 1970s and early 1980s, sociologists such as Christopher Lasch, Eva Moskowitz and Frank Furedi show that the vocabulary of therapeutics has infiltrated politics, popular culture, and work and school contexts such that 'terms like stress, anxiety, addiction, compulsion, trauma, negative emotions, healing, syndrome, mid-life crisis or counselling refer to the normal episodes of daily life' (Furedi 2004: 1). For these theorists, 'therapy culture' does not represent a particular interest in therapy as a clinical technique, but the cultural phenomenon where the form of thinking that characterises the relationship between individual and therapist becomes an instrument for shaping public perception on a variety of issues and social institutions. Furedi argues that this perspective constitutes a distinct view on the nature of human beings, whereby a person's emotional state is regarded as a problematic condition that defines their identity (2004: 22). By making the dysfunction of middle-class individuals and families a central narrative focus, the smart film strongly reflects this perspective. The 'therapeutic turn' thus provides a broad cultural frame for smart cinema's own shift in politics.

Sociological attention to the rise of therapy culture contextualises its development in terms of other changes in modern Anglo-American society. For Moskowitz, 'the story of the therapeutic gospel is the story of modern America. Its history is intimately bound up with the major developments of the twentieth century – the rise of the welfare state, the transformation of the public and private realms, the emergence of the military-industrial complex, and the increasing influence of television in American culture' (2001: 6). Many commentaries cast the shift to the interior as a moral problem, seeing that the singular focus on private life and an objective of self-realisation overwhelms attention to the larger public good by fostering the impression that the two are continuous. Furedi understands that the boundaries between public and private have been redrawn in a manner particularly relevant to the institution of the family. He identifies how the disapproval of the right to privacy that lies at the heart of the new emotionalism – where 'self' help typically implies helping oneself through external support and the public display of emotion – gives rise to a climate that is deeply suspicious about private behaviour.

At one level this creates a culturally derisive outlook on attitudes of stoicism and self-restraint, which are likely to be interpreted as repression. At a second, related level it creates strong pressure to open the private sphere up to public scrutiny. Amplifying and focusing the broad influence of psychoanalysis on modern Western culture, the contemporary therapeutic imagination is 'haunted by the belief that damage to the emotions is systematically inflicted on the individual within the family and during the course of day-to-day interpersonal relations' (Furedi 2004: 66). With this focus, these sociological analyses dispel the myth that therapeutic logic promotes closeness and connection between individuals, showing instead that it crystallises patterns of individuation and fragmentation by stigmatising relations of dependence. Furedi argues that the main accomplishment of therapeutic culture is this disorganisation of the private sphere, where the site that was once perceived as inviolate is now typically associated with repression, family violence and toxic relationships (2004: 68).

In this way, Furedi argues that the contemporary concern with the self is underpinned by anxiety and hesitation. Where a theorist like Moskowitz focuses on therapy culture as the 'worship of the psyche' that grounds contemporary Western society's belief in the centrality of self-esteem and happiness, Furedi concludes that it has constructed a diminished, emotionally deficit self with a permanent sense of vulnerability (2001: 21). It is arguably this sense of self that underpins the characters and situations of smart cinema. It is something indicated directly in casual references to therapeutic contact – in Roger Greenberg's (Ben Stiller) descriptions of advice received in the past from various therapists in *Greenberg* (Noah Baumbach, 2009), or Wendy Savage's (Laura Linney) awkward joke in *The Savages* (Tamara Jenkins, 2007) that she sometimes takes the medication – Xanax – that is advertised on the pen of the administrator who is admitting her father to a nursing home. For the most part, though, the films are not interested in dramatising the specific issues and treatment that arise from this collective vulnerability.[3] Instead, they share a concern with figures whose limitations are (ostensibly) amenable to therapeutic intervention. Characters are – often hyperbolically – depressed, repressed, anxious, addicted, phobic, narcissistic, dissociative, regressive and emotionally detached, and the cycle is in this way an effective fictional, cinematic expression of the genre of writing that Joyce Carol Oates once termed 'pathography' for its focus on 'dysfunction and disaster, illnesses and pitfalls, failed marriages and failed careers, alcoholism and breakdowns and outrageous conduct' (Oates 1988).

As will be discussed from various perspectives in Chapters 2, 3 and 5, it is the family that is largely represented as the source and site of these vulnerabilities. The figures of parents, siblings and other relatives are presented directly or implicitly as forces with enormous capacity to inflict emotional distress through attitudes of detachment, self-absorption, jealousy, tactlessness and derision. At a formal level, the family milieu itself is a force that expresses aversion by impacting significantly on character and narrative actualisation: from the monumental histories that curtail character maturity in Anderson's films (*The Royal Tenenbaums*, *The Life Aquatic with Steve Zissou* [2004], *The Darjeeling Limited* [2007]), to the anomie and repression that give rise to obsession, violence and absurdity in the suburban smart film (*The Safety of Objects*, *Donnie Darko*, *The Chumscrubber* [Arie Posin, 2005]), to the open depiction of 'toxic' patterns of influence between spouses, parents and children, and siblings (*Happiness*, *Your Friends and Neighbors*, *Margot at the Wedding* [Noah Baumbach, 2007]). In this way the concern with the transmuted categories of youth and adulthood in smart cinema expresses itself in terms of the vulnerabilities and aversions that anchor the notion of contemporary therapeutic culture. What this contextualisation makes clear is that the shift toward the 'personal' in the cycle is a move with thoroughly 'social' reflections and effects.

IRONY'S EDGE

For Sconce, the socio-cultural effects of smart cinema are achieved at the level of tone. As described above, he identifies the method by which the cycle critiques bourgeois taste and culture in the specific terms of irony: 'central to my analysis of the 'structure of feeling' informing this cinema and its audience . . . is the idea that irony, beyond existing as some ineffable cultural condition, is also a strategic gesture' (2002: 352). In this way, Sconce is primarily interested in Generation X in terms of its connection to a sensibility that bifurcates audiences into those who 'get it' and those who don't. Drawing on Pierre Bourdieu, he describes this strategy as a form of 'position-taking' by way of which the smart film distinguishes itself in relation to a larger aesthetic and cultural field of production.[4] As the product of directors born as late boomers or part of Generation X proper, Sconce thus classifies smart cinema as an expression of a generational shift in taste and prestige, and of the attendant tensions between older and younger cultural producers and critics.

Irony is here understood as a 'semiotic chasm' dividing a 'structure of feeling that sees everything, from *Scooby Doo* to paedophilia, in giant quotation marks' from 'a structure of feeling . . . that still looks for art to equal sincerity, positivity, commitment, action and responsibility' (358). Where critics such as Kenneth Turan perceive moral and political apathy in the trend and lament a time when audiences were given more than 'the horrific choice of getting things dark or getting them dumb' (Turan 1998), Sconce champions the ironic tone of the smart film as evidence of a transition in political cinema. In a careful extrapolation of the 'slacker' philosophy, he argues that the blank aesthetic should be read not as a disengagement from belief and commitment, but as a retreat from the 'moral map' of the social formation that judges ironic art as an illegitimate practice. Sconce thus identifies the smart film's semiotic intervention as a comment on 'the futility of pure politics or absolute morality' (2002: 368).

This book builds upon the observations made by Sconce to consider how the tone of smart cinema is achieved and the effects it gives rise to. Specifically, it is interested in how the phenomena of reference, quotation and blankness defines the sensibility not in terms of empty disaffection, but in terms of a strategic positioning in relation to the history of cinema and popular culture. Irony is investigated as a mark of distinction that classifies the smart sensibility as something that is not reducible to story, style or authorial disposition alone, foregrounding how the 'mark' of any generic sensibility is constructed discursively, as the perception of shareable elements appearing in differing assemblages.

If the notion of genre is conceived as a limit or law by which one recognises membership in a class, Jacques Derrida argues that the condition for the possibility of this law is the *a priori* of a counter-law (1992: 225). If a text or event is identified as belonging to a certain class on the basis of a set of identifiable traits or marks, then this counter-law is the *re*-mark that the text makes on the distinctive trait within itself. Derrida's argument on genre rests on the understanding that this supplementary mark does not itself pertain to any genre or class and that, therefore, genre-designations cannot be part of the corpus that they designate. As such, he formulates the hypothesis that a text would not *belong* to any genre: every text participates in one or more genres, but the mark by which it indicates this participation 'unmarks' it. The counter-law of genre gathers together the corpus but simultaneously keeps it from closing, thus both including and excluding it from an identifiable class. Derrida calls this inclusion and exclusion the *genre-clause*: 'a clause stating at once the juridical utterance, the designation that makes precedent and law-text, but also the closure, the closing that excludes itself from what it includes' (231).

Derrida's argument can elucidate the particular quality and potential of the smart sensibility. In Sconce's proposal, the 'smart' designation is a way of marking out a group of tonally similar films. At the same time, though, his very reliance on tone as a structuring element is a form of unmarking. By characterising 'smartness' in terms of a quality that is necessarily ineffable – and doubling this by characterising the tone itself in terms of the elusive notion of *irony* – Sconce effectively identifies the smart sensibility as a condition that cannot be identified with itself. Individual films 'participate' in this class discursively, and this placement is itself qualified by a shareable element that is highly unstable. Derrida's comments on the specific forms that the 'remark of belonging' may take are also instructive. The smart sensibility is characterised in terms of irony and reflexivity on the basis of the films' awareness of film history and their own place as cultural objects. As Chapters 1 and 3 will describe in detail, one of the distinctive *marks* of the smart film is the reflective stance it takes toward genre and authorship as classificatory discourses conditioned by semantic and syntactic laws. In this sense, the perceivable marks of genre or authorship in these films are also always re-marks on the designation that delineates membership in a generic or auteurist canon. This effect is an explicit thematisation of the 'remark of belonging' that prevents the smart film from fully identifying with the discourse(s) to which it 'belongs'.

A specific effect that this book seeks to describe, then, is how this 'remark of belonging' is enacted in the smart cycle. The concept has obvious resonance with the techniques of pastiche and quotation that are central to a postmodern aesthetic that distrusts ultimate positions of truth or reason. The chapters aim not to rehearse this position, though, but to describe how the smart film – as a particular tendency within the commercial/ independent field – might complicate such a designation. By examining how smart cinema recognises the contingency of its own terms as grounded in discourses such as authorship, classical narrative and genre, the book seeks to demonstrate the power of ironic expression as a positioning statement. It addresses what Linda Hutcheon describes as irony's 'edge': the affective dimension by which irony acts as a contextualising force that brings discourses into conflict. Hutcheon understands ironic art as a *perlocutionary* act that may create a distance from the discourse that it quotes, but that necessarily generates its own utterance in doing so. Rather than characterising irony as a detached position, she describes how its charge or 'cutting edge' produces a speaking position that is conditioned by relations of power. With a particular focus on the ethical implications of irony as a mode of presentation that *repeats* the discourse it ironises, she thus emphasises how the strategy has a discursive range of functions – from benign *reinforcement* to provocative *aggregation* – that are intuited differently in each interpretation (1995: 45). As such, Hutcheon concludes that the communicative space set up by irony is highly unstable, or even dangerous.[5]

Where Hutcheon is for the most part interested in the negative force of irony's power of repetition, the chapters that follow seek to describe some of the positive, aesthetic consequences that might arise in the process of quotation or 'remarking'. At one level this description acknowledges that the films oppose the traditions and practices that preceded them. Sconce, for example, cites the often hostile reaction that many of the smart directors had to film school as an experience opposing that of the 'movie brats' and, more explicitly, defines the narrative structure of the smart film as a direct departure from the European derived paradigm of art cinema, describing a shift from 'the modernist protagonist's search for meaning to the postmodern ensemble "fucked by fate"' (2002: 363). At another level, the study describes the stance taken toward these and other cinematic traditions in terms that are less oppositional, acknowledging how the smart film's tendency to 'stage' traditions may put these discourses at a distance, but also works to keep them in place. The films in which the smart sensibility can be perceived rely upon tonal detachment as a way of demonstrating their recognition of their own contingency. Beyond this, though, they also demonstrate their awareness of this recognition as their own utterance, and therefore of the contradiction at the heart of an ironic position. The following chapters aim to demonstrate how, rather than withdrawing from what it says, the smart film acknowledges the dual force of ironic expression.

When the ideas of Gilles Deleuze and Félix Guattari are drawn upon, it is in an attempt to describe the multiple effects and relations that this utterance gives rise to. Deleuze criticises irony for its movement of 'ascent' toward a unified principle or position of judgement. His poststructuralist philosophy is founded upon a rejection of the ironic logic that understands language as a system for representing the truth of a world that lies outside of it. Ideas, for Deleuze, do not exist *above* life as ideal forms but come *from* life as a flow of forces and desires. By abolishing the logic of height and depth, Deleuze conceives of Ideas as 'multiplicities', where 'multiplicity must not designate a combination of the many and the one, but rather an organisation belonging to the many as such, which has no need whatsoever of unity in order to form a system' (2004: 230). All of Deleuze's concepts – including irony itself – are founded upon multiplicity in this way: 'it is, perhaps, ironic to say that everything is multiplicity, even the one, even the many. However, irony itself is a multiplicity – or rather, the art of multiplicities: the art of grasping the Ideas and the problems they incarnate in things, and of grasping things as incarnations, as cases of solution for the problems of Ideas.' Against a pragmatic conception of irony as direct withdrawal, it is the multiplicity and creativity of Deleuze's 'superior irony' that this book seeks to mobilise in its discussion of the smart sensibility. It approaches the 'remark' of the smart film not as an expression of judgement or disengagement but as a pluralising, *affective* force.

AMERICAN SMART CINEMA

The book is divided into five chapters, each of which seeks to describe the sensibility of the smart film as a site of competing meanings from the perspective of one defining aspect – authorship, narrative, melodrama, music and suburbia. Importantly, the films discussed here are not intended to form a definitive group. A consequence of understanding smart cinema as something in which films 'participate without membership' is that the designation 'smart' can never be exact. Some of the films considered here come from Sconce's original group and some have appeared either after or alongside the films in that group. All demonstrate some evidence of the smart aesthetic in combinations that give rise to a formally and thematically self-conscious tone. As suggested above, though, this tone is principally understood not as a semantic end in itself but as evidence of the conflicted stance these films take toward cinema history. As such, each chapter discusses smart cinema in terms of the address it makes to a particular cinematic tradition or discourse. The films considered are designed not to define but to *demonstrate* the sensibility, and ultimately to suggest where else it may be perceived.

The first chapter explores where smart cinema might fit in contemporary debates around film authorship. Books such as those by Mottram, Mayshark and Waxman all focus on commercial/independent filmmaking as a field of contemporary American auteurs. This chapter considers how the directors' awareness of this discursive construction manifests in the films themselves. Drawing on the trilogy form as an important prop in the construction of historical auteur cinema, it considers how serialisation is formalised in the films of 'adjunct' smart directors Whit Stillman and Hal Hartley as a way of staging an auteur vision. A similarly dissimulative effect is then identified in the films of the auteurist 'unit' of Charlie Kaufman, Spike Jonze and Michel Gondry: *Being John Malkovich, Human Nature* (Michel Gondry, 2001), *Adaptation* (Spike Jonze, 2002) and *Eternal Sunshine of the Spotless Mind* (Michel Gondry, 2004). This latter section addresses how, in smart cinema as a type, the specific serialised forms of Stillman and Hartley open onto a broader self-consciousness around issues of synchronicity and repetition. This chapter seeks to provide an argument against the classification of these films as evidence of a contemporary climate of 'eclectic irony' (Collins 1993: 242) that puts itself at a remove from discourses of genre and authorship. Instead, it approaches the self-reflexive quality of films by Stillman, Hartley and

Kaufman as an *interrogation* of this climate: as a site of negotiation between ironic and sincere assertions that at once continues and narrates the tradition of auteurism.

Chapter 2 takes up Sconce's claim that smart cinema re-embraces classical narrative strategies by examining the structure of family dramas including *The Squid and the Whale* (Noah Baumbach, 2007), *Palindromes* and *The Safety of Objects* in relation to the models of classical and New Hollywood. These two narrative modes are approached by way of the *action-image* defined by Deleuze in *Cinema 1: The Movement Image*. The concern with issues of serialisation established in Chapter 1 is continued here in a discussion that posits smart cinema as a 'sequel' to the New Hollywood movement of 1967–75. Building on the links already established between New Hollywood and the contemporary commercial/independent field by Biskind and Mottram, the chapter argues that the *crisis* of action identified in the former era by both Deleuze and Thomas Elsaesser reappears in an inverted narrative format in the smart film. Linking smart cinema's own distortion of the classical three-part model (Situation, Action, Modified Situation) to the force of the 'toxic' family relations described above, this section describes how the episodic structure of the films transforms American film form by promoting an anti-causal conception of life as a random, continuing series of events.

The third chapter sustains this thematic focus to describe how the smart film can be read to take a revisionist stance toward the classical Hollywood genre of the domestic melodrama. Wes Anderson's 'augmented' family forms are discussed for the way that they rework both the narrative formula and tonal address of the 'aristocratic' variation of the family melodrama. Here, the 'blank' style of the smart film is referred back to the stylistic ironies found in the films of Douglas Sirk and, beyond that, to earlier examples of tableau presentation as a mode where 'telling' is subordinated to 'showing'. This chapter is concerned to specifically address the tensions that arise in smart cinema between self-conscious cultural knowledge and affect. By identifying these different scopic regimes in the address of smart film, it seeks to characterise the typical blankness of the sensibility in terms of a notion of critical pathos.

Chapter 4 examines the role that music plays in inflecting certain commercial/independent films with this melodramatic sensibility. This chapter discusses the peculiar 'musicality' of many smart films as a quality that exceeds the classical functions of popular music in film. In place of strategies of emotional expression and narrative commentary, evidence of a 'music-image' is identified in *The Royal Tenenbaums*, and in *Magnolia*, *Simple Men* and Terry Zwigoff's *Ghost World* (2001). Music is mobilised in these films as an excessive element that unbalances narrative flow by emphasising the plasticity of the image, but simultaneously re-directs the film itself into moments of revelation. This chapter describes how, bounded by their pop songs, these set-pieces mediate the cinephiliac discourse of 'privileged moments' in *figural* models in which affect is at once felt and qualified. This pluralising effect is described through reference to Deleuze and Guattari's work on music, where it is suggested that the force of the music-image is to transform the individuated structures internal to both image and song.

Chapter 5 turns once more to the narrative situation of smart cinema as drama couched in the minutiae of everyday family life. The identification of the 'suburban smart film' sub-cycle allows this final section to consider the wider cultural concerns of the smart sensibility by examining the position that it generates in relation to the literary and cinematic tradition of utopia/dystopia. Many of the films referenced in this book articulate the popular myth of suburbia as a typically inverted utopia: a depersonalised world that, extrapolated from consumer capital, is dominated by attitudes of despair, anxiety and violence. With reference to *Happiness*, *Your Friends and Neighbors*, *Magnolia*, *The Safety of Objects* and *The Chumscrubber*, this chapter describes the suburban smart film as a specific anti-utopian type concerned with the exposition of social fact. The implicitly conservative nature of this position is then challenged in a discussion of *Donnie Darko*. As a suburban smart science-fiction film, Kelly's feature mobilises a discourse on becoming that can be understood to animate a properly utopian dialectic. *Donnie Darko* harnesses all the conditions attended to in the study to demonstrate a radical smart film that indicates where the sensibility can be taken, and what it can do.

By seeking to release the notion of smart cinema from a fixed textual type to a constellation of forces and affects, this book necessarily implies that the sensibility can be felt in texts other than those addressed here. This project focuses closely on a small group of films in which a pluralising tone and a thematic concern with the family is particularly emphatic. While attending for the most part to Tamara Jenkins' film *The Savages* (2007) as a production in which the smart treatment of both aspects is crystallised, the Conclusion to the study also indicates how the sensibility might be felt in television texts. The rise of American post-network television has magnified the medium's perennial concern with the family in programs where a cinematic mode of address that favours its own type of blank performance and stylisation is evident. In this way, programs like *Arrested Development* (2003–6), *The Sopranos* (1999–2007), *Six Feet Under* (2001–5), *Weeds* (2005–) and *Big Love* (2006–) demonstrate a certain degree of overlap between the genre of 'quality TV' and smart cinema at the levels of both form and theme. Although a detailed consideration of this correlation is beyond the scope of this project, the comparison is drawn to indicate where further research may turn in a search for ongoing evidence of the smart sensibility.

Notes

1. For a detailed discussion of these industry developments see Justin Wyatt's 'The Formation of the "Major Independent" – Miramax, New Line and the New Hollywood'. Warner Bros' own specialty division – Warner Independent Pictures – closed in May 2008. One news report attributes the closure to the fact that Warner was 'too late to the game . . . by the time Warner Independent was founded in 2003, every other major studio had already established a specialty division' (Barnes 2008).
2. King's *American Independent Cinema* is especially valuable for its broad contextualisation of the independent field in terms of the historical avant-garde, the 1980s independent movement and individual filmmakers including Mark Rappaport and John McNaughton.
3. This is a task left to the emergent 'treatment genre' of television as demonstrated in 'quality' series such as *In Treatment* (2008–), *Tell Me You Love Me* (2007), *Huff* (2004–6) and – in a comedic vein – *Head Case* (2007–9).
4. King presents a similar contextualisation in *Indiewood: USA* when he draws on Bourdieu to identify how the 'distinction' of Indiewood cinema is partially constructed by techniques of niche-marketing: 'by choosing to view specialty rather than mainstream films . . . consumers are associating themselves (consciously or unconsciously) with a particular socio-cultural domain based on varying degrees of differentiation from mainstream cinema, culture and society' (King 2009: 12).
5. This conception of irony is taken up as an aesthetic and political strategy in Hutcheon's specific work on postmodernism: *A Poetics of Postmodernism: History, Theory, Fiction* and *The Politics of Postmodernism*.

1. AUTHORSHIP: WHIT STILLMAN'S 'YUPPIE' TRILOGY, *FLIRT, ADAPTATION*[1]

Contemporary discussions of film and authorship are broadly characterised by an attitude of unrest. Approaches to the topic self-consciously tread a line between recognising the myriad ways in which the field of study has evolved from the intentionalist position of the original *Cahiers du Cinéma* critics, and recognising the palpable ways in which the fascination with the auteur remains. In a 2001 piece titled 'Auteur Desire', Dana Polan describes the dual nature of this fascination as a drive to outline the desire *of* the auteur – a director's personal obsessions – and as the continuing obsession of the cinephile to understand films in terms of the person who signs them, a drive that demonstrates a certain desire *for* the auteur. The process of simply outlining the first type of desire has, of course, been challenged to a significant extent by the structural and poststructural turns in film theory. The insistence of classical auteurism on the director as a creative figure whose mysterious yet truthful voice must be deciphered by the auteurist has been displaced by more concrete attention to factors of industry and reception.[2] Even within these discourses though, contemporary work on film and authorship still, inevitably, demonstrates the second type of desire: the broad desire of the *auteurist* to, in Polan's words, 'give distinction to films according to their directors and to master their corpuses' (Polan 2001).

Given this continuity, the conceptualisation of advances in auteurism is often approached not in terms of an evolution in theory, but in terms of the practical evolution of auteurs themselves. The directors associated with the smart cycle provide a pertinent case study here, insofar as it is largely their discursive construction *as* auteurs that distinguishes them and their work from the Hollywood mainstream. Further to this, one of the hallmarks of the cycle's broadly ironic sensibility is a self-reflexive concern with the notion of authorship. To an extent, it is the distance that these directors put between themselves and the concept of the auteur that ultimately defines them in the terms of auteurism. An initial way to approach this cycle, then, is to take up the triangular schema by which Sconce locates the smart film at the 'intersection' of mainstream, art and independent film, and consider it in relation to 'art' cinema, and in particular the historical equation of this model with auteur cinema and national cinema. By examining how certain examples in the cycle take up this history as a point of reference, the smart film can be contextualised in terms of global cinema's broader transformation of these categories.

Auteurism and Serialisation

An individual director's terms of expression can only be traced through the appearance of successive films, so the basic notion of authorship is necessarily conditioned by patterns of continuity and repetition. This condition places the discourse of authorship in a relevant relationship to the specific industrial and textual models of repetition that emerge in sequels, series and remakes. Beyond their existence as highly commercial forms typifying the post-classical Hollywood 'disease' of 'sequelitis' (Hoberman 1985: 34), these types of films can also allow for the literal fulfilment of a highly personal vision beyond the boundaries of commercial concern. Particularly, where single sequels and film series involving more than three films tend to stick closely to industrially defined patterns of repetition (signified by titled numbers and/or repeat title terms),[3] the film *trilogy* provides a more interesting example of how serialisation can be opened up for the expression of a personal vision, and has subsequently been drawn upon by many widely recognised auteurs. As such, the trilogy is a compelling site in which to examine the relay between 'old' and 'new' conceptions of auteurism, where the smart film is understood as a sensibility that directly engages both.

In filmmaking practice and critical evaluation, the trilogy is an area where the condition of remaking that grounds all sequels is made explicit. Over the course of film history, critical discourse on film remaking has extended well beyond that on sequelisation and serialisation. Where the discussion of film sequels and serials has only recently begun to think beyond a direct, *acknowledged* model,[4] the discussion of film remakes has, from the outset, considered ideas of disguise, transformation and difference.[5] In thinking beyond a purely commercial motivation, recent work on film remaking can offer some guidance for a consideration of the auteurist dimensions of the film trilogy. For Constantine Verevis, there are at least two discursive categories of remaking that exist beyond an industrial model. If issues of production, distribution and exhibition define the industrial category of remaking, the *textual* category is concerned with the repetition of plots, structures and styles across films. Beyond this, the *critical* category of remaking is constituted by issues of reception and discourse, where extratextual elements of reviews, DVD extras, marketing campaigns and word of mouth can define a remake beyond the realm of acknowledged credits or clear textual signifiers (2006: 2). Like film remakes, the film trilogy can also be identified to exist in a commercial, textual and critical capacity.

The commercial or industrial trilogy is often an 'accidental' type, which arises when the drive to capitalise on a pre-existing audience with a single sequel is repeated. In this way, the '3quel' (Corliss 2007) is a frequently transient form, defining a series only until a fourth film is announced. Series including The Fast and the Furious,[6] X-Men,[7] Pirates of the Caribbean[8] and Spiderman[9] have all articulated and transcended the 3quel category in this way, while the three Rush Hour films offer an intact example (to date). As an *X-Men: The Last Stand* commentator notes, the third – and subsequent – films in these scenarios will often suffer from having to compete not only with an original hit, but with a sequel that surpassed this (Newman 2006: 84): the films are explicitly vying with their predecessors as an afterthought, rather than filling out a predetermined vision. Of course, the industrial category of trilogies includes examples that exploit the form's commercial potential *while* offering a coherent vision. Examples such as the Lord of the Rings,[10] Matrix[11] and both Star Wars[12] trilogies initially promoted themselves *as* a three-part series to build a sense of stature and anticipation designed to translate into box-office returns upon the release of the first and second sequels. In these examples, the trilogy functions as a specific prop in the auteurist marketing of films. The form builds and encapsulates a sense of intentional and authorial agency that, as Timothy Corrigan has identified, works as a 'brand-name vision whose aesthetic meanings and values have already been determined' (1998: 40).

If such industrial modes are largely confined to Hollywood, discursive textual and critical models of the trilogy are clearly identifiable in the fields of contemporary European and American auteur cinema. In the textual category of film remaking, the concept 'remake' is defined less by issues of acknowledgment and law than by issues of intertextuality. Beyond the direct examples of film remakes, which are stabilised through naming and/or copyright, the practice of 'remaking' can range from a film's direct quotation of another film to the repetition of a shot, scene or style, to more general repetitions of a popular story or myth (Verevis 2006: 19–21). Intertextuality can also be understood as the condition that constitutes a trilogy. In the commercial environment this occurs in an explicit way, with instalments pointing backwards and forwards to each other through mechanisms such as the 'to be continued' title. But, outside of this specific practice, a trilogy can be intertextually constituted in a more veiled way. The textual practice of the trilogy moves away from the direct intentionality of the industrial practice: rather than explicitly following up on an earlier hit or fulfilling the promise of another instalment, a director will – perhaps inadvertently – cast new scenarios in the terms of earlier concerns.

In some instances a director will return to a project when she or he finds that there is more to be said or done than the first film can adequately cover.[13] Projects such as Lars von Trier's 'USA – Land of Opportunities' trilogy; Nuri Bilge Ceylan's *Kasaba* (*The Small Town*, 1998), *Mayis Sikintisi* (*Clouds of May*, 2000) and *Uzak* (*Distant*, 2004); Nicolas Refn's *Pusher* trilogy[14] and Abbas Kiarostami's *Koker* trilogy[15] are all textually defined in this way. Interviewed upon the release of *Dogville* (2003), von Trier's rationale for wanting to continue his bare and highly stylised discourse on America with *Manderlay* (2005) and *Wasington* – the third film that has not yet transpired – extended only to his feeling that 'I think the world I've created is so inspiring I want to continue to live in it' (Bjorkman 2004: 27). Ceylan's continuation of the stories of earlier characters and repeat use of actors is even less determined: on *Uzak*, Ceylan comments 'this time I wanted to make a completely different film . . . but somehow it connected again. I couldn't get out of it yet' (Romney 2004: 23).

Refn and Kiarostami's projects have also emerged as a recurring interest in a group of characters and a particular environment, rather than an orchestrated narrative arc. Clear textual markers link the films together, but in no project other than Refn's is this signalled in the titles. The links between the films are instead 'found' at a critical level, indicating the way in which the textual category of the trilogy is also always a *discursive* category. This critical level also makes explicit the links between serialisation and film remaking. Articles and reviews on these and other trilogies tend to approach them as case studies of authorial remaking, with specific attention paid to the way in which the trilogy will often mark a maturation or perfection of the director's style.[16] In this way, the textual repetition is constituted as serialisation – a trilogy – entirely at a critical level. Even von Trier's trilogy – arguably the most commercial of the textual examples discussed – does not aggressively market itself intertextually: the posters for *Manderlay* do not mention *Dogville*, or use the 'USA – Land of Opportunities' tag at all.[17] Equally, in interviews, the release of a new instalment will often see the director far less interested in talking about the continuity between the new work and earlier films than about other aspects of the film or their practice more generally.[18] This points to the *flexibility* of the film trilogy as one of the most compelling aspects of the form; commentators seem far more comfortable interpreting three films with some internal consistencies as related (as a trilogy) than they do two (as a single, disguised sequel).

Gus Van Sant's *Gerry* (2002), *Elephant* (2003) and *Last Days* (2005) offer a contemporary American example on the outskirts of the smart cycle that can exemplify the fundamentally discursive quality of the film trilogy as a critical category. Van Sant's three films are loosely consistent in terms of their theme of the untimely death of young men, and their style, which is defined by 'long Steadicam tracking shots that shadow restlessly mobile protagonists from behind' (Dalton 2005: 66). As well as linking these three films to the formal blankness of the smart cycle, this stylistic mannerism is the most obvious sign of Van Sant's debt across these films to his mentor of sorts: Hungarian director Béla Tarr. All three films are also based on real life events, which they avoid referring to explicitly: with *Gerry*, a news story about a young man arrested for murdering his best friend after telling police a story about how they got lost in the desert together, with *Elephant*, the Columbine High School massacre, and with *Last Days*, the final days and suicide of Kurt Cobain.

Where these similarities were talked up in reviews of the various films, coming to a head (as is typical) with the release of the third, Van Sant played down the connections between the three, admitting only that they have 'death and youth similarities' and that they were made the same way – 'in one location and shot in order, with a minimal script and with an execution that promotes our idea of "reality"' (Taubin 2005: 17). Referring to the concept of a trilogy explicitly, Van Sant claimed that 'since there have been three films, then so far it's a trilogy. But not planned that way . . . [and] there may be another film on the way, so it could change.' The recurrent 'death and youth' theme in the subsequent *Paranoid Park* (2007) confirms this comment by extending the 'Death trilogy' (Taubin 2007: 55) into a type of quartet but, again, this impression is discursively controlled: critics commonly describe this film in terms of its aesthetic distance from the previous three films and its broader continuity with Van Sant's earlier work, thereby emphasising the previous trilogy even more decisively.[19] Other trilogies that have been constituted on account of even looser authorial repetition include Baz Luhrmann's *Strictly Ballroom* (1992), *Romeo and Juliet* (1996) and *Moulin Rouge* (2001) as Luhrmann's 'Red Curtain' trilogy, and Lars von Trier's 'E Trilogy' – *(The) Element of Crime* (1984), *Epidemic* (1987) and *Europa* (1991). The last example comes back full circle to the industrial category of the form, with von Trier's 'trilogy' constituted as such as a DVD release that patently stretches the texts to fit the form, by drawing only on the English titles of the first and third films.

THE TRILOGY: EUROPEAN ART CINEMA TO INTERNATIONAL ART CINEMA

The textual and critical dimensions of the film trilogy mean that it has formed a privileged model for the study of auteurism throughout the course of cinema history. Although, as has been demonstrated, a good deal of this work is currently going on around contemporary European and American auteurs, the most significant arena for the association has been the formal and narrative tradition that is understood as the European art cinema, where the trilogy form plays a specific function in the conceptualisation of national auteur cinema. In his collection of essays *European Cinema Face to Face with Hollywood*, Thomas Elsaesser outlines how cinema studies has traditionally defined European cinema in terms of three dominant discourses: *national* cinema, *auteur* cinema and *art* cinema (2005: 23). Each discourse, he suggests, functions as a 'paradigm of autonomy' with which European cinema – as a group of national cinemas – is distinguished from Hollywood. It is this conception of the sector that locates it as a point with which the smart film intersects.

One manner in which the auteur-based discourse functions to consolidate lines of autonomy lies in the way that perspectives internal and external to any given country tend to make one or two directors stand in for that nation – as autonomous, representative artists. One example of this tendency is the case of Ingmar Bergman: Elsaesser notes how, for decades, Bergman's films defined both to Sweden and to the rest of the world what 'Swedish' cinema – and identity – meant (15). Within European art cinema, Bergman is just one example of a director whose auteurist status owes something to the trilogy form. With their common themes regarding faith, shared actors, limited cast and spare style, *Såsom i en spegel* (*Through a Glass Darkly*, 1961), *Nattvardsgästerna* (*Winter Light*, 1963) and *Tystnaden* (*The Silence*, 1963) are typically understood as Bergman's 'Chamber' trilogy. Other familiar examples include Antonioni's *L'Avventura* (*The Adventure*, 1961), *La Notte* (*The Night*, 1962) and *L'Eclisse* (*The Eclipse*, 1962); Rossellini's *Roma, città aperta* (*Rome: Open City*, 1945), *Paisà* (*Paisan*, 1946) and *Germania anno zero* (*Germany Year Zero*, 1948); and Truffaut's Antoine Doinel films (which form a series rather than a strict trilogy).[20] All of these directors have been understood as auteurs in a way that is at least partially determined by the fact that they have all been nominated, at various times, as representative national voices. One of the places in which this is clearest is Deleuze's work on cinema: Antonioni and Rossellini are positioned as auteurs by Deleuze for the way that the images and situations in their work perform Italian neo-realism in terms of the formal aesthetic criteria that were, for André Bazin and for Deleuze, more significant than social content (Deleuze 1989: 1–9).

The trilogy form can be interpreted to play a specific function in this idea of national auteur cinema. On one hand, the trilogy offers an ideal framework within which to establish the moral vision and aesthetic language that constitutes a personal style or authorial signature. With an emphasis on the process of authorial *remaking* as semantic and syntactic repetition, critical delineations of the trilogies of the European art cinema offer precise examples of classical auteur theory as a process of investigation and decipherment. As Elsaesser has suggested elsewhere, a mere look at the filmographies of Godard, Antonioni, Truffaut, Wenders, Herzog and Kieślowski 'shows how important a prop the idea of the trilogy is for the self-identity of the European auteur' (Elsaesser 1994: 26). On the other hand, to return to Elsaesser's more recent work, the historical trilogy can be understood to work in a manner that goes beyond the personal: a regular cast of players and a consistent aesthetic approach can be seen to compensate for the European cinema's absence of pre-defined genres and stars. The repetition, which is typically interpreted as highly *individualist*, can be here read as the effort to link a particular directorial universe to cinema history (Elsaesser 2005: 136).

One of Elsaesser's key objectives in his *European Cinema* collection – implied in the book's subtitle – is to describe how European-Hollywood relations are no longer simply bi-lateral. In the face of global cultural capital and a festival circuit that enables the exchange of reputations across national borders, Elsaesser's interest is in the transformation of the three historical discourses on European cinema. One of the ways he traces this is through an evolving norm that he describes as the 'international festival film'. Here, he argues that the figures understood as contemporary European and American auteurs are no longer *national* auteurs: their work constitutes an 'international art cinema' that, by expressing similar concerns and styles across a wide spectrum of settings, 'gives a new meaning to regional or local attributes' (2005: 18). The group of directors who, for Elsaesser, seem to have more in common with each other than with directors of their respective national cinemas includes Lars von Trier, Wong Kar-Wai, Tsai Ming-Liang, Tom Tykwer, Abbas Kiarostami, Hal Hartley, Richard Linklater and Paul Thomas Anderson. Elsaesser characterises this 'mutation' both industrially and aesthetically, suggesting, firstly, that the lower cost of digital cinema has meant films are fulfilling functions in the domestic and public sphere that break down the conventional binary model of art/commerce through which the Europe/Hollywood opposition is usually understood, and, secondly, that the international art cinema is identifiable in terms of a stylistic repertoire that foregrounds a cinephile universe of film historical references shared with its audiences.

Both characteristics indicate how the group can also be relevantly linked on account of their demonstration of a type of 'new' auteurism. Elsaesser's argument on evolving technologies points to one of the most obvious ways in which the auteur has developed since the emergence of auteurism as a practice in the 1950s, which is in terms of his/her visibility. In an article titled 'Possessory Credit', Adrian Martin suggests that the contemporary commodification of auteurism demonstrates that there is no longer any doubt regarding auteur theory's original question as to whether filmmakers have their own recognisable style (2004b: 95). As alluded to earlier, Corrigan has discussed auteur theory as a form of marketing that calls auteurs into being according to precise institutional needs. Here, the 'commerce of auteurism' involves the simultaneous imposition of ideologies from without and self-promotional tactics from within. The 'celebrity' auteur figure that emerges from these tactics necessarily changes auteurism as a process insofar as the practice of decipherment is entirely eluded: directors now openly reveal their 'desire' in interviews, profiles, DVD commentaries, trailers and advertisements. The commerce of auteurism means that auteurs are now highly aware of themselves as an abbreviated image.

Beyond broad thematic commonalities that include an interest in issues of human relationships and personal identity, the group identified by Elsaesser is very much typified by this self-awareness, and the breakdown between art and commerce that it represents. As such, the 'international art cinema' can be understood as a force that, in addition to dissolving the national paradigm that has historically defined and distinguished European/Hollywood relations, collectively overwhelms the historical paradigm of auteur cinema as the personal expression of a singular creator. Hyper-conscious of the classical process of auteur theory as the decipherment of a personal vision, and of the way this is framed by contemporary technologies and ideologies, these directors necessarily take a distinctly reflexive approach to the whole concept of the auteur. They precisely demonstrate an earlier contention outlined by Elsaesser, where he suggests that what we mean today by 'auteur' is no longer about self-doubt or self-expression, but about the *dissimulation* of such signatures of selfhood, even when belief or doubt is passionately present (1994: 26).

As a sensibility tonally defined by irony, and as a cycle with a specific interest in confounding the discrete categories of art, independent and mainstream filmmaking, the smart film cannot avoid being considered in terms of this 'new' evolving norm, which is supported by the inclusion of Hartley and Anderson in Elsaesser's line-up. The self-conscious attitude to auteurism exhibited by the European and American directors alike manifests itself in various ways across their work and public personas: in film cameos, advertisements and other cooperative projects with which they involve themselves. Outside of the films themselves, examples could include Lars von Trier's Dogma initiative,[21] Spike Jonze's return to his skater roots with his 'lowbrow' co-operations in the *Jackass* projects[22] and, most overtly, Wes Anderson's American Express commercial, where he parodies himself while paying homage to Truffaut.[23]

Within the films, the attitude emerges as varying layers of self-reflexivity. This mannerism can be most adequately examined by reference to another contextualisation of the broad group of directors under discussion here. In a chapter titled 'Sincerity and Irony', Nicholas Rombes describes von Trier, Paul Thomas Anderson and Spike Jonze in terms of 'new punk cinema'. Arguing here that these – and other – directors are typified by an ironic stance inherited from punk, Rombes describes features such as *Breaking the Waves* (Lars von

Trier, 1996), *Magnolia* and *Adaptation* as new punk films for their ability to evoke a sincere emotional response while simultaneously creating possibilities for the audience to see through the mechanisms that elicit that response (2005: 74).

As will be specifically examined in Chapters 3 and 4, this double voicing is fundamental to the type of auteurism demonstrated in the international festival film and the smart film. Critical discourse on the directors associated with these cycles indicates how their films are open to at least two modes of reception. On one hand, they are capable of being received as classical auteurist products: 'well-made' works demonstrating consistent stylistic and thematic characteristics that collectively build a particular world-view.[24] On the other hand, perspectives such as Rombes' suggest that the key dimension of the films' critical appeal is the distance they exhibit toward their own skilfulness. From this angle, the most auteurist aspect of the cycles is an awareness, and unbalancing, of auteurism itself: the signature of these directors is, from the outset, a *narration* of their signature.

A specific dimension of this narration is the way these directors approach ideas of repetition and serialisation in their work. If the figure of the historical auteur (Bergman, Antonioni, Rossellini, Truffaut) can be discursively linked to the trilogy form in terms of the expression of an idiosyncratic moral vision that represents their nation, the auteurs of these new cycles distinguish themselves from this tradition by way of a distinctly self-reflexive approach to repetition and continuation. All these directors are highly conscious of the way they are positioned as auteurs by those commercial processes that force them to reveal the signatures which, for their European predecessors and *their* processes of serialisation, did have to be deciphered.[25] Subsequently, the international art cinema is an area where sequelisation is often thought imaginatively, both in practice and in discourse. To give just a few examples, Wong Kar-Wai's *2046* (2004) works as a 'disguised sequel' to his earlier *In the Mood for Love* (2000), Linklater's *Before Sunset* (2004) offers a real-time sequel to *Before Sunrise* (1995) and both Tykwer's *Run Lola Run* (1998) and Hartley's *Flirt* (1995) use a tripartite structure to explore three different versions of the one event. Von Trier and Kiarostami also work with the trilogy as a disguised sequel, as has been discussed. The remaining part of this chapter will subsequently turn to an examination of the way some directors who can be broadly linked to the smart cycle engage serialisation in their demonstration of 'new' auteurism's dissimulation of a signature.

The Smart Periphery

As the first two directors to be closely considered, Whit Stillman and Hal Hartley demonstrate the diversity of the smart sensibility as it is imagined by this book. Although three of Hartley's films, *The Unbelievable Truth* (1990), *Trust* (1991) and *Henry Fool* (1998), are included as 'postmodern screwball comedies' on Sconce's initial smart list (none of Stillman's are), both directors seem to maintain a certain distance from the phenomenon as it is evinced by other figures included there, particularly the likes of Wes Anderson, Paul Thomas Anderson, David O. Russell and Spike Jonze. As 'adjunct' figures, Hartley and Stillman exemplify the smart tendency as something open and partial. There are a number of ways of describing the distance between these directors and others outlined by Sconce. One is that Stillman and Hartley are around ten years older than the more central 'smart pack'; both born in the early 1960s and therefore, in the terms used by Sconce, 'late boomers' rather than part of 'Gen-X proper' (2002: 357). Another distinction, suggested by James Mottram, is that both Stillman and Hartley are resolutely 'East Coast' filmmakers (2006: xxii): both have resisted moving to the West and demonstrate a thematic and environmental concern with the East in their work. For Emanuel Levy, the two are firmly entrenched in 'The New York School of Indies'; geographically distinguished as, respectively, 'Upper East Side' and 'Long Island' (1999: 197).

A third, related, explanation could lie with the directions their respective careers have taken. Where each successive film by the central directors of the smart cycle seems to further perform the practical dimension of Palmer's concept of 'commercial/independence' by collapsing the two categories of 'independence' and turning their alternative visions into simultaneously commercial and critical successes, Stillman and Hartley have more obviously continued in the vein of independence that 'persists in a spirit of modernist negativity' (1988: 5). Stillman's 'Yuppie trilogy' is a particularly interesting example of the form in that the three films constitute his total output until 2011: the most recent, *The Last Days of Disco*, dating from 1998.[26] Both directors' 90s films secured them critical recognition, with Hartley in particular constructed as a leading figure in the 90s independent movement. Both too, though, avoided following up with larger-budget work: where Stillman is reported to have pursued adaptation and music projects without success,[27] Hartley followed 1997's *Henry Fool* with a series of non-narrative shorts (including *The Book of Life* (1998), *Kimono* (2000) and a series of video shorts in 2010) that recall those from earlier in his career. Compared to the cycle of films from *Trust* to *Henry Fool*, Hartley's post-1997 feature work, including the monster film *No Such Thing* (2001), *The Girl From Monday* (2005) and *Fay Grim* (2006) has also attracted minimal attention, and ensured that Hartley remains operative in a context largely removed from the contemporary smart scene.

Despite this industrial and physical distance, these two figures clearly demonstrate certain continuities with the other smart directors that will be discussed here. The smart quality in Stillman and Hartley manifests as a sensibility with literary roots. The two directors are frequently compared on the basis of their highly stylised dialogue, where their insistently verbal characters speak in arch, circular phrases inflected with philosophical and literary tones.[28] The off-kilter lucidity that typifies the dialogue of the smart film seems it owes much to this overtly 'talkie' tendency, with all films linked by a clear interest in dialogue over and above action. Both directors also demonstrate clear sympathies with the five 'signs' of the smart film as established by Sconce. Indeed, viewed objectively, Hartley's films seem to offer a textbook example of the smart film as a formal and thematic entity. Stylistically, his blank signature is constituted by terse, deadpan dialogue and by regular cinematographer Michael Spiller's clean, careful camerawork. Further, his films are all distinguished by a synchronous narrative structure that persists over and above the convoluted and often improbable twists of their plots (*Flirt* makes this characteristic most overt, as will be discussed). These plots, particularly in terms of interpersonal relationships, are often based upon chance encounters, and this thematic interest in fate and coincidence can also be extended to a formal narrative level, as exemplified by the 'wrong' shooting at the end of *Amateur* (1994). Finally, the general critique of American society that runs through all of Hartley's films manifests as an explicit concern with family dysfunction in *The Unbelievable Truth*, *Trust*, *Simple Men* and *Henry Fool*, while *No Such Thing*, *The Book of Life* and *The Girl from Monday* all broaden Hartley's critique of consumer society to a sometimes vitriolic attack on modern humanity as a whole.

The smart quality to Stillman's films is less pointed, with a slightly archaic variant of the sensibility emanating from the work by way of his understated and literary approach to filmmaking. His dialogue is written and delivered in a manner that is unmistakably minimalist, but it is inflected with an ambiguous earnestness rather than deadpan flippancy. In a similar manner, his blank approach to cinematography is less an arch cinematic statement than a theatrical trait, where sequences often appear as set pieces framed by a curtain opening and closing on a carefully organised stage. Thematically, the smart critique of family and consumption is broadened into a more general *enquiry* on human nature. Despite these idiosyncrasies, Stillman's work can be relevantly aligned with the smart film on account of his attitude to repetition and authorship. *Metropolitan* (1990), *Barcelona* (1994) and *The Last Days of Disco* provide a compelling example of the contemporary trilogy as a composite of textual and critical concerns. Specifically, the approach to serialisation taken by Stillman here demonstrates a particular functional status in relation to the notion of 'new' auteurism, for his particular brand of irony stages authorial remaking in terms of playfulness and disguise.

WHIT STILLMAN

In *Metropolitan*, Charlie Black (Taylor Nichols) describes his disappointment in Buñuel's *The Discreet Charm of the Bourgeoisie* (1972), which he finds an unfair and inaccurate portrait of a class which, for him, *does* have a lot of charm. Beginning from this premise, the broadest aspect of repetition across Stillman's three features can be framed generically: each film is a comedy of manners which, together, build a portrait to counter Buñuel's, describing the distinctive – if ambiguous – charm of the class. Stillman's tonal approach to this material is also highly consistent, with each film blending the satire typical of the comedy of manners with a distinctly affectionate attitude. The marker that most openly links the three films is itself somewhat hidden: the credits for the third film identify those actors who appeared in the earlier films under the titles 'from *Metropolitan*' and 'from *Barcelona*'. Following this contextualisation, the second and third films can be understood as disguised sequels that revisit the concerns of the first.

The strongest suggestion of sequelisation across the three films comes from the impression that the same set of characters evolves across different social settings. This is non-specific on two counts. First, the films don't seem to proceed chronologically. The period of each film is described hazily – 'not so long ago' (*Metropolitan*), 'the last decade of the Cold War' (*Barcelona*) and 'the very early 1980s' (*The Last Days of Disco*) – but both the political context and the relative maturity of the characters in *Barcelona* suggests it is chronologically the last film. Stillman supports this: 'my idea is that [*The Last Days of Disco*] is the last of three films, kind of a triptych. This is the centrepiece of the triptych that loosely connects the other two' (Pincus 1998). Second, the set of characters is not literally transposed. The protagonists of *Barcelona* – cousins Ted and Fred Boynton – are actors but not exact characters repeated from *Metropolitan*. In the earlier film, Taylor Nichols (Ted) plays Charlie, who is (as at least two Stillman characters are specifically described) 'a basically good person', if somewhat 'doleful and pontificating' (Fuller 1994: viii), and prone to backstabbing newcomer Tom Townsend (Edward Clements). In the second film, Nichols as Ted is a good deal more virtuous, repressed and anxious, with his scornful attitude toward his vocal cousin, his closeted Catholicism and his 'aspiration to free romance from the chains of physical beauty and carnality'. In *Metropolitan*, Chris Eigeman (Fred in *Barcelona*) also plays a nominally different character: Nick Smith, who is bitchier than his peers, and tends to be described by them as obnoxious and arrogant.

Effectively, though, Eigeman's Nick *is* repeated in *Barcelona* as Fred, and then again in *The Last Days of Disco* as the 'nightclub flunkey' Des. These three roles represent the clearest example of the sequelisation of a specific character, which is an impression significantly aided by Eigeman playing all

Figure 2   Mackenzie Astin, Kate Beckinsale and Chloe Sevigny in *The Last Days of Disco* (Whit Stillman, 1998). Courtesy October Films / The Kobal Collection.

characters. Nichols also appears in the third film, in a character-based cameo which is similarly overt: running into the advertising executive Jimmy Steinway (Mackenzie Astin) in 'the club', the unnamed Nichols character – whose Ted in *Barcelona* is a sales rep for the Chicago-based car company IHSMOCO – recognises Jimmy as a previous employee of ad agency Leo Burnett's Chicago office. When Jimmy enquires as to whether he is still with IHSMOCO, the Nichols character replies that he's now with the international side based in Spain: Barcelona is beautiful, he insists, but in human terms, pretty cold. The type of overt intertextuality represented by these repetitions is rare. Instead, the impression of sequelisation comes from the repetition of character *types*, such as those who flank Eigeman's ambiguously nasty character in each film. On one side is a straightforward 'bad guy' who, in each instance, is almost a caricature – the womanising baron Rick von Sloneker (Will Kempe) in *Metropolitan*, the anti-American journalist – also a womaniser – Ramon (Pep Munne) in *Barcelona* and the prejudiced nightclub owner Bernie Rafferty (David Thornton in *The Last Days of Disco*). On the other is a more complex and differentiated 'virtuous' figure, who functions to expose the foibles and pettiness of the respective social groups for what they are – the Austen-reading Audrey Rouget (Carolyn Farina) in the first film, Ted himself in the second, and the candid virgin Alice (Chloe Sevigny) in the third. Between these two extremes, all films depict a raft of characters at different degrees of 'basic goodness', who, Austen-style, pair up with the most clearly comparable type of the opposite gender by each film's end.

Beyond this consistent approach to characterisation, Stillman's periodisation is another aspect of his filmmaking that frequently sees these three films discursively constituted as a trilogy. All three films are concerned with the decline of an era. *Metropolitan* looks at an already 'reduced' New York debutante scene which will probably be the last one as the young characters have grown up knowing it: 'I don't want to just hang around watching the decline', insists Nick. And, indeed, by the end of the film the Sally Fowler Rat Pack (SFRP), as the group term themselves, has disintegrated, with various members pursuing outside relationships, leaving overseas or just reluctantly accepting the reality of their situation. Politically, *Barcelona* is concerned with the anti-American climate in Europe at the end of the Cold War, but this backdrop of social change is shadowed by more specific story elements also concerning various 'endings': Ted moving back to Chicago from Barcelona, his sales mentor Jack (whom he describes as 'one of those magnetic personalities from the World War II generation') falling ill and dying, and Ted and Fred, it is suggested, finally patching up their life-long feud and mutual distrust after Fred is shot and survives. *The Last Days of Disco* expresses its overt ending in its title, but the context of a group of recent graduates discovering the disco scene just as it is ending provides a backdrop for the way all of the characters' first or early-career jobs come to an end – either through being promoted (Alice) or fired (Jimmy, Josh, Charlotte, Des, Dan) – and for the way this signals to them a certain coming of age.

Formally, Stillman's films are linked by an understated approach to film style. None of the films offer a tightly structured plot, with the theatrical impression of a series of set pieces strongest in *Metropolitan*, where many scenes end on a fade to black. The rhetorical impression of life is also strongest in the first film, with every scene centring on carefully managed conversation rather than any suggestion of action. In some ways, *Barcelona* moves quite deliberately away from this approach, breaking its conversations up with overt action-based sequences such as the two bombs that go off – one in the film's first shot – and the assassination attempt upon Fred. The different approach in the sequel represents a change of heart for Stillman, who claims to have written *Metropolitan* under the conviction that life is an eventless affair and, in the interval between writing the next film, moved to the understanding that life does have melodramatic turns (Pincus 1998). The action in *Barcelona* is never represented in melodramatic terms, though, and, by *The Last Days of Disco*, Stillman appears to have reverted back to a belief in the essential rhetoric of everyday life, with the highest points of action in the third film being Alice's contraction of an STD, and Charlotte being taken to hospital in an ambulance with a hurt back.

Given the romantic slant to each comedy of manners, Stillman's condemnation of plot is most clearly apparent in his resistance toward narrowing the focus to two characters. In all three films, he suggests, the alleged interest of the story is in who is going to end up with whom, but 'it's the getting there that's interesting' (Pincus 1998). In the terms of *The Last Days of Disco*, each film is more concerned with 'the tremendous importance of group social life' – with the conversation as set-piece – than with the 'ferocious pairing off' of plot-based romantic involvements. Across the films, this avoidance of spectacle is matched by an extremely limited depiction of either sex or violent conflict: Stillman tends to cut to the aftermath of both, where characters dissect the event in dialogue. This helps to lend what one commentator describes as a rare and ideal quality to his characters (Bowman 2000: 15). The 'wild' potential of all three scenarios – a group of recently graduated friends, young Americans abroad, the 1980s nightclub scene – is radically underplayed.

Given his thematic concern with the young American bourgeoisie as anxious and at least partly pessimistic about their position in life, as well as the understated style with which this subject matter is presented, it is perhaps unsurprising that Stillman has attracted the interest of conservative political sectors. In 2000, *The Intercollegiate Review* devoted an issue to a symposium on Stillman's films, which praised the unostentatious, literary and even-handed portrayal of how 'the well born [also] suffer the disorientation of modernity, the loss of tradition' (Henrie 2000: 3). For these commentators, Stillman's films are of direct interest for the way in which they illuminate what an imaginative conservative cultural intervention might entail: they offer, as one contributor suggests, 'a hard but not unhopeful look at the prospects for innocence in our time' (Bowman 2000: 15). Regardless of whether this political interpretation does in fact represent the films fairly, the symposium gives an instructive example of the discursive constitution of a trilogy to an auteurist end.

The conservative work understands Stillman's formal and thematic chasteness in terms of an adversarial attitude to contemporary youth culture and a desire to hark back to an earlier cultural model. The effect of using declining eras as social backdrops is here understood as Stillman's nostalgia for an idealised past where there is still belief in the benevolence of American culture and power. In this forum, the films are read as rare and ideal works that are quite unlike anything else in contemporary American filmmaking. It can be argued that the consistencies in the work are here recuperated in terms of serialisation rather than simply authorial style in an effort to secure this particular vision as a form unto itself. Addressing the formal and thematic components of Stillman's filmmaking in terms of the trilogy form is an attempt to consolidate his peculiar chasteness as an auteurist vision which, rather than referring to an earlier cultural model, attempts to call a new model into existence. It is under the rubric of this approach that Stillman is frequently described as a Jane Austen for contemporary times, with the films read as attempts to discover the truth about human nature through the formalities of a specific class and era. This interpretation emphasises Stillman's Socratic strategy of using each character as a clearly defined type whose ideas and attitudes represent a particular world view.[29] From an auteurist perspective, this approach to serialisation can be taken further again, insofar as Stillman can be understood to deploy his disguised sequels in a particularly functional gesture. The films may appear to search for the truth about human nature but, in repeating this search three times, Stillman concludes that the human is *not* a definable type: it is a concept that can only exist as difference, resonating from continual re-framings and re-castings. Here, Stillman mobilises the trilogy form to iterate the Romantic idea that it is only through the continual effort to grasp the idea of the human that the idea itself can emerge.

Putting Stillman's serialisation at the service of classical auteurism in this way, though, is belied by the approach to repetition that is actually taken in the films, where Stillman simultaneously performs and effaces the gesture. The distance of Stillman's films from other contemporary examples of American art/independent cinema is frequently attributed to a perceived lack of cynicism,[30] and one of the ways this is apparent is in Stillman's refusal to condemn his subjects. His characters are highly articulate, informed and immaculately presented individuals, but their atypically serious attitudes and modes of expression are never didactically ironised. In both *Metropolitan* and *The Last Days of Disco*, male characters give impassioned opinions on the broad social contexts of the films before qualifying themselves: Nick Smith in the former film claims 'I'm not entirely joking', and Josh Neff in the second apologises, explaining that he's heading to a job interview and was trying to rev himself up, but that 'most of what I said, I believe'. This type of double-voicing characterises Stillman's approach to the trilogy form itself, where characters and scenarios are repeated with a certain wryness that at times appears almost bashful. Like Josh, Stillman *mostly* believes in the project he is undertaking, and the appropriateness of the 'triptych' form, but is aware of its overwhelmingly auteurist overtones. Although his approach does recognise that no one representation can ever adequately describe the human questions in which he is interested, his articulation of this signature concern seems to want to deflate its own philosophical grandeur.

One of the clearest ways this occurs is in Stillman's self-reflexive approach to his Socratic method of characterisation. His style of typecasting is echoed across the films by the attitudes of the characters themselves, who rampantly stereotype people. In *Metropolitan*, people are named 'titled (or untitled) aristocrats', 'West-siders' and 'public transportation snobs'. *Barcelona* alludes to 'Barcelona girls', 'plain, homely women' and – in the Spanish slang for

Americans – '*fasca*' and '*credos Yanquis*'. And *The Last Days of Disco* derides 'ad people', 'Harvard guys' and the 'Woodstock Generation'. This stereotyping is consistently countered, though, by the rhetorical dissection of other terms, including 'yuppie', 'preppie' and '*Estadouniedense*'. The self-aware strategy is most clearly articulated in *Metropolitan's* coining of the new term 'UHB' (Urban Haute Bourgeoisie) as 'a more sociologically precise alternative to preppie', and in *The Last Days of Disco's* group argument regarding whether or not *Lady and the Tramp* is a depressing tale of transparent character types.

As an authorial attitude that is recouped in other smart films that will be discussed here, Stillman's approach to serialisation is self-effacing without being overtly cynical. His characters are serialised as representations of particular world-views, but this is represented in small and affectionate, rather than grand and judgemental, terms. This modest attitude extends to other serialised dimensions of his three films. Deflecting a political reading of his tendency to return to declining eras, Stillman has insisted to one interviewer that, 'I just like pining for lost times . . . I can pine for this morning' (Murray 2006). The drive to repeat is here rendered as an accidental, rather than functional, approach to authorial remaking. The comment typifies how Stillman as auteur is ever-present on the *surface* of the text, where his double voicing specifies only that he, like his characters, is 'not entirely joking'.

Hal Hartley

For a number of commentators, framing Hartley's body of work in terms of serialisation is a way of consolidating his position in the auteurist 1990s American Independent movement. Geoff Andrew reads each of Hartley's films up to and including *Henry Fool* as part of a larger work in progress, where Hartley reworks his material in an effort to find fresh ways of looking at the subjects that obsess him (1999: 281). Similarly, Emanuel Levy understands each film as part of an ongoing process in search of a better understanding of the way we live (1999: 192). For both critics, this idiosyncratic 'process' exemplifies Hartley as a singular and somewhat mysterious creator: Andrew suggests that Hartley's work best embodies the spirit of contemporary independent filmmaking in America because his work is so far removed from the conventional genres as to be best understood as a genre unto itself (1999: 279). As already suggested in the discussion of Hartley's formal and thematic consistencies, this 'genre' is primarily distinguished by the deadpan, erratic approach taken in his filmmaking, and also by a regular cast of actors including Martin Donovan, Robert Burke, Bill Sage, Karen Sillas, Elina Löwensohn and Parker Posey. As discussed in relation to Stillman, the serialisation perceived in such dimensions is harnessed by these critics to demonstrate how Hartley calls a new model into existence. For other observers, the serialisation is read in more

Figure 3   Adrienne Shelly, Martin Donovan and Edie Falco in *Trust* (Hal Hartley, 1990). Courtesy Zenith/True Fiction / The Kobal Collection.

condemnatory terms. Ryan Gilbey acknowledges that the themes, actors and formal components repeated across *The Unbelievable Truth, Trust, Simple Men, Surviving Desire, Amateur* and *Flirt* position Hartley as an auteur, but discerns limited progress in this early (pre-*Henry Fool*) body of work, arguing how, for example, 'the struggle to forge an identity in the shadow of oppressive or infamous parents depicted in *Trust* and *Simple Men* became in *Amateur* simply the struggle to forge an identity' (1998: 8).

Despite the noted continuity across all of Hartley's films, it is the first three features – *The Unbelievable Truth, Trust* and *Simple Men* – that stand apart as an obvious textual trilogy, with their repeat use of the same actors as similar characters, their Long Island settings, and their overwhelming concern with family life as a 'bleakly unappealing prospect' (Andrew 1999: 290). It is generally understood that *Amateur* marks a departure in Hartley's career, in the way that its 'thriller' narrative makes some concession to genre filmmaking (Macnab 1997: 48), and in the way that Isabelle Huppert, unlike Hartley's regular cast of actors, brings star baggage from outside his typically hermetic world (Gilbey 1998: 8). The next film, *Flirt*, is positioned as the most academic and experimental of all the films. *Flirt's* explicit serialisation – depicting the same miniaturist relationship scenario three times across three different cities and casts of players – is again read by Hartley's auteurist commentators in terms of a personal vision: 'repetition has always been a feature of his work, but here it lies at the very heart of the film' (Andrew 1999: 304).

This condensation of Hartley's formal concern with repetition, though, functions as more than a dimension of auteurist style. As a self-contained trilogy, *Flirt* is a striking piece of choreography, but its serialisation maintains a certain distance from its own achievement. The (almost) exact repetition of the story throws Hartley's direction into stark relief as, after the first sequence, the viewer is watching for his execution rather than for content. As at least one review of the film notes, 'part of the pleasure in *Flirt* lies in waiting to see how a line you have already heard will be inflected, or what new backdrop Hartley will provide for a certain scene' (Macnab 1997: 48). In this way, the repetition in *Flirt* is the register through which Hartley 'double-voices' as auteur: the formal exercise showcases his idiosyncratic talent as a director, but ironises this by giving the viewer, in a sense, *only* this 'talent' to look at in the (second) Berlin and (third) Tokyo sequences.

Hartley makes the link between serialisation and auteurism that can be perceived in a general way here explicit in the 'construction' scene of the Berlin story. In each section of the film, the 'flirt' character – Bill (Bill Sage) in New York, Dwight (Dwight Ewell) in Berlin and Miho (Miho Nikaidoh) in Tokyo – asks for advice on their relationship scenario from a group of three anonymous characters. In New York Bill confronts a group of three men in a public toilet, in Berlin Dwight turns to a group of construction workers, and in Tokyo, Miho explains her situation to three women she is briefly imprisoned with for possession of a gun. In the first and third sequences of the trilogy the exchange is restricted to the diegetic world, and the anonymous characters offer their differential stances on the proper moral meaning of the romantic bind.[31] In the second sequence, the construction workers extend their discussion to the exercise of *Flirt* itself, referring back to the previous sequence and laying bare the directorial challenge of '[comparing] the changing dynamics of the same situation in different milieus'. The film's contained trilogy structure is here positioned as a process with which to decide a formal problem, namely whether or not a person's milieu *does* change the dynamics of a situation.

It is possible to understand *Flirt* primarily in terms of this problem, as a serious examination of Hartley's key concerns with identity and culture. In this understanding, the film's serialisation is a dimension of classical auteurism, from the position of both Hartley's desire and that of his commentators. However, the context of self-awareness that the trilogy's bare repetition gestures toward, crystallised within the construction scene, necessarily complicates this interpretation. For one thing, the model of the contained trilogy actively undermines the delineation of a clear moral vision. Each sequence concludes the common romantic scenario slightly differently, and never with any real clarity or resolution. Each sequence feels like a contained short film, and operates according to the codes of narrative and resolution typically found in this Hartley-favoured form. The viewer's expectation of these codes is well described by Geoffrey Macnab in an allusion to Chekhov's observation that, in a short story, you don't have to solve your characters' problems but merely state them correctly (1997: 48). *Flirt's* juxtaposition of the three short films 'solves' neither the diegetic romantic problem central to each nor the formal problem of the exercise itself regarding differing cultural milieus. Indeed, the express significance of the repetitive structure seems to be an active avoidance of conclusion or correctness in an attempt to merely *state* three possible configurations of the same event.[32] The trilogy form is drawn upon here not to build – or perceive – a coherent world view but, precisely, to argue for the impossibility of such a thing; something jokingly (perhaps) referred to in the self-reflexive scene when one of the builders asserts that 'the filmmaker' will fail in his project: 'he has already failed. But, in this case, the failure is interesting.'

It is as this 'interesting failure' that *Flirt* best exemplifies the role of serialisation and repetition in smart authorship. The functional role of serialisation that has been discursively conceived in relation to the European art cinema is evoked, but simultaneously commented upon. In *Flirt*, Hartley frames himself as auteur; he makes transparent both his own intention (desire) in terms of the formal exercise of the film, and the desire of his critics (auteurists) to perceive a particular worldview in his work. At the second level, *Flirt* works – in part – as a tongue-in-cheek rebuttal to those critics who accuse Hartley of repeating himself. At the first level, it is an academic exercise that admits, as Hartley has stated, that 'subject matter is not important to me . . . it is the quality of attention that is important' (Macnab 1997: 48). In this endeavour, *Flirt* recalls an acknowledged influence on Hartley – Jean-Luc Godard.

As a singular figure, Godard anticipates the complication of classical and 'new' auteurism as it is delineated in the international art cinema, and it is in Hartley's work that this connection is clearest. Despite the role that some of the French New Wave figures played in inaugurating classical auteurism as a theory, Godard's films tend to debunk the process by providing an up-front narration of the vision that the auteurist is supposed to 'find'. Unsurprisingly, Hartley and Godard are most often likened on account of the formal quality of their films, where an interest in camerawork, sound and performance pushes to the fore over narrative or subject matter. In 1994, Hartley interviewed Godard for *Filmmaker* and the introduction to the piece suggests Godard's 'slapstick, critical, and more often than not, adoring relation to images' as the dimension that most clearly 'shows the way' for Hartley (Bowen 1994: 14). A specific instance often attended to is Hartley's habit – more obvious in the earlier work – of freezing the onward movement of narrative with a dance sequence; a stylistic trait that is specifically attributed to *Bande à Part* (1964). In *Flirt*, the serial form freezes the narrative in a not dissimilar way, and provides an arena for the investigation – and re-investigation – of a formal problem. The function of the three scenarios, though, is experimental and not cumulative: rather than establishing an answer and a clear moral vision, the form delivers three inconclusive perspectives. The trilogy here works to mobilise one of Godard's much-quoted axioms: 'not a correct image, just an image' (*Pas une image juste, juste une image*). In line with Deleuze's take-up of the line, Hartley draws on the form to *question* rather than verify, where his authorship itself is the thing in question.[33]

SERIALISATION AND SYNCHRONICITY

Outside of the specific projects of these two directors, the stance on serialisation evident in Stillman and Hartley's tripartite works is a defining quality of the broader smart cycle's reflexive sensibility. Much of the motivation for the critical identification of the cycle's directors as contemporary American auteurs comes down to the way they all demonstrate significant thematic and formal repetition across their films. As suggested, though, it is the awareness and, in some cases, conscious dissimulation of this signature that makes up the cycle's particular take on auteurism itself. The approach that discursively constructs, for example, *Rushmore*, *Bottle Rocket*, and *The Royal Tenenbaums* as a (non-sequential) trilogy dealing with age and its progressive emotion[34] is qualified both by Anderson's subtle acknowledgement of his traits (apparent in places like the repeat cover art, done by his brother Eric, for the Criterion Collection DVD release of his films) and his open send-up of them (the American Express commercial). This acknowledgement of serialised concerns manifests in various ways across and outside of the films themselves, from Solondz opening *Palindromes* with the funeral of his earlier character Dawn Weiner from *Welcome to the Dollhouse*,[35] and later directly following up the characters from *Happiness* in *Life During Wartime* (2009), to Coppola claiming that *The Virgin Suicides*, *Lost in Translation* and *Marie Antoinette* 'do form a trilogy, even if I did not intend it',[36] to LaBute's theatre work, where *The Shape of Things* (2001), *Fat Pig* (2004) and *Reasons to Be Pretty* (2008) form their own trilogy, to Hartley's ten-years-later continuation of *Henry Fool* in *Fay Grim* (2006).

In his own description of the smart sensibility, Sconce couches this broad tendency toward repetition and serialisation in specific textual terms, as a dimension of the smart film's interest in synchronicity as a principle of narrative organisation. In a move again demonstrating the elasticity of the smart delineation, he refers beyond his core group of films and directors to another potentially 'adjunct' figure – Jim Jarmusch – and to Tom Tykwer who, as described, Elsaesser includes in the 'international art cinema' group. For Sconce, the simultaneous global taxi rides of *Night on Earth* (Jim Jarmusch, 1991), along with the repeated gallery scenes from *Your Friends and Neighbors* each 'draw attention to the synchronicities of their characters in time and space', while the tripartite structure of *Mystery Train* (Jim Jarmusch, 1989) and *Run Lola Run* foreground the fates of synchronicity as a formal and thematic strategy and *Donnie Darko's* time-loop strategy muses on the synchronicity of the universe (2002: 363). Appearing after Sconce's article, *Palindromes* is another film to include in this structurally synchronous group, with its eight different 'versions' of the character of Aviva all existing on the one narrative continuum.[37] In a broader capacity again, the 'ensemble' or 'network' narrative that will be discussed in Chapter 5 as a form especially typical of the suburban smart film also foregrounds the synchronicity of characters in time and space. For Sconce, the aspect of synchronicity relates directly to the smart film's interest in coincidence and 'the fundamentally random yet strangely meaningful structure of reality' (363) – an interest which, as described in the Introduction, he reads in terms of a shift away from the structuring 'search for meaning' in modernist art cinema toward a more listless and fatalistic sensibility.

The type of synchronicity Sconce is interested in is demonstrated in the Stillman triptych and in *Flirt* by way of explicit textual links – Ted from *Barcelona* appearing in-character in *The Last Days of Disco*, the builders in Hartley's construction scene likening the film's second scenario to the first – and by the broader patterns of thematic and structural repetition described that draw attention to a larger dramatic scenario. As suggested, though, the dimension of synchronicity is evoked in the films not to foreground how protagonists are acted upon by forces beyond their control – as it is in *The Sweet Hereafter*, *The Ice Storm*, *Donnie Darko* and *Magnolia* – but as a framework for the investigation of a situation (the 'UHB' set) or a formal problem (the influence of different cultural milieus) that announces itself as a directorial challenge. In the smart cycle, the links between serialisation, synchronicity and a type of self-aware auteurism that has been traced in these 'adjunct' figures finds its most unambiguous expression in the films written by Charlie Kaufman and directed by Spike Jonze and Michel Gondry: *Being John Malkovich*, *Human Nature*, *Adaptation*, and *Eternal Sunshine of the Spotless Mind*. Here, contained patterns of textual synchronicity open onto broader labyrinthine narrative structures that point not only to the concurrence of diegetic characters but to that of the films and their creation. As a partial result of the films' thematic satire of popular psychology, the strategy, which feels like a modernist exercise in *Flirt*, takes on a distinctly 'post-pop' sensibility (Mayshark 2007).

CHARLIE KAUFMAN, SPIKE JONZE, MICHEL GONDRY

These four films are read as a critical series on account of their common interest in the nature of reality and identity and their elaborate treatment of filmic time and space. Chris Norris describes the films as 'mind games' that we enter 'as if waiting for a dose of psilocybin to kick in: antennae up, alert to hidden patterns, warped inventions, alterations of expected reality' (2002: 20). In *Being John Malkovich* and *Eternal Sunshine of the Spotless Mind*, the thematic and formal concerns dovetail into literal 'adventures of . . . the brain', where the mind is used as a location in which to play out narrative. For Jesse Fox Mayshark, the cerebral orientation is existential: he argues that the films' questions about 'who we are and how we got that way' are all 'quests for transcendence of one kind of another – via love in *Eternal Sunshine*, art in *Adaptation*, science in *Human Nature* and, well, John Malkovich in *Being John Malkovich* – and the ways that those quests are invariably flawed and frustrated' (2007: 141). Again, these broadly serialised concerns are supported by specific textual instances of repetition and synchronicity: when, for instance, Craig Schwartz's (John Cusack) Heloise and Abelard puppet show in *Being John Malkovich* anticipates the title of *Eternal Sunshine of the Spotless Mind* (channelling a general concern with the plight of tortured lovers) or when, more openly, the making of *Being John Malkovich* is opened up as a parallel event to Charlie Kaufman's (Nicholas Cage) own adaptation in *Adaptation*, and Charlie's brother Donald (also Nicholas Cage) begins dating Caroline (Maggie Gyllenhaal), the make-up artist working on the earlier film.

The films confound classical auteurism in the first instance insofar as the signature concerns traced are largely based on Kaufman's scripts rather than on the direction of either Gondry or Jonze. Analyses such as Mayshark's are evidence of his own point that it has become common to talk about 'a Charlie Kaufman film' in the auteurist manner usually reserved for directors (2007: 137). As such, each director's formal execution of Kaufman's ideas tends to be received in atypically collaborative terms. The styles of Gondry and Jonze are generally distinguished along the lines suggested by Mayshark – 'Jonze is cooler and grittier, Gondry is warmer and dreamier' (138) – but each of the four collaborations with Kaufman demonstrate a common 'lo-fi' aesthetic, where low-key, analogue effects based on lighting, set changes and camera placement merge the fantastic and the monotonous. It is on the basis of this low-key approach to the extraordinary that Sconce includes *Being John Malkovich* in his core list of smart films, where, along with *Donnie Darko*, it is described as 'matter-of-fact surrealism' (2002: 350). For commentators such as Mayshark and Norris, this 'lo-fi' style is peculiar to the Kaufman/Gondry/Jonze unit itself.[38]

Another key dimension of the auteurist unit's style is a system of narrative re-framing that continually and abruptly pulls back from the patterns of understanding and identification set up between film and viewer. This approach provides an ongoing reinvention of the film's premise by incessantly transforming the temporal and spatial relationships between characters, as well as

Figure 4   Nicolas Cage and Meryl Streep in *Adaptation* (Spike Jonze, 2002). Courtesy Columbia Pictures / The Kobal Collection / Ben Kaller.

the viewer's relationship to the film. In the first, third and fourth films a story event clearly triggers this transformative process: in *Being John Malkovich*, the discovery of the portal into Malkovich's brain, in *Adaptation*, Charlie writing himself into his screen adaptation of Susan Orlean's book *The Orchid Thief* and in *Eternal Sunshine of the Spotless Mind*, Joel's memory erasure by Lacuna Inc. In each instance, the event is a platform for the free movement of the story between different spatial locations and temporal periods: for instance, between Craig's office block and wherever John Malkovich happens to be when someone goes through the portal in *Being John Malkovich*, or between Joel's apartment and the kitchen of his childhood home in *Eternal Sunshine*, when he and Clementine 'escape' into one of his early memories. In all the films, the impossible movement foregrounds how filmmaking itself is a construction of time and space. *Adaptation* makes the reflexive motif most overt by synchronising its narrative with Kaufman's own adaptation of Orlean's real life book: the character of Charlie Kaufman writing himself into his screenplay is contained by the real Charlie Kaufman writing himself into the screenplay of the Jonze-directed *Adaptation*. The effect of infinite regress finds its third expression when *Adaptation* itself coalesces with the film that the character Charlie writes himself into, and the hyperbolic Hollywood ending – gun fight, car chase, crocodile attack, romantic reconciliation, Charlie learning profound 'life lesson' – visualises the screenplay that Charlie presumably writes after consulting with famed screen-writer Robert Mckee and having his initial minimalist intentions for the adaptation quashed. By the end of *Adaptation*, the two versions of the adaptation of *The Orchid Thief* – Kaufman/Jonze's and 'Charlie's' – synch perfectly into one.

The *mise-en-abyme* effect produced by this narrative structure dissimulates authorial sincerity by literally revealing the fictional creation of the 'action' being watched. At this level, *Adaptation* can be understood in terms of a type of broad meta-genericity that identifies all filmmaking as an effect of its own vocabulary. Jim Collins has described how contemporary genericity recognises that any sincere generic impulse necessarily relies on other forms of generic representation in order to 'work' and, as such, operates with an acute awareness of how these traditions are circulated and received (1993: 248). Collins suggests that the 'action' of genre films such as *Thelma and Louise* (Ridley Scott, 1991) and *Batman* (Tim Burton, 1989) – and more recent and overt examples would include Wes Craven's Scream films (1996; 1997; 2000; 2011), Deborah Kaplan and Harry Elfont's *Josie and the Pussycats* (2001) and Shane Black's *Kiss Kiss Bang Bang* (2005) – is doubled: it describes both the character's adventures in the narrative, and the text's encounters with the semiotic array of contemporary cultural production (254). In focusing its narrative on its own construction, *Adaptation* taps into this meta-generic trend by announcing itself – and, by extension, all filmmaking – as a 'trick' on the audience. The tradition it foregrounds in this, though, is not genre but authorship – the perception of visionary, sincere filmmaking. By focusing on a character who wants to make a film that is not 'artificially plot-driven', Kaufman frames his own script as a meditation on what it feels like to be a screenwriter in this meta-generic climate.

Kent Jones has suggested that the film's creation of a freefall through narrative space is not so much an evocation of the idea that 'nothing is what it seems' as a dramatisation of the process of adaptation as the constant mutation between people and things (2002: 25). Beyond this, Kaufman's script can be understood as his own adaptation to a mass cultural situation where the irony of meta-genericity has become stable. As Rombes writes, 'Kaufman recognises that it is no longer a trick or a post-modern stunt to tell a serious story while, at the same time, telling the story of how that story was made' (2005: 80). By making himself the character who is struggling to create a 'sincere' adaptation of *The Orchid Thief*, Kaufman destabilises audience comfort with meta-generic self-reflexivity in a performative way: he structures *Adaptation* around emotional reversals that quickly follow moments of affective sincerity with narrative re-framings that make viewers question their emotional attachment to these characters. As Rombes notes, the result is that viewers become caught up enough in the story to be genuinely unsure whether the hyperbolic ending is ironic or something they are really meant to care about, despite the effort the film has gone to in elaborating the hollowness of all filmmaking, and Hollywood action films in particular (2005b: 79). In an interrogation of the stability of 'eclectic irony', *Adaptation* doesn't just disturb the transparent or 'said' meaning of film by showing its 'unsaid', but reverses this and disturbs our understanding of this 'unsaid' in turn. Susan Orlean has described Kaufman's screenplay as being about the ongoing, exasperating battle between looking at the world ironically and looking at it sentimentally' (quoted in Rombes 2005b: 78). The 'smart signature' that this battle gives rise to can be understood in literally dissimulative terms: as the ongoing negotiation between a climate of eclectic irony and the desire to say something sincerely.

At the beginning of his book on Joel and Ethan Coen, R. Barton Palmer articulates the attitude of unease alluded to at the outset of this chapter as the auteurist's necessary confrontation of the 'uncomfortable fact' that their approach is rather out of fashion (2004: 1). As Palmer goes on to describe, this confrontation has occurred on a broad scale as a transformation in the understanding of auteurism itself, which is no longer imagined as speaking an uncomplicated truth but as 'a shorthand method for explaining how films come to be what they are and come to say what they seem to say'. This chapter has drawn on such an understanding of authorship as a way of examining the dimensions of serialisation, synchronicity and self-reflexivity that in part define the smart sensibility. It has proposed that these effects are symptoms of the directors' awareness of both classical and commercial auteurism, and thereby function as part of the broad transformation in the concept itself. Palmer suggests that the Coens present a 'strange' situation insofar as the films strongly announce their authorship by way of their stylisation and conscious quotation of generic conventions, but the directors themselves occupy an 'anti-authorial position' in the industry by avoiding the brand of publicity that has made auteur-stars out of directors such as Steven Spielberg and Quentin Tarantino (2).

The three American auteurs closely discussed here have also avoided being constructed as 'personalities' for the strategic organisation of audience reception: Stillman and Hartley are highly reserved in their relationship to public life and the collaborative projects of Kaufman, Gondry and Jonze seem specifically designed to deflect the notion of a singular, bankable identity. As with the Coens, though, the films of these writer/directors all announce their authorship by way of their obvious stylisation, as well as in specific moments of textual self-reflexivity that conjure the tradition of auteur cinema. This chapter has argued that it is *in* this stylisation, and in particular in the reliance on the dimension of serialisation, that the ongoing formal and thematic concerns that find them discursively constructed as auteurs in the classical sense are acknowledged. This announcement materialises as an attempt to qualify the 'personalities' that emerge from their work. It is not an anti-authorial, self-effacing technique that puts everything they say in quotation marks and, as in the meta-generic tradition, determines a stable unsaid meaning, but an attempt to do the exact opposite: to pluralise and intensify what *is* said in a positive narrativisation of auteurism itself.

NOTES

1. Some sections of this chapter were originally published as 'Remaking and the Film Trilogy: Whit Stillman's Authorial Triptych', by Claire Perkins, in *Velvet Light Trap* 61, pp. 14–25. Copyright © 2008 by the University of Texas Press. All rights reserved.
2. A good overview of film studies' response to structuralist and poststructuralist challenges toward authorship can be found in David A. Gerstner and Janet Staiger's introductions to *Authorship and Film*.
3. A close examination of the new films reviewed in *Sight and Sound* between January 2002 and December 2006 discovers only two examples of films that can be approached as 'direct' sequels that don't acknowledge their predecessor in their title: *Russian Dolls* (Cedric Klapisch, 2005; *The Spanish Apartment*, 2002) and *The Devil's Rejects* (Rob Zombie, 2005; *House of 1000 Corpses*, 2003).
4. See Carolyn Jess-Cooke *Film Sequels* (2008) and Jess-Cooke and Constantine Verevis, *Second Takes: Critical Approaches to the Film Sequel* (2009).
5. Even the early taxonomic surveys whose usefulness is questioned by contemporary theorists admitted a significant degree of flexibility to the concept 'remake' that is still not accorded to that of the 'sequel'. For instance, Michael Druxman's 1975 survey *Make It Again, Sam: A Survey of Movie Remakes* stipulates three general categories of remaking specific to pre-1975 Hollywood: 1. the *disguised* remake, in which a new film does not draw attention to its earlier version; 2. the *direct* remake, in which a new film makes some alterations to an original property but does not hide the fact that it is based on an earlier production; 3. the *non*-remake, in which a new film creates an entirely new plot but goes under the same title as an original property (13–15).
6. *The Fast and the Furious* (Rob Cohen, 2001), *2 Fast 2 Furious* (John Singleton, 2003), *The Fast and the Furious: Tokyo Drift* (Justin Lin, 2006), *Fast & Furious* (Justin Lin, 2009), *Fast Five* (Justin Lin, 2011).
7. *X-Men* (Bryan Singer, 2000), *X2* (Bryan Singer, 2003), *X-Men: The Last Stand* (Brett Ratner, 2006), *X-Men Origins: Wolverine* (Gavin Hood, 2009).
8. *Pirates of the Caribbean: The Curse of the Black Pearl* (Gore Verbinski, 2003), *Pirates of the Caribbean: Dead Man's Chest* (Gore Verbinski, 2006), *Pirates of the Caribbean: At World's End* (Gore Verbinski, 2007), *Pirates of the Caribbean: On Stranger Tides* (Rob Marshall, 2011).
9. *Spider-Man* (Sam Raimi, 2002), *Spider-Man 2* (Sam Raimi, 2004), *Spider-Man 3* (Sam Raimi, 2007), *The Amazing Spider-Man* (Marc Webb, 2012).
10. All directed by Peter Jackson – *Lord of the Rings: The Fellowship of the Ring* (2001); *Lord of the Rings: The Two Towers* (2002); *Lord of the Rings: The Return of the King* (2003).
11. All directed by Andy and Larry Wachowski – *The Matrix* (1999); *The Matrix: Reloaded* (2003); *The Matrix: Revolutions* (2003).
12. *Star Wars* (1977); *Star Wars: The Empire Strikes Back* (1980); *Star Wars: Return of the Jedi* (1983); *Star Wars Episode I: The Phantom Menace* (1999); *Star Wars Episode II: Attack of the Clones* (2002); *Star Wars Episode III: Revenge of the Sith* (2005).

13. In some cases this recognition does actually determine the form initially. Theo Angelopoulos' trilogy-in-progress – *Trilogy: The Weeping Meadow* (2004); *Trilogy 2: The Dust of Time* (2007); *Trilogy 3: Return* (forthcoming) – provides such an example, destined as it is to chart the history of Greece from the early years of the last century to the present (see Roddick 2005).
14. *Pusher* (1996); *With Blood On My Hands: Pusher II* (2004); *I'm the Angel of Death: Pusher III* (2005).
15. *Khane-je doust kodjast* (*Where is the Friend's House?* 1987); *Zendegi va digar hich* (*And Life Goes On . . .* 1991) and *Zire darakhatan zayton* (*Through the Olive Trees*, 1994).
16. Jonathan Romney's article on Ceylan, for example, describes how 'the path from *Kasaba* to *Uzak* reveals a filmmaker whose register is subtly expanding, with a melancholic moral perspective, a sharp, understated wit and a keen eye for the revealing, ostensibly empty moments of everyday living' (Romney 2004).
17. See http://www.impawards.com/2005/manderlay Accessed January 5, 2007.
18. See, for instance, J. Hoberman's interview with Refn (Hoberman 2004).
19. Amy Taubin writes: 'There are familiar Van Sant elements – adolescent anxieties, androgynous boys, a looping, nonlinear narrative – but *Paranoid Park* differs from the director's three previous films (sometimes referred to as "the Death trilogy") in that its structure is not a formal device imposed from the outside but rather springs from the boy's consciousness, evoking both a typical adolescent's fragmented attention span and the evasions and fixations of a nice kid whose life has spun out of control' (2007: 55). See also Peranson 2007.
20. Examples of the delineation of these groups of films as 'trilogies' or critical series can be found in much of the writing that locates these directors as central to the European Art Cinema. See, for instance, Ian Cameron and Robin Wood's *Antonioni*; Robin Wood's *Ingmar Bergman*; Don Allen's *François Truffaut*; Peter Brunette's *Roberto Rossellini* and Ruth Ben-Ghiat's chapter on Roberto Rossellini's 'Fascist War Trilogy'. Sam Rohdie alludes briefly to the discursive process itself in his *Antonioni* as part of a description of how Antonioni's work was appreciated in the 1950s (1990: 2) and, as Elsaesser notes in his 'Putting on a Show' piece, Bergman qualifies his original endorsement of *Through a Glass Darkly*, *Winter Light* and *The Silence* as a trilogy in the preface to Vilgot Sjöman's *Diary with Ingmar Bergman* in *Images – My Life in Film* by describing it as a 'rationalization after the fact': 'the "trilogy" has neither rhyme nor reason. It was a Schnapps-Idee, as the Bavarians say, meaning that it's an idea found at the bottom of a glass of alcohol' (Bergman quoted in Elsaesser 1994: 25).
21. See Nicholas Rombes, 'Sincerity and Irony' for a detailed discussion of Dogma and irony.
22. For a description of Jonze's early directorial projects see Mayshark 2007: 138–9.
23. The commercial, performed on the set of a fictional Anderson film, includes a character called 'François' and uses the score from *La Nuit Américain* (1973), Truffaut's own film about filmmaking.
24. With regard to the smart cycle, this style of commentary is generally typical of the recent work that includes the films in the context of a larger 'American independent' or 'Sundance' movement. See Mottram 2006, Geoff King, Andrew 1999, Levy 1999.
25. On this authorial awareness in relation to Wes Anderson, see Devin Orgeron's 'La Camera-Crayola: Authorship Comes of Age in the Cinema of Wes Anderson' (2007).
26. After a thirteen year absence, Stillman's *Damsels in Distress* is planned for a 2011 release: http://blogs.indiewire.com/theplaylist/archives/first_look_at_whit_stillmans_damsels_in_distress_starring_greta_gerwig_adam/

27. Stillman is reported to have been attempting to adapt Christopher Buckley's *Little Green Men* and secure funding for a Jamaican music project titled *Dancing Mood*: http://theplaylist.blogspot.com/2010/06/whit-stillmans-new-project-damels-in.html
28. See, for instance, Levy 1999: 194, Andrew 1999: 281–2 and Gilbey 1998.
29. On this strategy, Stillman mentions British writer Thomas Love Peacock, 'where every character is a point of view. And [*The Last Days of Disco*] is trying to be a naturalistic real-world view of something like that' (quoted in Pincus 1998).
30. See, for instance, Graham Fuller's introduction to the Faber screenplays of *Barcelona* and *Metropolitan* or Nichols, 'Whit Stillman's Comic Art' (2000).
31. Hartley's self-conscious Socratic style here is similar to that which Stillman uses on a broader scale.
32. The same understanding could be applied to the film that is structurally and contemporaneously most comparable to *Flirt*: Tykwer's *Run Lola Run*.
33. See Deleuze in 'Three Questions about *Six Fois Deux*': 'Godard has a beautiful axiom: Not a correct image, just an image. Philosophers, too, should say it, and find some way to act on it: not correct ideas, just ideas. Because correct ideas are always ideas that conform to dominant meanings or established passwords; they're always ideas that verify something, even if this something is yet to come, even if it is the future of the revolution. Whereas "just ideas" are a becoming-present, a stammering in one's ideas that can only be expressed in the form of questions, which tend rather to silence their answers, or else to show something simple, which shatters all the proofs' (1992: 35).
34. See Rumsey Taylor, 'Wes Anderson's Tragic Comedy' (2004).
35. The *Sight and Sound* review of *Palindromes* describes it as 'a sort-of sequel to *Welcome to the Dollhouse*, opening with the funeral of that film's protagonist Dawn Wiener and featuring Dawn's brother Mark, again played by Matthew Faber' (Rayns 2005: 74).
36. See Siegfried Morkowitz, 'Sofia Coppola's *Marie Antoinette* rocks Cannes festival' (2006).
37. In narrative order, 'Aviva' is played by Emani Sledge, Valerie Shusterov, Hannah Freiman, Rachel Corr, Will Denton, Sharon Wilkins, Shayna Levine and Jennifer Jason Leigh.
38. This view is supported by the critical reception of Kaufman's directorial debut, *Synecdoche, New York* (2008), where it is the nihilism and despair of the work that is generally emphasised. See, for instance, Norris' *Film Comment* review: 'the epiphanies . . . are brutal – far from the life and love-affirming sentiments of *Adaptation* and *Eternal Sunshine*' (Norris 2008).

2. NARRATIVE: *THE SQUID AND THE WHALE, THE SAFETY OF OBJECTS, PALINDROMES*[1]

Hollywood Renaissances

In his introduction to a collection of essays originally written for a retrospective of 1970s American films at the 1995 Vienna Film Festival, Alexander Horwath claims that 'if you have come of age as a cinema-goer during the heyday of New Hollywood cinema – sometime between *Bonnie and Clyde* and *Taxi Driver* – you've probably experienced the main brands of post-1970s American cinema by necessity as less rich, less intelligent, less political, as retrograde' (2004: 9). Horwath here typifies the widely held position that regards the birth of the New Hollywood in the late 1960s and early 1970s as a 'Renaissance' in American filmmaking. As expressed by theorists including Noel King and Thomas Elsaesser, this critical position understands the historical period as 'a brief window of opportunity when an adventurous new cinema emerged, linking the traditions of classical Hollywood genre filmmaking with the stylistic innovations of European art cinema' (King 2004: 91). Generally regarded as an interim between the decline of the Old Hollywood studio system and the reassertion of a similarly conservative system enabled by a new formulaic blockbuster form, the Hollywood Renaissance is approached as a unique time by its supporters in that its dissident ethos was underwritten by a Hollywood keen to hit upon a new formula for success. As associated with directors including Arthur Penn, Robert Altman, Monte Hellman and Peter Bogdanovich, the cinema described by Andrew Sarris as one of 'alienation, anomie, anarchy and absurdism' (quoted in King 2004: 20) represented not just a change in filmmaking, but a radical transformation of *commercial* filmmaking.

Insofar as it understands this era as a type of finite Golden Age, there is an unmistakably pessimistic undertone to the Renaissance position. Steve Neale has challenged its dominance in discourse on contemporary American cinema, arguing that it produces 'a partial and misleading picture' of history (Neale 2006: 91). Citing the box office success of musicals (*Funny Girl*, William Wyler, 1968) war films (*Tora! Tora! Tora!* Richard Fleischer/ Kinji Fukasaku, 1970) and family-oriented films (*The Jungle Book*, Roman Davidov, 1967) during the late 1960s and early 1970s alongside films such as *Bonnie and Clyde* (Arthur Penn, 1967) and *M*A*S*H* (Robert Altman, 1970), Neale contests the perception that audiences were solely endorsing the violent and formally innovative Renaissance films. Further, he attempts to diffuse the view that this era marked a revolutionary break with traditional ideological values by looking back to the breaches generally acknowledged to have been made by earlier American films such as *Anatomy of a Murder* (Otto Preminger, 1959) and *Psycho* (Alfred Hitchcock, 1960) (2006: 106–7). In this way, Neale combats the culturally pessimistic perception of the Renaissance as a finite and singular impulse. A perspective that looks forward for evidence of the impulse in later American cinema can support this challenge.

The books by Biskind, Waxman and Mottram referred to in the Introduction all echo the enthusiastic claims of the Renaissance theorists in their discussion of the changes in Hollywood during the 1990s and the emergence of a critically and popularly successful commercial/independent strain of 1990s American cinema. Biskind openly describes his account of this period as 'a sequel, of sorts, to *Easy Riders, Raging Bulls*, my history of that exuberant, fecund decade, the 1970s, that gave us the so-called New Hollywood' (2004: 1). For Biskind, the key aspect of the 1970s legacy is the emergence of many of the directors here linked to the smart cycle – Wes Anderson, Spike Jonze, Paul Thomas Anderson, Alexander Payne, David O. Russell – as 'a loose collection of spiritual and aesthetic heirs'. Mottram opens his book similarly, describing the 'Pizza Knights' – a monthly film group comprised of a representative sample of these directors – as the 'spiritual descendents of the so-called maverick filmmakers of 1970s Hollywood' (2006: xv), and claiming that his book centres on the question: 'are we returning to an age where formerly independent directors are using studio funds to further their own idiosyncratic vision? In other words, is this the dawn of New Hollywood Part II?' And, in the piece already quoted, Horwath suggests that 'during the past fifteen years many of the (few) important American films still had their reference points . . . in the culture of the Seventies' (2004: 10). Supporting this, he gestures to a handful of these directors – Paul Thomas Anderson, Wes Anderson, Richard Linklater

– along with some cross-overs from the earlier generation – Robert Altman, Martin Scorsese, John Sayles.

The concept of sequelisation that Biskind and Mottram elaborate is largely founded in industrial terms. Both – particularly Biskind – are essentially concerned with the position of these directors in relation to Hollywood, and in how they triggered a transformation of the 1980s studio model. Horwath, by contrast, is more interested in textual issues of transposition. The 'reference points' he refers to in the 1990s films include personnel, aesthetics and attitudes from the 1970s: it is New Hollywood as style and subject matter that, he argues, is still locatable in films made after 1977. Biskind and Mottram's sweep of contemporary directors is also necessarily broad, with a focus to the 'larger' figures – Quentin Tarantino, Steven Soderbergh, David Fincher – whose films have been at the forefront of the industrial transformations. As it has been described thus far, the smart sensibility can be identified in many but not all of the films Biskind and Mottram are interested in. Given its distinctive type of stylistic blankness and its interest in the politics of the white, middle-class American family, it is perhaps Wes Anderson and Todd Solondz who best demonstrate the sensibility – directors who are respectively passed over by Biskind and Mottram.[2] With an eye to Horwath's textual grasp of sequelisation, and in line with the discursive ideas of serialisation already introduced in Chapter 1, this section is concerned with the smart film as a narrower and imprecise tendency within the broad 'Sundance' generation upon which to trace interests sequelised – continued, transformed – from the 1960s and 1970s.

'The Pathos of Failure': Crisis 1

The historical and industrial emergence of New Hollywood cinema has been thoroughly documented by theorists including Thomas Schatz, Tino Balio and Jim Hillier, who describe the economic and social conditions that allowed the first films of this period to innovate in ways those of Old Hollywood could not.[3] What these authors also emphasise is the short-lived nature of this innovation: the Golden Age of American cinema is widely understood to draw to a close by the mid-1970s. Various commentators mark the specific point of closure with various films, but *Jaws* (Steven Spielberg, 1975) and *Star Wars* (George Lucas, 1977) are two productions commonly understood to signify how the complex and contradictory narratives and attitudes of the late 1960s and early 1970s are re-mythologised into discourses that stamp out all formal and political dissonance. For Horwath, the shift in popular cinema in the US marked by *Star Wars*' mythical and militant narrative mirrors the specific modes of repression and displacement also evident in American public life from 1977 onwards (2004: 11). Schatz, from an industrial perspective, describes how the marketing and release strategies for *Jaws* revived and redefined Hollywood's blockbuster tradition (Schatz 1993: 80).

In both social and industrial accounts, however, it is film form and narrative that is referred to for the most tangible evidence of the shifts from Old Hollywood to New, and then to *New* New Hollywood, or the blockbuster image. The tone of cultural pessimism discernable in Horwath and King's discussions essentially comes down to an identification of the minimal challenge to classical form and narrative offered by films produced through mainstream channels after the mid-1970s. This is a position supported by the work of film form theorist David Bordwell, who argues that the 'intensified continuity' of closely framed and rapidly edited contemporary blockbuster form may represent a significant shift in filmmaking style but doesn't depart from classical principles. Classical continuity practices controlling action and screen space are not fragmented by blockbuster form but intensified: Bordwell argues that, with faster cutting and fewer establishing shots, practices securely linking cause and effect onscreen are called upon to be less ambiguous than ever (2002: 16). As such, one way to think the emergence and decline of the first New Hollywood films is to look at how mainstream American filmmaking witnesses, in this period, the respective waning and renewal of classical form and narrative, or of the classic American action-image.

Elsaesser's 1975 article 'The Pathos of Failure: American Films in the 1970s' gives what is still regarded as the definitive account of the transformations films such as *Two-Lane Blacktop* (Monte Hellman, 1971), *California Split* (Robert Altman, 1974) and *The Conversation* (Francis Ford Coppola, 1974) effected upon Hollywood filmmaking in the 1967–75 era. One of the most enduring aspects of Elsaesser's piece is the way in which his summation of the unmotivated heroes and direction-less journeys of these films anticipates what Gilles Deleuze describes as 'the crisis of the action-image' in his *Cinema 1: The Movement-Image*, published in France eight years later.[4] Although initially identifying signs of this crisis in the post-war American cinema that he describes as 'outside Hollywood' – films by Robert Altman, John Cassavetes, Martin Scorsese and Sidney Lumet – Deleuze ultimately locates the crisis in the 'freer' cinema of post-war Europe. In particular, he derives the logic and signs of the 'time-image' that the crisis gives rise to from a particular consciousness that he argues is specifically absent from American films, where the 'empty frame[s]' of the great genres of action-image cinema cannot be overcome (1986: 205–11).

In Deleuze's description, the time-image emerges in Italy around 1948, and then in France and Germany at progressive ten-year intervals. The cinema of these nations ushers in a modern image in the shape of different temporalities: the Neo-realist, New Wave and New German movements all register a shift in the relationship between movement and time. Time is no longer recouped by movement as something linear and chronological, but comes to the surface of the image in its own right, enveloping the situation and controlling its progression. The image of these new movements is not realist as it is no longer anchored by a strong sensory-motor schema: the situations of Visconti or Godard do not extend directly into action but possess a reality of their own. Primarily invested by the senses, this reality constitutes a pure optical and sound situation to which action is connected in an oneiric way. It is as if, writes Deleuze, 'action floats in the situation, rather than bringing it to a conclusion or strengthening it' (1989: 4).

Elsaesser sees a direct link between the New Hollywood films and the directors with whom Deleuze is principally concerned, identifying the malaise of this cinema as something familiar from 'cinematically self-conscious European directors' (2004: 279). As a key characteristic, the waning of physical action is interpreted as the result of a search for a new form of narrative free from 'the parasitic and synthetic causality of a dramaturgy of external conflict', the search 'for a mise-en-scène that can take a critical stance' (283). The new form arises from the way in which the conventional, external motif of the journey is complicated by the protagonist lacking a corresponding internal drive. Elsaesser comments on how, in *Two-Lane Blacktop*, the journey is introduced in an off-hand way – the potential goal of the race to Washington is '[toyed] with', inciting no real interest for either the characters or the film narrative. Intrigue is played down in other dimensions too; most notably in the way action avoids the potential conflict between the male characters over the single female. As Elsaesser notes, all the points at which the spectator could potentially become absorbed by a plot are played down, resulting in an 'anti-action' film. *Bonnie and Clyde* and *Badlands* (Terrence Malick, 1973) are structured around similarly itinerant journeys, where the criminal couples' goal of escape is neutralised by the implicit knowledge of their eventual capture. *The Conversation* – through the figure of Harry Caul (Gene Hackman) – provides what is perhaps the most adequate metaphor for the way in which these films forego the intrigue of conflict or suspense by emptying conventional suspenseful motifs of their dramatic interest: Caul's blank-faced approach to his audio surveillance work is to listen to the quality of the recording, and not the content of the conversation he records.

This lack of drive infiltrates practically all of the Renaissance films as a stylisation of despair or helplessness. Attitudes of obsession, guilt and anxiety recur across the various scenarios, emanating from figures who are neither psychologically nor emotionally motivated. Unlike the protagonists of classical Hollywood, these figures have no 'case to investigate . . . name to clear . . . woman (or man) to love [or] goal to reach' (Elsaesser 2004: 281). For Robert Kolker, it is loneliness that defines the era. The bitterness of a film such as *Night Moves* (Arthur Penn, 1975), he suggests, 'comes from anxiety rather than anger, from a loneliness that exists as a given, rather than a loneliness fought against . . .' (1980: 19). Tracing images of paranoia, isolation, oppression and claustrophobia in films including *The Parallax View* (Alan Pakula, 1974), *The Wild Bunch* (Sam Peckinpah, 1969) and *The Conversation*, Kolker describes the sixties and seventies as a type of *noir* revival, where these favourite themes of the 1940s cycle resurface after the more reassuring films of the 1950s. The emotional paralysis that permeates a film like *Night Moves* renders any attention to details of an investigative plot useless: 'the plotting becomes less important than the searching itself' (65).

Other commentators also attend to this formal and thematic paralysis. In his discussion of James Toback's *Fingers* (1978), Adrian Martin picks up on a connection to Hitchcock that Deleuze also sees in the Renaissance films,[5] and describes a 'realm of cinematic fiction centred on obsession rather than action' (2004a: 310). American films of the early 1970s are, for Martin, all about 'guys relentlessly pursuing some dream-ideal' in the form of a woman, a hallucination or a memory. The crisis of the action-image, in this interpretation, emerges from the way a melancholic male is placed at the centre of an action plot: again, the external motif of plot is disabled by the internal protagonist's obsessive personality, which makes action 'less and less possible' (312). In Jimmy, the protagonist of *Fingers*, Martin sees the dissolution of sensory-motor continuity incarnate. For Christian Keathley, the Renaissance films are an explicit response to Vietnam: he describes them as a 'post-traumatic' cycle that replays the war experience's defining realisation of powerlessness. Themes of disaffection, alienation and demoralisation encode the 'opening up of the interval between perception and action as a traumatic event' (2004: 296). The crisis of the action-image in these films is described for Keathley by the repeated fate whereby a character is left not dead, but wounded and powerless. The endings of both *Chinatown* (Roman Polanski, 1974) and *The Candidate* (Michael Ritchie, 1972) clearly represent the frozen state in which so many Renaissance figures are caught: between perception and action, or action and reaction; trapped, as Keathley describes it, 'in the affection-image'.

For Elsaesser, the rejection of personal motive in the 1960s/1970s cycle of American films, along with their liberal outlook and unsentimental approach to American society, reflect a larger ideological rejection. By 'essentially . . . manag[ing] to transform spatial and temporal sequence into consequence, into a continuum of cause and effect' (2004: 280), classical Hollywood form posits a fundamentally affirmative attitude to the world based upon faith in the value of positive action. Finding a loss of this confidence in the Renaissance films, Elsaesser also sees a larger rejection of purposive affirmation and moral pragmatism. Beyond issues of industrial similarity, it is the transposition of this textual and ideological effect to the contemporary smart film that is of interest here. As the model of 'realism' that the Renaissance films undermine, the

Figure 5   Al Pacino and Gene Hackman in *Scarecrow* (Jerry Schatzberg, 1973).
Courtesy Warner Bros / The Kobal Collection.

classical action-image is, for Deleuze, defined not by recourse to real events, but by a relationship between milieus and behaviour, or situation and action (1986: 141). The key point of continuity between the two cycles is that both put this particular model of realism under erasure, and thereby mark two disparate points in the breakdown of the American cinema as a universal and triumphant model.

Jerry Schatzberg's 1973 film *Scarecrow* is representative in many ways of the formal and thematic concerns of the Renaissance cycle. The film traces the journey of two drifters who meet in the opening scene while attempting to hitch a ride: Max (Gene Hackman) and Francis (Al Pacino). Max, who has just got out of prison, is initially hostile to Francis – whom he calls Lion, after his middle name, Lionel – but soon asks him to be his partner in a carwash business he is heading to Pittsburgh to set up. The film demonstrates the classic Renaissance journey in that this destination is vague and somewhat absurdly envisaged; it is the movement itself that is the dramatic focus, marked out by three understated narrative developments. The two visit Max's sister Coley (Dorothy Tristan) and, after getting into a fight while out with her and a friend one night, spend a brief time in prison. Upon release, they travel to Detroit en route to Pittsburgh so Lion can visit the five-year-old son he has never seen. When they arrive in Detroit, Lion decides to telephone first and is lied to by his ex-partner, who tells him the child was stillborn. Soon after, Lion suffers a type of fit, descends into a catatonic state and is hospitalised. In the final scene, Max buys a round-trip ticket to Pittsburgh, apparently intending to return and look after his friend.

In both the Renaissance and smart cycles, the crisis of the action-image is identifiable as a specific type of exaggeration, where the logic of the respective images is no longer simply a narrative device, but structures the characters' very reality. The crisis-image that emerges is not a straight subordination of the old sensory-motor schema, but a systematic deformation that simultaneously evokes and transcends its connective principles. Deleuze describes two forms of the action-image: the *large form* and the *small form*. The large form image is structured by the schema of Situation, Action, Modified Situation (SAS') which, very broadly, organises the manner in which a situation (milieu) provokes responsive action that eventually modifies – or restores – the original situation.[6] The sensory-motor capacity of the small form image is, by contrast, founded upon a reversed schema of Action, Situation, Modified Action (ASA'), where the situation must be deduced *from* initial action. The small form image is less stable, as the situation is 'not given as an in-itself . . . [it] always refer[s] back to struggles and modes of behaviour always in action or in transformation' (1986: 163–4).[7] Insofar as its journey structure displays some fidelity to this differential logic, the model of realism that *Scarecrow* 'erases' is that of the small form action-image.

A film concerned principally with a journey will almost always reject the large form SAS' model by refusing the primacy of a milieu. A character may be forced out of a situation and onto the road by certain milieu forces but, once into the journey, it is action that is the defining element: it is movement and transformation *from which* each new situation along the way appears, and not vice versa. Typifying Renaissance form, *Scarecrow* transposes this structural 'index of lack'[8] to its narrative, which is not developed in close detail. Relying upon the spectator's *deduction* of information, the action on screen is elliptical, with no clear establishment of where the characters are at any one moment, where they are heading or what they are thinking or feeling. Each new location emerges from their movement in an unheralded way, and eventually gives rise to the action of new movement as they continue on. Their movement itself is depicted in dialogue-free montage sequences that show Max and Lion clambering up or down the sides of trains, picking fruit at sunset, distributing notices on the windscreens of parked cars, eating over a campfire. The sequences are temporally indistinct: they form ellipses in the film in which the audience are held at a distance from the narrative, not granted access to the details of the situations, in much the same way as they know little about either of the main protagonists, and where their various quirks and attitudes emerge from.

The analogies Deleuze draws on to describe the classical type of the small form image include a knotted rope, a broken line and a skeleton; each one describing how the action is still structurally encompassed, but in an unpredictable way (1986: 168). Each sequence in *Scarecrow* appears discrete – the action cannot be determined by and in a preceding scene – so it is the film's *fidelity* to the small form image that can begin to describe the idiosyncratic character of its journey-form. However, it is only with its distortion of the classical image that this new form is fully realised. For Elsaesser, the new journey-form represents American filmmaking attempting to deal with the technical problem of just how to depict the unmotivated hero as a new type of ideological protagonist (2004: 287). *Scarecrow*'s opening scene offers a remarkably pure example of the formal qualities of this type of journey. Like all road movies, the film alternates between sequences of travel and periods of relative stasis in the destinations reached. The opening scene confuses these sequences in a way that is typical of the narrative as a whole: Max and Lion emerge *in action* – on the road trying to hitch a ride – but this action consists of nothing but waiting. The two characters merely pass time, Max almost motionless and Lion clowning around on the spot in an effort to win him over. As is typical in the small form image, action functions as an index of lack by disclosing a situation not explicitly established by the film (Max and Lion hitching). But, stretching a handful of shots over at least five minutes, action emerges as a more literal index of lack: it functions not only as the suppression of a narrative situation, but as the suppression of the whole dimension of character motivation.

In contrast to the journeying heroes of the Old Hollywood genre films, neither Max nor Lion have any real goals beyond getting a ride. Their (indirect) movement toward Pittsburgh functions to disguise their real lack of motivation, as do the peculiar façades of commitment both characters display: Lion obsessively carries with him a lamp intended for his child, and Max keeps compulsive track of his funds. Their arbitrary destination is propped up by Max with a combination of clichéd dreams (the carwash will have a deep freezer full of steaks and a radio playing the hit parade) and absurd fixation (it has to be in Pittsburgh because his money is in a bank there). Their forward movement is neutralised, consistently failing to bring about situations that challenge and eventually realise character desire. Action is, in this way, ineffectual: an independent variable that seems to exist quite apart from the journey itself. Action loses all ability to logically link to a situation: each scenario is not disclosed as somehow pre-existent but is created anew in each instant, existing only in and of itself *as* a continuous type of action.

One way in which this crisis is emphasised is in the motif of *looking*: repeatedly, at the point where action could be expected to trigger a new situation that is in some way expected, the characters step out of the action and, along with the spectator, simply *regard* it. When Max asks Lion to distract a store cashier while he steals a birthday present for Coley, Lion creates an hysterical scene by running manically down aisles and throwing stock in the air, and Max can only stare after him transfixed, unable to carry through with his shoplifting plan. Similarly, once Lion buddies up with a guard in prison, Max's refusal to engage with – *act* with – him is primarily represented through his blank and silent stares: from a truck with the other prisoners as he watches Lion washing a police car; as he is working in a pig pen and Lion approaches with news about being the talent show director; at mealtime in the prison cafeteria when Lion approaches him with a cigar and yet another effort to humour him. Further, Lion's own staring – first in a bar striptease scene, and later as he experiences his fit – express, in their catatonic nature, the absolute breakdown of action and its capacity to connect to a situation.

Deleuze describes the specific crisis of the small form action-image by suggesting that 'ellipsis ceases to be a mode of the tale, a way in which one goes from an action to a partially disclosed situation: it belongs to the situation itself, and reality is lacunary as much as dispersive' (1986: 207). In Max and Francis' stares this elliptical reality is clear: action is no longer an *index* of lack that discloses the situation to the spectator, but, unmotivated by character desire, is lack itself. It cannot adequately disclose anything to the audience or to the characters and, in this peculiar idleness, the situation is delayed and lost. When *Scarecrow* literalises the crisis of the form by having Max purchase a round-trip ticket in the last scene – committing to a perfectly circular form of movement – the 'necessary and rigorous' line that anchors the sensory-motor dimension of the small form image is severed altogether.

'JOINT CUSTODY BLOWS': CRISIS 2

In *A Cinema of Loneliness*, Kolker (asking the reader to suppress chronology for the sake of imagining the relationship of the fictions) observes how Gene

Hackman as Harry Moseby survives *Night Moves* only to emerge 'older, more frightened, and even more lonely, as Harry Caul in . . . *The Conversation*' (1980: 68). Although these attitudes are represented in a fundamentally different way, the objective of finding a specifically textual type of sequelisation to films such as *Scarecrow* and those referred to by Kolker can be supported by observing the way that Hackman emerges older, more frightened and lonelier again twenty-eight years later, as Royal Tenenbaum in Wes Anderson's *The Royal Tenenbaums*. This coincidence in Hackman's performances gestures toward the way in which the anxiety-based attitudes that are largely stamped out of studio-based filmmaking in the late 1970s and through the 1980s re-emerge in smart cinema. This coincidence is structured as a *transposition*, though, and the process by which this occurs can again be encapsulated by the shift from *social* to *personal* politics of power. In both the New Hollywood and smart cycles, anxiety represents a certain critique of bourgeois taste and culture, but this is borne out in essentially different terms.

Both thematically and formally, this shift is clearest in the respective approaches of each cycle to characterisation and genre. Where the Renaissance films tend to cast their apathetic protagonists as unattached drifters or obsessive loners, the similarly anxious figures of the smart film are typically tethered to a family and/or house and/or career: generically – as will be discussed further in Chapter 3 – the shift can be broadly determined as a move from the road movie to the family (melo)drama. In many smart films, the fear and loneliness no longer belongs to the outlaw or drifter but to alienated professionals, suffocated housewives and disaffected teenagers, and the violent outbursts and escape motifs of the first cycle are translated into the smothered, insular themes of adultery, divorce and abuse. This generic movement indicates how the formal crisis of action in the smart film is enacted upon a fundamentally different image from that of the Renaissance crisis. Both cycles are more concerned with the observation of character behaviour than with a strongly attenuated plot, but the family setting of the smart film means the characters are less likely to be thrown together in an attempt at flight and transformation than to be struggling with a configuration that is eternal and familiar. As has been discussed, the small form inclinations of the Renaissance image stem principally from the fact that the earlier films don't begin with meaningfully constructed milieus: the story comes from the forces implicit in the action which is seen, not in the history which is not. By contrast, the portraits of dysfunctional American families that the smart film depicts evoke the large form action-image (SAS') in relying heavily upon its initial step of establishing a milieu as a situation whose forces bear down upon the protagonists (Deleuze 1986: 141).

As was discussed at length upon its release, Noah Baumbach's *The Squid and the Whale* is based in part on the divorce of the director's own parents – novelist Jonathan Baumbach and *Village Voice* film critic Georgia Brown – in

Brooklyn in 1986. The film's representation of the Berkman family makes clear that Baumbach is 'someone who grew up with postmodernism and Godard' (Quart 2005: 28) and, aside from Hartley, his films bear the smart cycle's most palpable traces of the French New Wave's influence. Baumbach admits that his two earlier features *Kicking and Screaming* (1995) and *Mr Jealousy* (1998) make direct reference to the earlier movement through their reliance on the characteristic anti-realist techniques of voice-over narration, irises and jump cuts (2008: 29). *The Squid and the Whale* – as well as the next two features, *Margot at the Wedding* and *Greenberg* – eschew this type of stylistic allusion in favour of an observational style that attempts to put the audience directly into the scene. *The Squid and the Whale* film is captured on handheld Super 16 and takes a straightforward approach to the staging and framing of its sequences, which mostly focus on conversations involving combinations of the four Berkman protagonists – Bernard (Jeff Daniels), Joan (Laura Linney), Walt (Jesse Eisenberg), sixteen, and Frank (Owen Kline), twelve. The intimacy of the style is well-suited to the typically smart material – one review describes the roving camera as evoking the 'primal anxiety of a child listening to his parents whispering angrily in an adjacent room' (Malcolm 2005) – but it departs quite radically from the staged aesthetic that is evident elsewhere in the smart cycle.

In particular, the style of *The Squid and the Whale* directly opposes that of its producer Wes Anderson: as Baumbach himself comments, Anderson's work is more 'absurdist and idiosyncratic', and part of what he enjoys about working with Anderson (Baumbach co-wrote *The Life Aquatic* and *Fantastic Mr Fox*) is the chance to be engaged in films which, stylistically, he wouldn't make himself (Quart 2005: 29). On *The Squid and the Whale's* style, Baumbach has said that 'the idea was to film with a handheld camera but as steadily as possible . . . so that you'd have some feeling of a human hand in there. I wanted it to feel lived-in but also very immediate and not awash with nostalgia' (Winter 2005). The distance between this directorial ambition and Anderson's is most obvious in the conversation set-pieces that both tend to favour: in Anderson, characters are statically isolated in meticulously constructed space, and the use of multiple cameras maintains the set-up exactly across shot/reverse-shot sequences. The technique is well exemplified in *The Royal Tenenbaums* in a scene that will be discussed further in the next chapter, where – across the vast divide of their grand dining room table – Royal tells his three children that their mother is leaving him. Each set of characters occupies a static space that is exactly reversed, explicitly pitting Royal against Margot (Gwyneth Paltrow), Richie (Luke Wilson) and Chas (Ben Stiller).

In Baumbach's own 'family conference', when Bernard and Joan confront Walt and Frank with the news of their separation and the impending joint custody situation, the characters sit in a rough circle and the camera roves amongst them, the framing of each character subtly different in each instance.

Figure 6   Jesse Eisenberg, Owen Kline, Laura Linney and Jeff Daniels in *The Squid and the Whale* (Noah Baumbach, 2005). Courtesy Samuel Goldwyn Films LLC / The Kobal Collection.

The effect is similarly observational, but replaces Anderson's polished remoteness with a sense of pace and immediacy. This tempo has been perceived by some as another New Wave influence: upon the film's release, David Denby commented in *The New Yorker* that *The Squid and the Whale* can be likened to Louis Malle's 'scandalous family drama' *Murmur of the Heart* (1971) in terms of its coherence, intimacy and speed: 'this is a middle-class American "Murmur" – not as daring or perverse, perhaps, but more tender and enveloping, and better acquainted with failure' (Denby 2005). For the purposes of the argument here, the speed and intimacy of Baumbach's film can be read as a tendency which, while departing from the typical formality of the cycle, precisely expresses the smart film's approach to action and narrative. This effect can again be framed in terms of the differential sequel that the smart cycle offers to the New Hollywood. The influence of the European art cinema is again felt, but where the former American cycle expresses this influence in terms of a 'malaise' that stretches and slows the narrative, Baumbach channels those exuberant New Wave aspects that *invigorated* filmmaking practice.

The Squid and the Whale is best described as a 'fast-moving series of short, pointed vignettes' (Scott 2005) examining how each member of the Berkman family deals with the change the separation brings to their lives. The internal tension with which the film is concerned is established from the competitiveness of the opening family tennis match, where Bernard and Walt play Joan and Frank.[9] Post-separation, these battlelines are maintained, with Walt supporting his father's new life 'across the park' and taking on Bernard's pompous literary attitudes as a way of dealing with other people, and Frank siding with Joan, who has had affairs, and quickly begins dating his admired tennis coach, Ivan (William Baldwin). Grounded by a pedantic joint custody arrangement where the boys spend exactly half their time with each parent, *The Squid and the Whale* traces, among other things: Walt's doubtful relationship with his classmate Sophie (Halley Feiffer) and crush on his father's student Lili (Anna Paquin), who Bernard himself starts dating when she moves into his spare room; Frank's 'acting out' by drinking, swearing and masturbating in public; Bernard's slight, rejected attempt to reconnect with Joan; Walt's plagiarism of a Pink Floyd song and subsequent trip to an educational psychologist, and Bernard's eventual collapse and hospitalisation from alleged exhaustion. The film ends with Walt rejecting his father for the first time, leaving him alone in hospital and claiming he wants to 'even things out' and stay with Joan some more.

The Squid and the Whale expresses the very essence of smart narrative action in that its story consists of a series of moments that appear at once dense and incidental, and that succeed one another quickly and unpredictably. Similarly to the Renaissance films, the smart cycle is not concerned with a traditional three-act structure tracking the purposive development of a plot. Conversely to the earlier cycle, though, the smart film doesn't suppress information about its characters and context; techniques including voice-over, montage and titles are commonly used throughout the narrative to often exaggerated effect, establishing and embellishing details in a swift and detailed way. This information-heavy approach indicates the cycle's reliance upon the Situation or milieu of the large form action-image. The trappings so easily rejected by the Renaissance characters – job, home, school, parents – in favour of obsessive flight (literal or figural) are the very substance of the milieus sketched in the opening sequences of the smart film.

This reliance is demonstrated most clearly by the ensemble narrative structure that will be discussed further in Chapter 5. Films favouring this structure – such as *Short Cuts*, *Magnolia*, *Happiness*, and *The Chumscrubber* – put the viewer directly into their interconnected characters lives by depicting them at work or school and with family. Outside of the ensemble structure, Tracy Flick (Reese Witherspoon) in *Election* and Max Fischer (Jason Schwartzman) in *Rushmore* are firmly identified in terms of their position and ambitions at school through voice-over and montage. *Safe* begins with unhappy housewife Carol White (Julianne Moore) pulling into a suburban garage with her husband and then cuts straight to the two making love expressionlessly in an example of one of smart cinema's 'stock shots' (Sconce 2002: 364). And, upon waking up on Carpathian Ridge after an episode of sleepwalking, the opening of *Donnie Darko* sees its titular character descend to a suburban street and kitchen where a sign on the fridge explicitly asks 'where's Donnie'? Characters are introduced not in terms of their individual quirks – as Max and Lion are – but in terms of their milieu: the smart protagonists are inherently *connected*, part of a situation that restricts their movement and, cinematically, recasts the possibility of action.

The first three sequences of *The Squid and the Whale* involve all four members of the Berkman family: they play tennis, drive home through the leafy streets of their Park Slope neighbourhood, and eat dinner together. In each sequence, the forces implicit in their family milieu become more visible. The effect of this in the dining sequence gives some insight into why Sconce describes the 'awkward dining shot' as another of smart cinema's stock techniques (2002: 364). These sequences – and expressive examples can be found in *The Royal Tenenbaums, The Safety of Objects, The Ice Storm, Welcome to the Dollhouse, Happiness, Storytelling, Donnie Darko, Your Friends and Neighbors, Magnolia* and *Punch Drunk Love* – establish the milieu and its pressures by articulating the dynamic of the family unit, where everyone has a role to play and there is usually an undercurrent of conflict.

The Safety of Objects opens on a typical weekday morning, cutting between the breakfast scenarios of the narrative's four families to quickly establish a good deal of character information: Esther Gold's (Glenn Close) attachment to her comatose son Paul (Joshua Jackson), who a slow pan reveals is sitting at the table in his wheelchair; the financial hardship but close intimacy of the Jennings family, where the daughter Sam (Kristen Stewart) sulks because her single mother Annette (Patricia Clarkson) can't afford to send her to camp, but manages to coax her younger, deaf sister Rayanne (Haylee Wanstall) to copy her and swallow a mouthful of cereal; the distance between the members of the Train family, where the children fight downstairs over a box of cereal while the mother Susan (Moira Kelly) stays in bed and the father Jim (Dermot Mulroney) makes a quiet exit to work; and the subtle kookiness of the Christianson's, where the mother Helen (Mary Kay Place) chatters to her tomboy daughter Sally (Charlotte Arnold) and her friend Sam about the calorific value of Pop Tarts and the necessity of loving and respecting oneself. The cutting between the four suburban scenarios escalates as the focus zeroes in on those details that reveal most about the characters and their interconnection: Julie Gold (Jessica Campbell) masturbating in the backyard instead of watching Paul as instructed by her mother; Helen practicing Tai Chi in her living room; Jim's disenchantment when he is told one of his lawyer colleagues has made partner over him; and Esther trailing Annette, who it will be revealed was in a relationship with Paul before his accident.

Demonstrating a significant insularity, the conversation in the dining sequences typically involves issues internal to the milieu – work, school, family interaction. When external issues are raised it is principally to support the illustration of the unit's dynamic. In *The Squid and the Whale*'s own example, the relative quality of Charles Dickens' works comes up as dinner discussion, but primarily to convey, with tremendous economy, the relationship between the teenage Walt, his arrogant father and his candid mother. As one review describes, this scene is an early sign of how Walt is morphing into his father, and Linney beautifully underplays Joan's horror at watching her son become the enemy (Longworth 2005). Meanwhile, Frank – the younger son – is distracted by the cashew he has put up his nose.

In his discussion of the large form action-image, Deleuze illustrates the SAS' schema by exclusive reference to American genre films, including the documentary, the psycho-social film, *film noir* and the Western (1986: 143–6). In each example, the image develops slightly differently, but each genre is nonetheless 'solidly anchored' in a milieu that acts as the 'Encompasser': 'the milieu and its forces incurve on themselves, they act on the character, throw him a challenge, and constitute a situation in which he is caught' (141). In the genres mentioned by Deleuze, the milieu often has a quality of openness: the situational forces of the Fordian milieu, for instance, are framed by the constant presence of the land and the immanence of the sky. The smart film presents a converse and exaggerated Encompasser by referring back to the family melodrama where, as Douglas Sirk has commented, everything 'happens inside' (Elsaesser 1987: 52). The smart film amplifies this stifling milieu by squaring its closed family units off into clearly separate entities, something clearly expressed in the titles of *The Safety of Objects*, which introduce the various families in a diorama where they figure as tiny, cut-out groups depicted inside their fenced premises. The set-up conveys how, like the other films that deal with a number of proximate and interconnected families, the relationship between these separate units is grounded in terms of suspicion, hostility and open competitiveness. The families of the smart film tend to regard themselves as individually *empowered* units – something simultaneously encouraging and encouraged *by* their carefully divided proximity.

This type of empowerment is described by Baumbach in a conversation with Phillip Lopate, where he suggests that the sense of separation and insularity conveyed in the Brooklyn location of his film reflects that felt by the Berkmans, who tend to regard themselves as 'somehow smarter and better' than other families (Lopate 2006). *The Squid and the Whale* is the only smart film to actually put this sense of empowerment in (faux) intellectual terms[10] – with Bernard and Walt dividing the world into philistine and non-philistines

– but its effect can be seen elsewhere across the smart cycle. This supports Baumbach's claim that he is trying to represent the way that *all* families regard themselves as somehow smarter and better than others, in a manner that has less to do with education per se than with a quality created by the insular family unit. The attitude can be felt in the patronising smugness with which Cynthia Stevenson's proud housewife Trish treats her depressive and directionless sister Joy (Jane Adams) in *Happiness*, or the superior distance Donnie's mother Rose (Mary McDonnell) keeps from the hysterical and god-fearing PE teacher and neighbourhood mother Kitty Farmer (Beth Grant) in *Donnie Darko*.

The sense of empowerment is externalised to the point of parody in Posin's *The Chumscrubber*, where the cookie-cutter mothers (Terri, Carrie, Jerri[11]) of the various suburban developments openly vie with each other to keep up the appearance of their respective families. The endeavour reaches its pinnacle when Terri (Rita Wilson) and Carrie (Glenn Close) clash in their cul-de-sac over parking requirements for the family events they have organised for the same day – Terri's wedding to mayor Michael (Ralph Fiennes) and Carrie's memorial service for her son Troy, who commits suicide at the beginning of the film. In all of these instances, the smart cycle refers back to the family melodramas of the 1950s, where the biggest fear of the individual societal units is also what their counterparts think of them. In both cycles, the isolating effect of keeping up this 'smarter, better' façade is ultimately what is communicated. In her suppressed loneliness and anxiety to please, Glenn Close's Carrie could even be a twenty-first-century evocation of Jane Wyman's similarly tragic Cary Scott in *All that Heaven Allows* (Douglas Sirk, 1955).

The smart film's articulation of this attitude is one element that affects its treatment of the classical action-image. Insofar as the family unit puts itself into a type of exile from the neighbours it regards as inferior, the family shifts from being an entity that is simply closed to being, in Baumbach's words, an 'outsider' (Lopate 2006). As a consequence of understanding themselves only in terms of the unit, the members of the smart families are cast as quasi-aristocratic *types*: the Tenenbaums, the Berkmans, the Savages. In Baumbach's fifth feature, the surname of the misanthropic, under-employed protagonist who house-sits for his wealthy brother, is the film's simple title: *Greenberg*.[12] These milieus make limited claims to universality: they are hyperbolically local and obsessively detailed, and it is as though the sheer weight of their history and detail is more powerful than the characters, who are finally unable, or unwilling, to effectively modify them.

As an amplified Encompasser, then, the family milieu functions as a stifling situation that its characters cannot extricate themselves from. In Deleuze's specification, the *action* (A) in the SAS' structure of the large form image consists of the character(s) responses to the milieu forces that bear down on them. This action cannot happen, though, before the characters become capable of it: there is necessarily a 'big gap' between the initial situation and the action that finally modifies it (1986: 154). Action, when it occurs, is driven by the power of actualisation through which the character(s) acquire a new mode of being, and the sensory-motor advance of the form hinges upon the condition that it is *only* at this point that they are able to effectively modify or restore the initial situation. In the smart film, the hyper-milieu impacts severely upon the characters' potential for this type of purposive actualisation.

The divorce theme of *The Squid and the Whale* offers a literal example of how this occurs. The film's vignettes can be read almost entirely in terms of contrasts between the new and old situations, where the characters' navigation of the post-divorce situation is meted out in small, and larger, discrepancies from the historical family milieu. Bernard struggles to replicate the family home – claiming that it was important for him to get a place like Joan's, and that he is going to cook and run the house as the boys are used to – but, initially, both sons can focus only on differences: the further distance from school, what will happen to the cat, their father's unwelcome 'surprises' of a ping pong table, a poster of a tennis pro who Frank dismisses as an 'asshole', and a tiny, absurd writing desk designed for a 'leftie'. Some discrepancies are confronted (Bernard feeding the cat generic food instead of Purina) and some merely observed (the ease with which Bernard always finds a park directly outside his new house rather than having to search endlessly as he does in Park Slope). The physical restriction of the family – represented most fully in the figure of Bernard, who is constantly driving back and forth between houses with the boys, loitering on Joan's doorstep while waiting for them or double-parking in the street – poignantly expresses the manner in which all four Berkmans are inhibited in their potential to develop a new mode of being. Joan is most active in her efforts to establish this, but her attempt has shadows of the historical milieu cast all over it: a jealous Bernard belittles her relationship with Ivan ('why is your mother dating all these jocks? Very uninteresting men', he comments to Frank) and her publishing success is palpably traversed by the resentment of both Bernard and Walt. Walt's own effort to establish a relationship with Sophie develops entirely in 'Berkman' terms: he seduces her with empty literary clichés and promptly breaks up with her on his father's advice that it's good to 'play the field' at his age. Even Frank's desperately *anti*-Berkman behaviour (drinking, masturbating) cannot avoid a precocious self-awareness: 'do you think that you and I are philistines?' he asks a visibly taken-aback Ivan, after a conversation with his father.

This restricted potential for character actualisation necessarily impacts upon the causal schema of the large form action-image. The textual sequelisation that is being traced here between the Renaissance and smart cycles rests upon a conception of the erasure of a classical model of realism by way of an exaggeration or amplification of its indices. In the Renaissance cycle, the structural index of lack is transposed from a narrative device to the suppression of motivation. As suggested, this broadly amounts to a stretching-out of sensory motor form: action slows down to the point where it can no longer link or disclose situations. In the smart cycle, the milieu is amplified to the point where it inhibits rather than triggers character actualisation. In an inverse experimentation to the Renaissance cycle, the effect of this can be characterised as the *speeding-up* of sensory-motor form.

In his own discussion of the breakdown of the action-image in the American Renaissance cycle, Deleuze comments on how chance becomes the sole guiding thread in these narratives, meaning 'sometimes the event delays and is lost in idle periods, sometimes it is there too quickly' (1986: 207). This schema offers a fitting description of the differing forms of experimentation between the Renaissance and smart cycles. A film such as *Scarecrow* is clearly dominated by 'idle periods' that obscure its events – the fight that lands Max and Lion in prison, Lion's fit – and add up to the impression that little really takes place. By the film's end, though, organic change has unmistakably occurred in the characters, who have effectively acquired a new mode of being: Max, most clearly, has learned the importance of human contact and made a friend whom he plans to look after, tempering his early-stated position that he doesn't love or trust anybody. The smart cycle exhibits little of the Renaissance idleness: as the swift-moving series of vignettes described, the films are marked by the rapid and detailed introduction of a number of characters who are almost immediately involved in a disparate series of events. In a precise inversion of the earlier cycle, much appears to happen to the characters, but these encounters do little to change, or actualise, them. Sconce also emphasises this quality when he identifies that the favoured narrative structure of the cycle 'is no longer the passive observer of an absurd world who eventually experiences some form of epiphany, but rather a range of characters subjected to increasing despair and/or humiliation captured in a rotating series of interlocking scenes in which some endure while others are crushed' (2002: 362).

In the smart film, then, the 'event' is 'there too quickly'. This phenomenon is clearest in the films that are founded upon the cycle's general interest in issues of chance and coincidence – *Donnie Darko*, *Magnolia*, *The Sweet Hereafter* – where the event is not impelled by the protagonists at all but happens *to them*, and tends to occur early: a falling jet engine, a bus crashing into a lake. The 'coincidence' films highlight the way in which action in the smart film is never something the protagonists really become capable of. These narratives do not trace the actualisation of hero's power, so there is no 'big gap' between the initial situation and a form of definitive action that will modify it. Rather, the gap exists between the action – or series of actions – and the *modified* situation, and the defining characteristic of the form is that the degree to which this gap is filled at all is always ambiguous. In classical terms, the action (A) occurs too early, and the majority of the narrative is an examination of a modified situation that has not been purposively or adequately built toward. In *The Squid and the Whale*, character action attempts to respond to the claustrophobic milieu forces early in the narrative: the family conference at which the separation is announced and Bernard's subsequent move both happen within the first ten minutes of the film. Walt describes the accelerated schema – from his perspective – in the scene immediately following the conference. He confronts his mother in the bathroom, asserting that 'this is a great family' (Situation) and 'I don't know why you're screwing it up' (Action). Within this logic, the overwhelming part of Baumbach's film is concerned with the physically modified situation as a discrete series of examples; it is, in the terms of the film's tagline, an examination of how 'joint custody blows' (Situation').

By altering the distances implicit in the classical large form schema, *The Squid and the Whale* comments on the implausibility of the form as a model of realism. The contained and linear SAS' schema is displaced by several small moments that express the forces of the hyper-milieu. This structure demonstrates how the film is anchored by the schema at a micro rather than macro-level: each vignette is effectively a distinct SAS' formation in which the characters' inter(action) affects or *modifies* them in some way. Sometimes this modification resurfaces explicitly in their behaviour: when Frank confronts Ivan with the prospect of being a philistine or Walt suddenly turns on Sophie for being difficult, the upshot of previous moments comes out, as unmistakably as the cashew that Frank shoves up his nose in the first dinner scene is coughed out in a later drinking spree. Because the outcome of one vignette rarely leads logically into the premise of the next, though, the smart characters seem to run in place, and the end scenarios of the films suggest that – while some characters may find liberation, many do not.

Varying directorial styles and critical interpretations cast this in different ways. The perception of *The Squid and the Whale* as Walt's recognition of his parents as 'neither gods nor monsters but as screwed-up, very foolish adults' (Denby 2005) suggests that the film's collection of disparate experiences *do* produce a certain sense of insight, for Walt at least. Part of the reason this is so marked, though, is that it is starkly contrasted to the concurrent lack of change in his father, who responds to Walt's attempts to break away with typical blustering pomposity, promising that he will put some new posters up in his son's room, and lend him his first edition of *The Naked and the Dead* 'as a present'. This type of character blindness is a signature effect of Solondz and LaBute's takes on the smart film, where they favour protagonists that never achieve any level of recognition through their experiences, and simply continue on in their wilful and destructive patterns.[13] The endings of *Happiness* and *Your Friends and Neighbors* are exemplary in this manner, mobilising the two 'stock' scenarios of the smart film – a family meal and a sexual coupling – to demonstrate the zero degree of development that the savage events of the narrative have produced in their characters.

The narrative style of Solondz's *Palindromes* makes the point even more unambiguously. In a move sequelising *Welcome to the Dollhouse*, it opens at the funeral of that film's awkward and unhappy teen protagonist Dawn Weiner (Heather Matarazzo). Signalling upfront *Palindromes'* signature lack of belief in transformation, Dawn has committed suicide, and her brother Mark's (Matthew Faber) deadpan eulogy blackly emphasises the lack of progress she achieved when alive: 'Dawn went through many stages in her short life, but one thing that never changed was her love of music. Even when she was told again and again she had no real talent.' Before this title sequence, the film's dedication – 'in loving memory of Dawn Weiner' – indicates the extra-textual resonance of the finality for Solondz, who claims the melancholy nature of the 'sequel' was unintended, 'in so far as I begged Heather Matarazzo to reappear as Dawn in subsequent work of mine, but she refused. She said she never wanted to play this character again. So I had to let go, to say, "it's over"' (Matheou 2002: 29).

The 'official' sequelisation that is achieved in making Aviva – the thirteen-year-old protagonist of *Palindromes* – Dawn's cousin is shadowed by the looser connections forged by Solondz's serial characters, many of whom are archetypes familiar from films before and after *Palindromes*. A lack of faith in the possibility of change is again openly indicated here, especially in the emphatic repetition of what Kate Bernstein has called 'the selfish, overbearing, superficial, slightly dumb suburban Jewish mother' (2005: 54). who appears as Mrs Weiner (Angela Pietropinto) in *Welcome to the Dollhouse*, Trish Maplewood (Cynthia Stevenson) in *Happiness*, Fern Livingston (Julie Hagerty) in *Storytelling*, Joyce Victor (Ellen Barkin) in *Palindromes*, and Trish (Allison Janney) in *Life During Wartime*. These cheerfully tactless housewives encapsulate the force of the family milieus that bear down upon Solondz's characters as a series of blunt expectations and stultifying judgements. Seeing a 'glimmer of hope' in the 'fresh start' that her sister Joy is attempting in life, Trish in *Happiness* feels she can finally confide to her that the whole family never believed she would amount to much, and that she really needs to start eating red meat to clear up her skin. In *Palindromes*, Joyce is desperate to map her own experience onto her daughter: when Aviva becomes pregnant with a much wanted baby, she urges her to be brave 'like Mom', who aborted a baby years earlier and 'never felt as relieved as when I got rid of that little Henry'. It's not a baby, she assures Aviva, 'not yet . . . it's like it's just a tumour'. When Aviva does go through with the abortion and complications lead to an emergency hysterectomy she takes flight from the family milieu, hitchhiking a ride with a trucker who sodomises her then abandons her to her ongoing journey.

While these character types, attitudes and scenarios are all typical of

Solondz's style, *Palindromes* goes further than any film in expressing a lack of change at a formal level. The film makes tangible a story composed of short vignettes by breaking its narrative up into nine sections, each introduced with a title card that emulates a new baby announcement, with the name of a key character from the sequence spelled out in Solondz's signature cursive font on a pink or blue background. The sections are further distinguished in the way that the protagonist Aviva is played by a different actor in each instance, from the small black girl who opens and closes her story (Emani Sledge), to the young male actor Will Denton in a brief, dialogue-free section in the middle, to the adult performers Sharon Wilkins and Jennifer Jason Leigh. Upon the film's release, many reviews interpreted the strategy as evidence of Solondz's political comment on the 'hot' issue of abortion, understanding that 'the employment of diverse actresses articulates visually that every single "type" of woman in the country is immersed in the complex political debate being waged over her body', and that the different performers 'bring out inherent prejudices within viewers as we find ourselves reacting differently to the very same character depending upon the actress playing her' (Bernstein 2005: 54).

Solondz's employment of the structural model of the palindrome is here understood to express the blank morality for which he is infamous: 'just like Aviva's name, her desire to be a mom, and the situation – as well as the film itself – can ... be read as a sort of palindrome, similarly unclear forward or backward as to what the correct position is' (53). At a narrative level, the palindromic structure similarly informs the film as a whole and its separate sections. The vignette approach precisely demonstrates the distinction of smart narrative style, for Solondz experiments within the confines of a strict linear narrative. Each section represents a discrete SAS' form where specific action changes the situation with which it begins, and the different actors emphasise the break that each section subsequently makes from the previous one. For instance, the 'Henry' section starts with Aviva (Hannah Freiman) throwing up from morning sickness, and ends with a static long shot of her parents weeping over her in a hospital bed after assuring her she is 'good as new' after her botched abortion. The scene cuts to a pink 'Henrietta' card and a close-up of a new Aviva (Rachel Corr) trying to hitch a ride.

Overall though – of course – nothing changes in the film. After her stay at the nightmarish, fundamentalist home of 'Mama Sunshine' (Debra Monk) and subsequent involvement in the murder of her abortionist, Aviva is transported directly back to her own family home, where her mother is imperiously organising the guest list for her upcoming birthday party. Aviva is here played by Jennifer Jason Leigh, whose disconcerting performance of a thirteen-year-old's insecure mannerisms neatly expresses how age and experience do nothing to affect the powerful influence of family expectations and attitudes. At Aviva's urging, Joyce reluctantly includes Mark Weiner, who is facing a charge of

Figure 7   Ellen Barkin and Jennifer Jason Leigh in *Palindromes* (Todd Solondz, 2004). Courtesy Extra Large Pictures / The Kobal Collection / Macall Polay.

child molestation, and it is Mark who again verbalises the film's message. Approached only by Aviva, he bitterly espouses his worldview that 'people always end up the way they started out. No one ever changes. They think they do but they don't.' The palindromic motif is here cast as a life sentence – a hopeless form of tautology ('she is she; you, you') that is performed in the next and final sequence, where Aviva again has sex with the boy who made her pregnant in the first place. As Judah – who has changed his name to Otto – rocks sweatily on top of her beside a stream in a forest, the reverse shots of Aviva's face cycle through all the performers who have played her, finishing on the young black girl who appeared first, who lisps direct to camera 'I have a feeling . . . that this time I'm going to be a mom.'

The sequence supports the political interpretations of *Palindromes* in the way that it emphasises Aviva's conceptual power – in place of a three-dimensional character, she is rendered as a problem that looks different from diverse perspectives. In a narrative analysis, the strategy is a precise expression of the force of the encompassing milieu – Aviva is a blunt exemplar of a narrative system where physical action (here literal transformation) results only in repetition and stasis. Walt in *The Squid and the Whale* expresses the effect in a plainer moment of paralysis. After he leaves his father in the hospital, he runs through the streets of New York to the Museum of Natural History, and the film ends on his silent contemplation of the squid and whale diorama that an earlier sequence has revealed terrified him as a child. His stare could be interpreted as a triumphant conquering, but this possibility is rendered ambiguous by the sequence, which cuts from a close-up of his blank look to a long shot from behind that dwarfs him in relation to the enormous display. The moment again refers *The Squid and the Whale* back to the blank, paralysed stares that end many of the Renaissance films, as well as to the family melodrama, which, as Elsaesser identifies, most often 'records the failure of the protagonist to act in a way that could shape the events and influence the emotional environment, let alone change the stifling social milieu'. Without the catharsis of direct, externalised action, the conflict, and even the redemption, of smart characters necessarily turns inward, where it cannot escape the terms of their situation. Elsaesser suggests that the protagonists of the family melodrama 'emerge as lesser human beings for having become wise and acquiescent to the ways of the world' (1987: 55). Walt's stare and the various faces of Aviva indicate how the smart film also confers a negative identity on its characters: if they recognise anything, it is typically only their powerlessness in the face of their world.

For some commentators on *The Squid and the Whale*, this narrative style demonstrates the failure to adequately develop a plot beyond the film's initial set-up. What this chapter has suggested, though, is that this observational vignette style is the narrative foundation of the films in which the smart sensibility can be felt. The fact that the Berkmans 'certainly don't solve their problems in the course of the 88 minute film', as one review complains (Dermansky 2006), can be read as a comment on the improbability of the characters' acquisition of 'a new mode of being' in the classical mode. The 'setting of the scene' in these films refers less to the *construction* of an initial milieu than to the early emergence of a modified situation, in which action of some description has tried to respond to pre-existing pressures. It is not that 'nothing' happens beyond this point, but that the new situation itself is subtly transformed and reviewed by subsequent SAS' sequences. The modified situation (S') is not a static outcome but a process, where it is clear that the pressures bearing down on the initial milieu (S) have *already* produced it as a modified situation of its own – a downward spiral, in the case of *The Squid and the Whale* and most of the other family-oriented smart films, from the historically – and already ambiguously – content family milieu (represented, in Baumbach's film, by Walt's 'happy' memory of Joan taking him to the Natural History Museum).

The fact that the milieus onto which these films open continue to exert their power throughout the narrative positions the outcome not as something final but as another point of potential transformation. The form is distinctly *restless* insofar as the characters are inhibited by their closed milieu but not frozen by it: they are constantly railing against its forces in patterns of advance and retreat. In this way, the smart film does not attempt to convey something universal about the world but is a snapshot of lives that simply *continue*. The absence of any one, definitive point of action promotes an anti-causal conception of life as an unpredictable and continuous series of events: the form is not finite (SAS') but can more accurately be described in terms of a *flow* – S'AS'. . .

Intensified Discontinuity

In both cycles of American filmmaking under examination here, experimentation at the level of film form is achieved through a certain *intensification* of classical form; specifically, by an exaggeration of the signs of the small and large form action-images. In the New Hollywood cycle, the first sign of the small form image – the elliptical index of lack – moves from being an active device through which situations are linked and disclosed to being a characteristic of the characters' drifting reality. Its sensory-motor dimension is slackened and connections between behaviour and events are consequently loosened, and details suppressed. The index collapses at the level of action, but is intensive at the level of form more generally, where it produces a new style of critical American filmmaking. In the smart cycle, the signs of the large form image are more literally intensified, but similarly disabled in terms of their overall effect: the encompassing milieu becomes a *hyper*-milieu whose forces inhibit the protagonists' attempts to respond to it. In the characters' incapacity to act strongly and decisively, the smart film transforms American film form from a three-act structure with a late, modifying point of action to a series of discrete sequences that ultimately describe the failure of an early attempt at modification. In a similar effect to the New Hollywood experimentation, the signs of classical form are no longer a structuring device but '[belong] to the situation itself' (Deleuze 1986: 208).

By way of conclusion, these intensified 'crises' of the American action-image might be considered in terms of the periods in which they emerge. The New Hollywood films mark the end point of the Old Hollywood studio system, with its reliance upon the solid schemas of classical form to produce features at a high rate. The evaluation of the New Hollywood period as a time of American auteurism essentially consists of a belief in the films as *expression*, over and above the bottom-line concerns of the Hollywood industry. These films were produced and distributed in the industry's effort to reconnect with a film-going public who were no longer interested in Old Hollywood style: their brief, in essence, was to alter the old style action-image. Once the industry hit upon blockbuster form as a new and more reliable formula with which to address their commercial concerns, the visibility of the New Hollywood style declined. For Hollywood, the experimental period that put the action-image into crisis functioned primarily to trigger a new action-image – New Hollywood 2: the blockbuster image. One way to think about the emergence of the smart film is to consider it as a direct response to fifteen years of this high-concept, formulaic and excessive style. The directive didn't come from the industry, and the cycle by no means *replaces* dominant form, but the smart film's 'brief' nonetheless resembles that of the New Hollywood: to, in turn, put the blockbuster action-image into crisis.

These respective 'briefs' can perhaps explain the different shape that the crisis of the action-image takes across the New Hollywood and smart cycles. The latter group of films are responding to a dominant action-image that is spectacular and knowing: today's popular American cinema is, in Bordwell's words, 'always fast, seldom cheap, and usually out of control' (2002: 16). For some commentators, the contemporary blockbuster form itself represents a 'crisis', with its overwhelming effects, speed and general lack of story creating a fragmentary and narratively incoherent 'post-classical' American cinema.[14] As described earlier, Bordwell argues against this position by describing contemporary visual style in terms of tactics that are designed to compel attention and sharpen emotional resonance, thereby representing 'traditional continuity amped up, raised to a higher pitch of emphasis' (16). Essentially, he claims, the acceleration of classical Hollywood style in no way compromises its basic sensory-motor foundations. Bordwell's position throws the smart cycle's own intensification of classical film form into sharp relief. The smart film shares the contemporary blockbuster's general concern with pace and the communication of a large amount of information quickly.[15] This is well represented in the restless quality of films discussed in this chapter, where the narratives move in short scenes composed of short shots. As has been described, though, this formal acceleration is not matched by an intensification of continuity. In a manner that both recalls and inverts the New Hollywood's approach to film narrative and style, the smart film intensifies classical principles in such a way that they *disable* the sensory-motor connections of classical continuity. Where the intensification of the blockbuster exists at the level of stylistic tactics and amounts to the consolidation of classical form, the intensification of the smart film exists at the level of form itself, and amounts to the American cinema's second significant cycle of experimentation.

NOTES

1. Some sections of this chapter were originally published as 'Sequelizing Hollywood: The American "Smart" Film', by Claire Perkins, in *Second Takes: Critical Approaches to the Film Sequel* edited by Carolyn Jess-Cooke and Constantine Verevis, the State University of New York Press ©2010, State University of New York. All rights reserved.
2. Biskind makes only two brief references to Anderson (21, 387). Mottram defines his 'Sundance Kids' as a uniquely West Coast phenomenon, excluding directors such as Solondz and Hal Hartley because 'they have remained camped out on the East Coast, largely avoiding entanglements with the studios' (Mottram 2006: xxii).

3. See Balio *The American Film Industry* (1985); Hillier, *The New Hollywood* (1993); Schatz 'The New Hollywood' (1993).
4. This connection is made by Constantine Verevis in 'A Cinema of Seeing' (1997).
5. Deleuze suggests that Hitchcock introduces the mental image into cinema by surrounding an action with a set of relations that vary the subject, nature and aim of the action: 'what matters is not who did the action – what Hitchcock calls with contempt the *whodunit* – but neither is it the action itself: it is the set of relations in which the action and the one who did it are caught' (Deleuze 1986: 200). By making relation itself the object of an image, the mental image or relation-image closes the set of action, perception and affection-images and pushes the movement-image to its limit. For Deleuze, this functions as a prelude to the crisis of the traditional image of cinema.
6. For full detail on the five laws that define the large form action-image see Deleuze 1986: 141–59.
7. For full detail on the two laws (indices) defining the small form action-image see Deleuze 1986: 160–77.
8. Deleuze uses this term to describe how an action discloses a situation which is not given: 'since the situation is not given for itself, the index here is an index of lack; it implies a gap in the narrative, and corresponds to the first sense of the French word *ellipse*' (Deleuze 1986: 160).
9. Baumbach's taste for this metaphor is again demonstrated in the croquet game in his next feature – *Margot at the Wedding*.
10. An interesting adjunct effect can be found, though, in the Whit Stillman trilogy discussed in Chapter 1. Stillman's films are similar to Baumbach's own *Kicking and Screaming* in that the 'units' do not involve family but groups of college-educated friends. It has been commented about both Stillman and Baumbach that the sound of fully articulate people speaking can be, at first, a little embarrassing (see Matthews 1995). The connection between Stillman and Baumbach is further emphasised by Stillman regular Chris Eigeman – who rarely appears in any other film work – performing in Baumbach's earlier features.
11. This technique of using phonetically similar and interchangeable names for characters also appears in Neil LaBute's *Your Friends and Neighbors*, which also features a Terri, Cary and Jerry, as well as Mary, Cheri and Barry. In LaBute's film the empowered units are made up of couples rather than extended families, and the competitiveness is sketched in more viciously sexual terms.
12. As will be discussed further in Chapter 3, this effect directly recalls Orson Welles' preoccupation with 'the magnificence of the Ambersons' in *The Magnificent Ambersons* (1942).
13. LaBute supports the idea of the characters 'running in place' when, on his director's commentary for *Your Friends and Neighbors*, he reveals that the sequences were re-shuffled several times in post-production before the final order was reached.
14. Bordwell notes that this position is extrapolated in several essays in Neale and Smith's collection *Contemporary Hollywood Cinema*, especially in Elizabeth Cowie and Thomas Elsaesser's pieces.
15. Bordwell comments that the independent sector also demonstrates aspects of intensified continuity, suggesting that David Cronenberg and Allison Anders, in particular, subscribe to the style (2002: 21). More interestingly, he suggests that 'when an independent goes mainstream' – for some, an apt description of the smart niche – their cutting is likely to accelerate: he traces the gradual decrease of Jarmusch's average shot lengths from the one-take scenes of *Stranger than Paradise* (1984) to a 6.8 second ASL in *Ghost Dog: The Way of the Samurai* (1999).

3. MELODRAMA: *THE LIFE AQUATIC WITH STEVE ZISSOU, THE ROYAL TENENBAUMS*

'I wonder if the three of us could have been friends in real life. Not as brothers, but as people.'

Jack Whitman (Jason Schwartzmann),
The Darjeeling Limited (Wes Anderson, 2007)

Sconce describes three 'stock shots' in smart cinema: the 'awkward couple' shot, where a strained couple are captured in tableau form separated by blank space, the 'awkward coupling' shot, where a camera placed directly above the bed records expressionless sex, and the 'awkward dining' shot, where maladjusted families are shown trapped together over food (2002: 364). All three shots express the interpersonal alienation within the white middle-class that is a key dimension of these films. As was suggested in the previous chapter, the dining sequence is the most consistent example; it appears – in varying manifestations – in almost every film discussed here, as the most upfront index of the family dynamics that lie at the centre of each work. As the signature smart shot, it points up how an interest in the force of family relations is a key dimension of this sensibility.

Across the body of smart films there are directors who repeatedly deal with the dynamic between blood relations or their substitutions: Wes Anderson across *Bottle Rocket, Rushmore, The Royal Tenenbaums, The Life Aquatic, The Darjeeling Limited* and *Fantastic Mr Fox*; Todd Solondz across *Welcome to the Dollhouse, Happiness, Storytelling, Palindromes* and *Life During Wartime*; Paul Thomas Anderson across *Boogie Nights, Magnolia, Punch*

Drunk Love and *There Will Be Blood*; Noah Baumbach across *The Squid and the Whale*, *Margot at the Wedding* and *Greenberg*, and Tamara Jenkins across *The Slums of Beverly Hills* (1998) and *The Savages*. Beyond these specific directors, films such as Arie Posin's *The Chumscrubber*, Rose Troche's *The Safety of Objects* and Ang Lee's *The Ice Storm* demonstrate isolated examples of the thematic fixation. And in those smart films that don't explicitly deal with the subject of the family dynamic, the unit itself remains a central force: in, for example, *Adaptation*, *Election* and *Donnie Darko*. Supporting the idea that smart cinema is underpinned by the logic of contemporary therapeutic culture, all of these directors have a certain obsession with characters who, in James Mottram's description, are 'psychologically scarred by their families' (2006: 354). In all smart films, the family is utilised not to enhance an external complication but is itself, as social institution, the basis for conflict.

Chapter 2 has already linked the smart film to the historical trend of the family melodrama on the basis of its narrative arc, arguing that the S'AS' . . . schematic of the cycle recalls the melodrama's typical pattern of resignation to those rituals of social and family life that cannot be modified, much less escaped. There are at least three broader points on which the two cycles can be compared.[1] First, both are usually considered a mode or sensibility rather than a strict genre. As numerous commentators have indicated, the strict definition of 'melodrama' (music + drama) describes, in the first instance, the typical Hollywood mode of address. For Linda Williams, 'melodrama is a peculiarly democratic and American form that seeks dramatic revelation of moral and emotional truths through a dialectic of pathos and action. It is the foundation of the classical Hollywood movie' (1998: 44). And Steve Neale notes that Thomas Elsaesser uses the term 'family melodrama' to identify a canon of melodramas that he focuses on as the basis for a discussion of ideology, class and Oedipal conflict (2000: 184). Second, and in a related capacity, both cycles are the product of discursive construction. The (family) melodrama as a form with an inherently ironic mode of address emerged not at the time of the films' release in the 1940s and 50s, but with the Marxist and psychoanalytic rediscovery of the films in the 1970s.[2] Third, the discursive organisation of both modes has ultimately been founded upon the identification of close connections between the formal dimension of the films and conventions of theme, plot and setting (Schatz 1981: 243). The 1970s critics' deduction of ironic strategy in the films of directors such as Douglas Sirk was based most significantly upon issues of *mise-en-scène* and broader ideas of film style. Similarly, the identification of the smart film as a critically ironic mode understands the dimensions of blank cinematography and tone as central to the thematic evaluation of white, middle-class life cycles. Accordingly, the following discussion of the smart film as a type of revisionist family melodrama likens the two cycles on the basis of broad conventions of setting, plot and characterisation, but argues that the smart film's revisionism is felt most significantly at the level of style and tone.

THE FAMILY MELODRAMA

The genre of melodrama is syntactically based upon a notion of victimhood. In Schatz's description, 'melodrama' before WWII – when understood in more specific terms than the broad processes of dramatic articulation and musical punctuation – described a narrative formula depicting a virtuous individual or couple 'victimized by repressive and inequitable social circumstances, particularly those involving marriage, occupation, and the nuclear family' (1981: 222). In addition to the arch stylisation of this schema in the films of Sirk, Vincente Minnelli and Nicholas Ray, the post-war period also saw the rise of narrative conflicts reflecting the real life transformations of the middle-class family unit as the clearest representation of America's patriarchal and bourgeois social order. These well-documented post-war changes – suburbanisation, the pluralisation of women's roles between the labour market and the home, increased mobility, greater education – manifested themselves in the themes of the 1950s melodramas, positioning them more overtly as *family* melodramas.[3] In this period, the 'typical' Hollywood melodrama emerged as a narrative tracing the identity crisis of an individual whose divided domestic and occupational commitments provided a rational basis for confusion and anxiety (243).

The key to the 1970s constitution of melodrama as a critical genre was the perception of a strategy of double-voicing in these narratives. Critics such as Elsaesser and Paul Willemen attended to Sirk's films for the way in which form, style, rhythm, camera movement, colour and *mise-en-scène* was mobilised to constitute an 'extra link' in the usual chain of representation. The additional level of signification parodied the stylistic procedures that traditionally conveyed the self-righteous petit bourgeois world view of the American melodrama (Willemen 1991a: 272). In identifying the animation of an anti-utopian dialectic, the rediscovery of these films was based upon the perception of a specific social function, where aesthetic form retroactively disclosed the distortions and contradictions of 1950s affirmative liberal culture. Although these distortions were already emerging in the melodramas of the 1940s,[4] Sirk's auteurist commentators saw the distinction of his films to lie in their sophistication of this double-voicing technique. The 'blissful' ending in Sirk is animated by the textual effects of the narrative as a whole, which overstate melodrama's generic codes, and put forward an hysterically wrought *mise-en-scène* that relies on dimensions of excess and incongruity. As Bruce Babington and Peter Evans note, the basic case for Sirkian irony postulated a 1950s majority audience who understood the surface meanings of the films, and a minority audience who responded to the subtextual effects critiquing American bourgeois ideology (1990: 48). Although this view comes under attack from feminist and anti-auteurist perspectives on melodrama,[5] the broad position recapitulated by Babington and Evans is that Sirk's highly self-conscious films are still 'best explained by conscious ironic intent' (49).

THE SMART FILM VICTIM

On the basis of both the victim narrative and the tonal strategy of double-voicing, the smart film is directly comparable to the family melodrama. The narrative formula of the latter cycle, as summarised by Schatz, classically involves an interrelated family of characters, a repressive small-town milieu, and a preoccupation with America's socio-sexual mores (1981: 224). The smart film succeeds this formula with minimal transformation: the family of characters is central, the repressive small-town milieu is (typically) replaced by a repressive suburban milieu, and a concern with American socio-sexual politics is again the most obvious theme. Within the parameters of this formula, the smart narratives are also concerned with characters who are victims of social circumstances involving the nuclear family, marriage and occupation. The vulnerabilities of these characters are pure expressions of the terms of therapeutic culture: maladjusted and taunted teenagers – *Donnie Darko*, *The Chumscrubber*, *Election*; spouses distanced by boredom, dislike and deceit – *The Life Aquatic*, *Happiness*, *The Squid and the Whale*, *Magnolia*, *Me and You and Everyone We Know* (Miranda July, 2005); and characters who seem at best disgruntled with their occupations – *Punch Drunk Love*, *I Heart Huckabees* (David O. Russell, 2004), *Being John Malkovich*, *The Safety of Objects*.

The shift in the smart film toward a personal politics of power can in this way be read as a shift away from overtly political narratives toward the concerns of the melodrama's own structure of feeling. For Schatz, a paradox emerges in this genre when the melodrama moves its thematic focus to the family as institution, and the attendant politics of emotion and communication. Once this occurs, family crisis becomes the dominant narrative conflict. Because the institution itself is the dominant social structure, though, the narrative cannot appeal to forces beyond the family to resolve the conflict (1981: 228). There is no force within the social structure that can be violently eliminated as in other genres and, as was described in Chapter 2, the range of 'strong' action is limited by this closed world: 'the characters are, so to speak, each others' sole referent, there is no world outside to be acted on, no reality that could be defined or assumed unambiguously' (Elsaesser 1987: 56). The family melodrama is most interesting for the uneasy coexistence of criticism and affirmation that emerges from this isolated focus.

Figure 8   Dermot Mulroney and Glenn Close in *The Safety of Objects* (Rose Troche, 2003). Courtesy IFC Films / The Kobal Collection / RAFY.

A paradox can also be seen in the smart film's depiction of the family as institution, in that it mostly insists upon the nuclear incarnation of the unit in an era where this is somewhat archaic.[6] The cycle's attention to the personal politics of emotional dysfunction within the nuclear family presents a strong case for the redundancy of the institution but, like the 1950s melodramas and those 1960s films that openly thematised their critique – *The Graduate* (Mike Nichols, 1967), *You're a Big Boy Now* (Francis Ford Coppola, 1966) – the smart film's reliance on the unit as an unshakable context presents it in at least partially affirmative terms. The distinction between all three cycles lies in the way this critical-affirmative trajectory is articulated. Sirk's elevation as auteur was based upon his ability to produce an ironic critique within the strict confines of the classical Hollywood system – to recognise, as he said himself, that 'irony doesn't go down well with the American public' (quoted in Willemen 1991a: 269). The historical and industrial contexts of the 1960s and smart cycles, though, represent the degrees of freedom afforded by the evolution of New Hollywood films that were discussed in the previous chapter. Specifically, both latter sets of films emerge from areas that are, in varying ways, adjacent to the dominant studio concerns. Where Sirk faced an audience favouring the clearly delineated narrative positions of 'for and against', the irony of New Hollywood and the smart film embodies a mode of address that is popular and desired. Irony functions here not in a Socratic sense, to communicate a meaning diametrically opposed to what is expressed, but as a tonal dimension that pluralises everything it says. Subsequently, the smart film's critique of the nuclear family is not concealed in an apparently positive representation but is right on the surface, where the very *fact* of the unit is at once ironic and affirmative.

THE FAILED DISCIPLINARY SOCIETY

Chapter 2 described the way in which the smart film inherits a formal lack of pragmatic motivation from the New Hollywood films of the late 1960s and early 1970s. At the level of theme and subject matter, this 'crisis-image' is put in more explicit terms. Where the 1950s melodramas concealed their critique of the family in an affirmative image, and the New Hollywood films expressed their own by, for the most part, directing their narratives away from the unit altogether, the smart film makes its own critique the very substance of its narrative. From the contested issues involving paedophilia, abortion, serial adultery, incest, misogyny and rape in *Happiness*, *Your Friends and Neighbors*, *Palindromes*, *The Sweet Hereafter* and *In the Company of Men* to the broader themes of unhappiness and failure that manifest in the many stories of separation and death, the so-called anti-humanist tendency of the films is directly embodied in family-based themes. The critique put forward by these family portraits is most clearly articulated in their rejection of the overarching schema of moral reason that ultimately codes all interaction in more generic 'family features' and teen films toward a secure and righteous identity. It is at this level that the cycle is clearest in its representation of the socially inscribed nature of ageing, and of 'post youth' as a reconceptualised perspective on exactly what constitutes adulthood and maturity.

One way of approaching this representation at a political level is to read it in terms of what Deleuze discusses as the disintegration of the disciplinary society. Drawing on Foucault's analysis of the institutions of family, school, factory, and prison, and arguing that they reach their height at the outset of the twentieth century, Deleuze stresses the analogical structure of each: the individual passes through and exits one society before 'starting again' in the next. These historical disciplinary societies organise 'vast spaces of enclosure', and aim to compose a productive force whose effect will be greater than the sum of its component forces (1995: 177). In the case of the family, this general project of ordering and distribution exists in the perception of the institution as the locus in which identity is assigned. For Deleuze, these disciplinary societies undergo a generalised crisis in the second half of the twentieth century, where they are replaced by control mechanisms that operate not as enclosed and discrete units but as global systems made up of inseparable variations. Hence, the factory is replaced by the corporation; the school by perpetual training. Where, in the disciplinary society, one finishes and starts again, the new control mechanisms operate by modulation, which mean, effectively, 'you never finish anything' (179).

Where the New Hollywood's movement away from the family as situation can be read to encode this generalised crisis, the smart film describes the attempt, and failure, to *reinstate* the family as disciplinary society. One of the most striking, and clichéd, aspects of the cycle is the archaic quality of the representations: the traditional role play, family rituals and neat suburban settings all hark back to the pristine situations of the 1950s popularised by television. The punch line of the cycle, of course, is the incongruity produced once the films start examining the darker issues subtending this façade. In its reference back to the narrative formula of the family melodrama, though, and this genre's own double-voicing strategy, the smart film indicates how this disciplinary 'norm' has never been anything but a façade or illusion.

The most exact expression of this illusion from a director that Sconce names as smart is Todd Haynes' 'rewriting' of Sirk in *Far From Heaven* (2002).[7] Beyond this direct examination, the illusionary norm is dramatised elsewhere in the smart cycle in the modulated roles and scenarios that result from its attempted reinstatement. One of the most obvious modulations is observable in the signature representation of children and teenagers as precocious and articulate, and adults – particularly parents – as comparatively naïve. In *Punch Drunk Love*, the teenage-like Barry Egan is still taunted by his sisters as 'Gay Boy' before embarking upon an awkward, first-love-style romance; in *The Safety of Objects* Jim Train quits his corporate job to participate full-time in a mall competition to win a car, and in *Being John Malkovich* puppeteer Craig Schwartz is mocked by Maxine (Catherine Keener) for 'playing with dolls'. Other films present the converse instance of wise or driven children and teenagers: clear in the surprising insight that Frank Berkman has unwittingly inherited from his paranoid family in *The Squid and the Whale*; in the careful and serious way that Sylvie (Carlie Westerman) collects and stores homewares for her marriage trousseau in *Me and You and Everyone We Know*; in Billy's (Rufus Read) frank questions about sex to his father in *Happiness*, and in Judah's Hal Hartley-tinged comments about his parents in *Palindromes*, who are too busy to help with his feature film: 'People are unreliable. They have no faith.'

In *The Chumscrubber*, a film that will be addressed further in Chapter 5, the tendency takes the form of a running gag where the teenagers keep calmly explaining the complicated drugs and ransom case in which they are involved to adults who, involved with their own obsessions, dismiss it as unlikely or uninteresting. The adults' unhappiness in this film is consistently represented in their reduction to a child-like state, from the town mayor having a life-changing epiphany and painting blue dolphins all over his fiancée's walls, to a father

Figure 9   Mary Lynn Rajskub, Emily Watson and Adam Sandler in *Punch Drunk Love* (Paul Thomas Anderson, 2002). Courtesy Ghoulardi/New Line/Revolution / The Kobal Collection / Bruce Birmelin.

attempting to confide in a twelve-year-old boy about his marriage breakdown. *The Chumscrubber* also demonstrates the numb attitude to cruelty and promiscuity that is often embodied in this reversed tendency: when, for example, two teenage boys openly lust after their friend's flirtatious mother, or a self-obsessed bride-to-be fails to notice her son has been kidnapped by teenagers who amuse themselves by daring each other to stab the boy. The structure of *Palindromes* discussed in Chapter 2 takes the reversal further again by casting Jennifer Jason Leigh and Sharon Wilkins as the thirteen-year-old Aviva in two of the vignettes.

This representational trend is one method that demonstrates the failure of the smart family as a disciplinary society: it is described not as an enclosed space through which its children pass and exit in order to 'start again' as adults, but as an interminable and undifferentiated state where, as Tilda Swinton has said in regard to *Thumbsucker* (Mike Mills, 2005), the adults are in search of the same things as the children (Byrnes 2005). These worlds of precocious children and stunted adults demonstrate, to return to Deleuze's terms, the family as control mechanism: as a 'metastable [state] of a single modulation, a sort of universal transmutation' (Deleuze 1995: 179). By juxtaposing this phenomenon with hyperbolic illusions of the family as a traditional, enclosed unit, the smart film demonstrates how the family is not containable in the cast of the disciplinary society, something the codified mise-en-scène of the family melodrama was already attesting to in the 1950s.

THE AUGMENTED FAMILIES OF WES ANDERSON

In *American Independent Cinema*, Geoff King summarises the genre conditions of the independent sector as a process in which two different tonal registers are brought into conjunction to produce an incongruous and destabilising effect (2005: 183). He alludes to Solondz' habit of blending the comedic modality with painful material, as well as to John Cassavetes' juxtaposition of a melodramatic crime/gangster narrative in *The Killing of a Chinese Bookie* (1976) with everyday routines and preoccupations. The smart film as it has so far been discussed in this chapter can be explained in terms of this strategy insofar as it brings together a traditional representation of the family with the reality of a dysfunctional scenario. The offbeat quality that distinguishes the sensibility is embodied in the incongruous effect created when an illusionist norm is juxtaposed with the family as 'metastable state'. A further incongruity is created in the way that this juxtaposition in fact renders the dysfunctional family functional. As Adrian Martin has written in a chapter addressing TV shows including *The Addams Family* (1964–6), *Married with Children* (1987–97), *Roseanne* (1988–97) and *The Simpsons* (1989–), 'the central irony of most of our so-called dysfunctional comic families [is that] they function very well indeed' (1994: 72). If these families are united by a common principle that inverts them in relation to a fantasy notion of a family that would maintain social order, Martin suggests that – once inverted – the units are in fact quite resolute.

In the context of television, this is attributed to a principle of populism and 'anti-social sanity' whereby the families' shared resignation to their imperfect scenario keeps them together. Where a film like *Little Miss Sunshine* (Jonathan Dayton and Valerie Faris, 2006) demonstrates the populist apotheosis of this tendency in contemporary commercial/independent film, the smart sensibility expresses the paradox in less categorical terms. For example, the family meal that concludes *Happiness* may present units that *have* broken apart – both fathers lost to divorce and jail – but the blind and indomitable spirit remains as Trish and her mother (Louise Lasser) pester Helen (Lara Flynn Boyle) to find them new men, and nine-year-old Billy triumphantly announces that he has mastered the technique of masturbation taught him by his absent, paedophiliac father.

As suggested at the beginning of this chapter, Wes Anderson is one director included in the smart cycle whose films demonstrate a highly consistent concern with issues of family dynamics.[8] However, the families in Anderson's films depart from the paradigm of *Happiness* and *The Chumscrubber* in a number of ways. First, only one of the films – *Rushmore* – demonstrates the consistent suburban setting with its fixtures of home, school and work; the others extend to rural Texas (*Bottle Rocket*), New York (*The Royal Tenenbaums*), Italy and Haiti (*The Life Aquatic*) and India (*The Darjeeling Limited*). Second, the families are not as resolutely nuclear as in the films discussed so far. The family unit as the basis for narrative conflict is an augmented form comprised of blood relations, but also of friends, partners, colleagues, teammates and mere acquaintances. The unit in *Rushmore* is most fully expressed not in the blood example of Herman Blume (Bill Murray) and his two sons Ronny (Ronnie McCawley) and Donny (Keith McCawley) but in the unit that embodies the teenage Max, Herman and Rosemary Cross (Olivia Williams), a primary teacher from Rushmore who both Max and Herman fall in love with. The 'composed' family is also demonstrated in the oceanographic unit that Steve Zissou (Bill Murray) builds around himself in *The Life Aquatic*. When Ned (Owen Wilson) introduces himself to Steve ('probably' his father) at the age of thirty, Steve invites him to join the 'pack of strays' that is Team Zissou – a group consisting of various marine/filmmaking personnel that have been with Steve for many years, as well as his wife Eleanor (Anjelica Huston), 'the brains behind Team Zissou'. On the particular 'adventure' that the narrative is concerned with, this group extends to include Ned, a group of interns from the University of Alaska, a 'bond company stooge' (Bud Cort), a pregnant journalist putting together a story on Steve (Cate Blanchett) and, eventually, Steve's oceanographic 'nemesis' Alistair Hennessey (Jeff Goldblum).

In this way, Anderson's families openly flout the illusionist norm. Various hangers-on complicate even the units with a secure blood basis: the Tenenbaum ensemble includes Eli Cash (Owen Wilson), childhood friend and Margot's sometime-lover; the butler Pagoda (Kumar Pallana) and Henry Sherman (Danny Glover), Etheline's fiancée. Similarly, the unit of Peter (Adrian Brody), Francis (Owen Wilson) and Jack Whitman in *The Darjeeling Limited* is expanded for the mid-section of the film, when the boys are invited to join the intimate mourning rituals of the family whose son's drowning they witness. Within Anderson's 'ensemble' families, the modulation of roles described above is also apparent, often to the point of hyperbole. All of Anderson's characters are child-adults, from Dignan (Owen Wilson) in *Bottle Rocket* with his hand-drawn seventy-five year life plan, to Eli, who sends reviews of his books to Etheline for encouragement, to Steve, who treats his boat *The Belafonte* and all its equipment like so many toys. The conversely shrewd children are represented in Max Fischer, in the young Tenenbaums, in Chas Tenenbaum's thoughtful children Ari (Grant Rosenmeyer) and Uzi (Jonah Myerson), and in Klaus Daimler's (Willem Defoe) nephew Werner (Leonardo Giovannelli) in *The Life Aquatic*. The trend is particularly emphatic in the case of those adults who are parents: Herman, Royal, Steve, Etheline, and Patricia Whitman (Anjelica Huston) are all depicted as being, at least part of the time, too self-interested to express much concern for their offspring. When they do, the results are mixed. The conflicted theme is openly alluded to by Anderson in *The Life Aquatic* character of Jane Winslett-Richardson – who reads Proust to her unborn baby and is trying to curb her habit of swearing before it is born, but who is pregnant to her married boss, and still 'hits the sauce' (drinking Steve's Campari).

Of all Anderson's characters, the adult Tenenbaum children are the perfect emblems of the modulated trend. Along with their father Royal, none of the children have been able to survive the world outside the family unit. The 'family of geniuses' that once was – Richie a champion tennis player since the third grade, Chas possessing 'an almost preternatural understanding of international finance' since the sixth grade and Margot a grant-winning play-wright in the ninth grade – is confined to the film's seven minute prologue, the climactic end of which conveys that 'virtually all memory of the brilliance of the young Tenenbaums had been erased by two decades of betrayal, failure and disaster'. As the story begins – twenty-two years later – Richie has bombed out of international tennis and, travelling alone on an ocean liner, has 'never been so lonely in [his] life', Margot has been secretly married and divorced and has not completed a play in seven years and, after surviving a plane crash that killed his wife the previous summer, Chas has become 'increasingly concerned' about the personal safety of his sons. Where Eli, Etheline and (Margot's husband) Raleigh St Clair (Bill Murray) are all experiencing modest success, Royal is grouped with his children as a failure: having been disbarred and briefly imprisoned from his position as a prominent litigator in the 80s, he is broke and being evicted from the hotel that he lives in. Most crushingly, it is suggested, none of his family has spoken to him in three years.

The narrative of *The Royal Tenenbaums* traces the return of the trio, and Royal, to the family home in New York. While the arrangement of the family may contradict the more typical nuclear unit, this trajectory precisely expresses the smart cycle's overall concern to *reinstate* the family. The once-great Tenenbaum children are recalled in the miniature trappings of their bedrooms, which remain exactly as they did two decades earlier, and in their appearance, where they physically embody themselves as children. In all of Anderson's films, costume functions as a way of defining the ensemble families. For the execution of their crimes in *Bottle Rocket*, the unrelated 'brothers' Dignan, Anthony (Luke Wilson) and Bob (Robert Musgrave) all don matching yellow jumpsuits, and Team Zissou are visibly described by their mismatched pale blue wardrobes, insignias and red hats, which work in stark contrast to the pristine, white-on-white get-up of Operation Hennessey.[9] In *The Darjeeling Limited*, the boys wear matching train-issue pyjamas – which themselves recall those in *The Life Aquatic* – and each carries a piece of their father's animal print luggage set. In *The Royal Tenenbaums* Richie and Margot wear the same outfits that they did as children: a casual brown suit with a tennis kit, and a striped Lacoste dress with loafers and a fur coat.[10] In each instance the one 'adult' addition – sunglasses and heavy black eyeliner – make them look even more like children dressing up as adults.

As in other smart films, the dysfunctionality of *The Royal Tenenbaums'* narrative setup of grown adults moving home *en masse* is rendered functional by the film. Once the children are 'inverted' back into their childhood space they proceed quite happily: Chas, for instance, seamlessly continues working from his old bedroom, employing Ari and Uzi as assistants. When compared to the more satirical suburban smart films, this trajectory does tend to evoke something like the populism alluded to by Martin. Royal and his children do not regain the heights of their historical achievements by way of moving back home, but they do discover the bonds that never existed or could not be admitted in the past. The most hyperbolic expression of this comes in Royal and Chas' acceptance of one another, while Richie and Margot's admission of their quasi-incestuous lifelong love provides the very kernel of 'functional dys-functionality'. By the time Royal really passes away, he has ingratiated himself to at least some extent with every member of the augmented Tenenbaum clan, something best expressed by Henry when he tells his fiancée's ex-husband that 'I don't think you're an asshole Royal . . . I just think you're kind of a son-of-a-bitch.' Like the eventual sighting of the jaguar shark towards the end of *The Life Aquatic*, the film's epilogue brings the whole 'family' together at a funeral that, it is agreed, Royal would have found 'most satisfactory'. In a final slow-motion display of solidarity, each member walks out of the family crypt – and the film – one by one, and the last shot is of the gate's insignia as Pagoda pulls it closed: *Tenenbaum*.

The Royal Tenenbaums and the Aristocratic Tradition

At one level, the populism of *The Royal Tenenbaums'* ending is undercut by its wry humour, as evident in the way Chas, Ari and Uzi swap their usual red track-suits for black ones, and in the inscription on Royal's headstone – which reads 'died tragically rescuing his family from the wreckage of a destroyed sinking battleship'. At another level, though, the ironic details perfectly complete the family portrait as the unit imagined by Royal. The distance introduced by this humour does not undermine but enhances the curiously residual nature of the Tenenbaum family as depicted at the film's end: it expresses their very mode of being as 'the greatest family that never was' (Jones 2001: 24). In the film's regal ending, the family is idealised as a functional dysfunctional unit: they could not work their lives out beyond the parameters of the unit but have done so inside it, with everyone squared away into smaller modules under the eclectic banner of 'Tenenbaum'. Within this enclosed space, they 'work' perfectly. The false notes in the grand sense of (en)closure can again be referred back to the endings of the 1950s family melodramas. Although the smart cycle as a whole has been likened to this historical tradition in terms of its narrative formula and dramatic conflict, *The Royal Tenenbaums* generically recalls the mode more so than any other smart film. As Mottram has observed, 'while *Punch-Drunk Love* upturns the romantic comedy and *About Schmidt* uses the road movie by way of investigating the theme of the family, *The Royal Tenenbaums* actually sets itself up as a household melodrama' (2006: 342). This occurs in two broad ways: first, at the level of narrative formula, where the film reworks the 'family aristocracy variation' of the melodrama; and second, at the level of stylistic irony, where Anderson revises the distanciation techniques used by the 1950s directors. The remainder of this chapter will examine these two levels of revisionism in *The Royal Tenenbaums*, focusing on the transposition of the family melodrama's key dimension of affect.

In his chapter on the genre, Schatz identifies a number of elements that emerge in early family melodramas of the 1940s but are refined in later examples by Sirk, Minnelli and Ray. Some of these generic elements include: the figure of a dying patriarch in a female-dominated household; the narrative search for a father/lover/husband by anxious offspring; a male intruder-redeemer figure who regenerates and stabilises the family; a focus on the household as the locus of social interaction; the depiction of marriage as a social ritual that solidifies a couple's position within a community (rather than providing an escape from it); a narrative that traces the courtship of a widowed mother as well as, or instead of, her post-adolescent daughter; and the haunting of this courtship by the previous lover's ghost, usually in the guise of children and a class-bound home (Schatz 1981: 229–33). In articulating what he describes as the 'family aristocracy variation', Schatz suggests that the narrative-thematic core of the family melodrama is a metaphoric search for the ideal husband/lover/father that, 'as American mythology would have it, will stabilize the family and integrate it into the larger community' (1981: 235). The division dramatised by the narrative is between socioeconomic security and emotional or sexual fulfillment, with the female characters put in a position where they must opt for one or the other. Schatz sees the dilemma intensified in films including *Written on the Wind* (Douglas Sirk, 1956), *Giant* (George Stevens, 1956), *Cat on a Hot Tin Roof* (Richard Brooks, 1956) and *Home from the Hill* (Vincente Minnelli, 1960). In these films, the family's status is enhanced by its role within the community, with the dramatic conflict based on a contradictory view of marriage as a means of liberation from unreasonable familial demands, and the only way of perpetuating the family aristocracy.

The Royal Tenenbaums' return to the aristocratic tradition is typically described by reference to two sources that Anderson admits he was inspired by: J. D. Salinger's Glass family – who appear in *Nine Stories* (1953), *Franny and Zooey* (1961), *Raise High the Roof-Beam, Carpenters* (1963) and *Seymour: an Introduction* (1963) (Romney 2002: 13) – and Orson Welles' *The Magnificent Ambersons* (1942) (Smith 2001: 28). Welles' film exemplifies the aristocratic tradition as a narrative form that traces succeeding generations of a family who creates and controls the socioeconomic climate around them. Like the Hadley family in *Written on the Wind*, the Ambersons are an 'inescapable ideological given' (Schatz 1981: 235). In both films, the empowerment of the family unit that was discussed in Chapter 2 is literally performed, with the social community a direct extension of the family estate that revolves around Major Amberson (Richard Bennett) and Jasper Hadley (Robert Keith). The concern for both patriarchs regarding the relay of power from one generation to the next is motivated by the spoiled, depressive and confused temperaments of the heirs – George Amberson Minafer (Tim Holt) and Kyle and Marylee Hadley (Robert Stack and Dorothy Malone) (237). Schatz identifies how in the typically affirmative narratives of the aristocratic genre – such as *The Long Hot Summer* (Martin Ritt, 1948), *Cat on a Hot Tin Roof* and *Giant* – an 'intruder-redeemer' figure will enter the scenario as someone who resolves the various family conflicts and returns the heir to the patriarch's favour. The roles are transposed by *The Magnificent Ambersons*, which sees the intruder figure – Eugene Morgan (Joseph Cotton) – *incite* conflict amongst the family when he returns after eighteen years to be with the woman he has always loved – George's mother, Isabel Minafer (Dolores Costello). After Isabel's death, though, the conflict is eventually resolved when George and Eugene make peace. By contrast, Schatz notes that in *Written on the Wind*, Sirk sustains the subversion of convention beyond the film's end: the tension remains unresolved amongst the family members, and ultimately destroys them (1981: 238).

The appeal of *The Royal Tenenbaums* lies in the way it brings this variation of the family melodrama into conjunction with a metastable family to produce a contemporary version of the uneven aristocratic society. It has already been suggested that Anderson's film departs from the suburban smart film in terms of its setting and family organisation. The key way in which *The Royal Tenenbaums* distinguishes itself from this mode (as has been said for Baumbach's *The Squid and the Whale*, and applies also to Jenkins' *The Savages*) is in its depiction of the family unit as an isolated society. As Schatz writes, the typical 1950s melodrama undercuts the 'ideal' of the family as an autonomous human community by situating it within a highly structured social milieu that ultimately determines the family roles. The suburban setting and network-narrative style of a film like *The Chumscrubber* recalls this approach, updating small-town America as an 'extended but perverted family' in which class-consciousness, gossip and reactionary attitudes have stamped out any 'human elements' of love, honesty or generosity (Schatz 1981: 227). By contrast, the augmented Tenenbaums *do* function as an autonomous community: their aristocratic impression stems from the way the wider society appears as an extension of their peculiar values, rather than a climate that attempts to repeal them. Finally, these 'functional dysfunctional' values do appear more conducive to 'human' attitudes than the suburban smart film allows, a phenomenon that significantly contributes to the construction of critical pathos that will be discussed in the next section.

As in the aristocratic films discussed by Schatz, the Tenenbaum family estate – 'the house on Archer Avenue' – functions as the seat of dramatic action, and as the locus for social-familial ritual. The prologue describes the house almost purely in terms of the children's ritualised activities: each bedroom is set up as a shrine to its occupant's discipline (Chas' archived financial magazines, Margot's library of plays, Richie's tennis trophies), the ballroom houses Richie's obsessive drawings of Margot and doubles as her ballet practice space, and a blackboard timetable keeps track of everything. In both the past and the present, the house also functions as the logical space for all events: Margot's eleventh birthday party and the performance of her first play, Etheline's bridge gatherings, and finally her marriage to Henry. The house is also where Richie attempts suicide, and is where Eli crashes his car, in the film's highest moments of action. As practically every description of *The Royal Tenenbaums* attends to, the film's production design is overwhelming, building up a private, rarefied universe: a 'homemade, handcrafted world [with] a strong aroma of 6th grade shop class, of ashtrays made for your mom found in the back of the closet 20 years later' (Jones 2001: 26). Supporting the impression of the Tenenbaums' control over their socioeconomic climate, the detail of the family home is extended to the depiction of New York, which appears in similarly miniaturist terms as a collection of details that are at once obviously invented and entirely plausible: the battered Gypsy Cabs and Green Line buses, the *Côte d'Ivoire* ocean liner and Arctic Line terminal, The Lindbergh Palace hotel, Brook's College, the 375th Street Y and Windswept Fields.

In Anderson's reworking of the constellation of characters outlined by Schatz, the key revision is that there is no feudal monarchy to inherit: the emphasis is not on the transfer of real power but on the reinstatement of a kind of imagined 'royalty'. The most significant evidence for this royalty is the historical genius of the young Tenenbaums which, having abated, makes them inadequate heirs to their own power. Both Chas and Richie are hyperbolically 'tormented' figures – Chas by the death of his wife and Richie by his love for Margot – and Margot's background file positions her as similarly 'frustrated', both artistically and sexually. Royal as patriarch *is* close to death as the story begins but doesn't know this yet, and fakes 'a pretty bad case of cancer' in an attempt to ingratiate himself with his family once he has been evicted from the Lindbergh Palace. By forcing himself upon the Tenenbaums in this way (only Richie is warm to him) Royal himself functions as the intruder figure and, despite his stated desire to 'make up for lost time' with his children, initially equals the distant and somewhat tactless father he was twenty-two years earlier. As the story proceeds, though, he begins to impersonate the father he never was, and by the film's end, as outlined, has in a sense fulfilled the intruder's purpose and redeemed the family. As Anderson has commented,

> I started thinking of the Luke Wilson tennis player character as trying to bring the family back together, but in the end, it's the father that really does it. Luke's character has a warmth towards everyone which nobody else has, his feelings towards the family are less conflicted, but the one who made stuff happen was the most complicated and conflicted, the father. (Smith 2001: 28)

Etheline and Margot perform the parallel mother/daughter courtship with Henry and Richie. In both cases, their previous lovers unsubtly hamper the romance, until both Royal and Raleigh resign themselves to the situation and step aside. As a result of the wider community appearing to function in the idiosyncratic terms of the family, neither romance is especially impeded in social terms. The implication of Margot and Richie's incest is barely alluded to, except by a jealous Eli, who labels the relationship 'sick and gross', and later by Royal, who concludes that it's 'still frowned upon . . . but then what isn't these days, right?' The film's revision of the historical aristocratic scenario naturalises Etheline's situation even further. In the 1950s examples, the mother figure is caught in early middle age between her socially prescribed role as a mother and her reawakened individual and sexual identity, and is typically forced to opt for either socioeconomic security or emotional fulfilment (Schatz 1981: 233). By setting the story at a later point in the family's history, *The Royal Tenenbaums* ensures that Etheline's courtship of Henry is not untimely at all: she has fulfilled her role as mother-domesticator many years earlier, raising a family of geniuses whose talent declined through no fault of her own. At the beginning of the story she is not trapped by a domestic situation but is a successful archaeologist and bridge teacher, and Henry is already her friend and business manager.

What is untimely for Etheline is all three of her children returning to live under the same roof for the first time in many years. Even within this scenario, though, only the vaguest class and race-based objections are raised: Chas insists upon referring to Henry only as 'Mr Sherman', and Royal, clearly jealous, describes him in passing as 'that old black buck'. Even though Etheline doesn't appear to contemplate Royal as an alternative partner, the connotations of the two figures are clearly confused, with Henry the suitor positioned as the sensible socioeconomic prospect (he even couches his proposal to her in terms of a tax benefit) and Royal the husband offering an emotional engagement, albeit a slight and conflicted one (two of the rare times that Etheline appears moved are in scenes with Royal: first in her tearful response to his initial lie that he is dying and second in the park scene where Royal thanks her for raising their children, and then asks 'how's your love life?').[11]

As has already been outlined, the paradox that arises from making the family unit the basis for conflict in the genre of the family melodrama is that the existing family structure is ultimately called upon to act as both the problem and its eventual resolution. As Schatz notes, the only external motivation for resolution in the aristocratic tradition is the influence of the redeemer figure. *The Royal Tenenbaums* concentrates this paradox further by ensuring that *all* characters are part of the family unit: by setting the family up as an expanded, isolated form from the beginning there is no appeal to outside forces at all. This has the effect of intensifying the generic conventions. The conflict and resolution of the scenario is literally written in the terms of the unit as a tautological form. For one thing, the family name itself becomes the focus of reinstatement: with no real money or status attached to it, it is the imagined power crystallised in the very name 'Tenenbaum' that is simultaneously sought and evoked by the narrative. The twisting of the roles also produces a concentrated effect, with Royal doubling as both patriarch and intruder-redeemer. Part of the redemption brought about is, classically, the clarification of the daughter's sexual identity but, as described, this only occurs for Margot with her admission of her love for Richie, her brother. If the move to the family melodrama in the 1950s was marked by a rejection of the external complications that the family conflict had previously enhanced, the smart film's revision of the genre turns inward again, and writes *all* roles in terms of the family, where they become a subject as well as a function.

CRITICAL PATHOS: DISTANCIATION AND AFFECT

Kent Jones pegs the bittersweet tone of *The Royal Tenenbaums* well when he describes its sadness as 'the longing to "restore" a family that was never that happy in the first place to a glory that never was' (2001: 26). This tone can also be identified with Anderson's revision and intensification of the conventions of the family melodrama. As alluded to at the beginning of this chapter, Sirk, Minnelli and Ray's reliance on techniques of irony and distanciation in their films demonstrate how this genre was itself 'never that happy'. Alongside its revision of the genre's narrative formula, *The Royal Tenenbaums* can be interpreted to revise this dimension of the family melodrama's stylistic approach as well.

As has already been outlined, it was the 'double-voicing' strategies of Sirk's films that saw them, and the melodrama as a whole, reconsidered in the 1970s. For Willemen, Sirk's approach relies upon an adaptation of the stylistic features of both expressionism and symbolism, sharing with these movements a characteristic rejection of the conventions of illusionism. In his films, this rejection manifests not in a refusal of the generic rules imposed by the studio system but in their intensification. Specifically, Willemen outlines four ways in which Sirk stylistically magnifies the emotionality of the melodrama: by the deliberate use of symbols as emotional stimuli; by setting the action in an 'echo-chamber' reminiscent of a stage; by using choreography as a direct expression of character; and by the use of baroque colour schemes (1991a: 269–70). For Willemen, this stylisation rejects illusionism by introducing a distance between the film and its narrative pretext. In the second strategy, for instance, the mobility of the camera describes the plot and implicates the viewer at an emotional level, while the overwhelming use of long-shots and mid-shots creates a vast space that keeps the characters at a distance (Willemen 1991b: 276). As 'deliberate and systematic' uses of stylistic procedures that characterised the studio filmmaking of the era, Willemen argues that the key aspect of this distanciation is that it opens a space between Sirk and the spectacle he presents, not between the audience and the spectacle. On the whole, he observes, Sirk's melodramas mercilessly implicate the audience in the emotionally engaging surface action, and their parodic *intensification* goes unperceived.

Where Willemen postulates an audience who either does or does not perceive the strongly marked stylisation, and whose engagement is subsequently critical *or* emotional, other critics have identified more modulated receptions of Sirk's work. In their *Movie* article 'All that Heaven Allowed: Another Look at Sirkian Irony', Babington and Evans suggest that the Sirkian system is simplified by any model of response that hinges on an 'either/or (tears/intellect)' division. Instead, they argue that melodrama demands a model of 'critical pathos', where affect exists in a mutually qualifying relationship with detachment, and is not destroyed by critical understanding (1990: 49–50).[12] To exemplify this response, they address the 'unhinged' behaviour of Marylee Hadley (Dorothy Malone) in *Written on the Wind*, which is typically understood to mobilise overt irony as a function demonstrating the characters' limited capacity for self-knowledge. Babington and Evans suggest, though, that the artificial context created by the film's emotional turbulence and violence does not cancel out but *generates* pathos; in this instance, for 'the realities of female frustrations turned to perversity within the bounds of [the] inflexibly patriarchal family' (53).

They argue that Marylee's histrionic scenes – created through dramatic gestures, sentimental music and symbolic settings – be approached not simply as an example of hyperbole that distanciates its own spectacle, but as part of an 'uneasily suggestive' structure of ironies mingling the sexual with the infantile: 'Marylee is at once almost dementedly perverse and the character most wholly, if distortedly, alive and rebellious in her brash vulgarity and colourful sensuousness' (55). Similarly, they suggest that the *covert* ironies in *All that Heaven Allows* produce a response that is ambiguous rather than purely intellectual. Here, the ironic *deux ex machina* that Laura Mulvey perceives in the film's conclusion, along with the attendant symbols (doves, a deer, Wedgwood china), are described as functions that *confuse* the viewer's perspective: their distanciation 'is structured . . . to produce a response along the following lines: "would that this beautiful image were simply true, but it tells us more about our psychic longings than about the reality principle"'. In this way, Babington and Evans conclude that Sirkian irony is finally *more* pessimistic than his auteurist critics allow.

SMART PATHOS

By emphasising a 'psychic longing' at the heart of Sirk's ironic processes, Babington and Evans argue that the dimension of affect cannot be eradicated from a critical response to his films. For these critics, the most taboo aspect of Sirkian melodrama is not the detached revelation of the contradictions in bourgeois ideology, but the larger worldview that underpins this: the 'pessimism that things are "All that Heaven Allows", "Written on the Wind" or an "Imitation of Life"' (1990: 50). The key tone in this position is, for them, not apathy but a yearning for transcendence. It has already been suggested that longing is also the defining tone of *The Royal Tenenbaums*. Like other examples in the smart cycle, this film deals with 'therapeutic' issues of depression, anxiety, melancholy, boredom and impatience. More so than other examples, though, it also deals openly with the issue of nostalgia: the longing for the past that, elsewhere in the cycle, is generalised and ironised by suburban imagery. As something partially distanciated through cinematography and performance, Anderson's articulation of nostalgia in this film (as well as others) encapsulates the smart film's paradigmatic tone as a confusion of parody and sincerity. In its generation of affect *through* stylistic irony, *The Royal Tenenbaums* demonstrates its own version of critical pathos.

For Sconce, it is the *erasure* of affect that is a 'centrepiece' of the smart film. The first characteristic of the cycle that he addresses is the cultivation of 'blank style', as 'an attempt to convey a film's story, no matter how sensationalistic, disturbing or bizarre, with a sense of *dampened affect*' (2002: 359). As he describes, this blankness is achieved not through a feigned attempt at verité, but through a series of careful stylistic choices mobilised to signify dispassion and disinterest. Where the stylistic ironies of melodrama are readable in strategies of excess and intensification, those of the smart film manifest themselves in these minimalist patterns of framing and editing. Drawing on the example of *Safe* (Todd Haynes, 1995), Sconce outlines how these patterns include: a camera and characters that mostly remain stationary, meaningful set décor, cuts that are measured, unobtrusive and wholly subordinate to character and dialogue, and a form of 'tableau' presentation that isolates its protagonists in static long-takes shot with straight-on, level framing (2002: 359). Together, these techniques support the rejection of 'intensified continuity' that was discussed in Chapter 2. As Sconce writes, the patterns create a sense of disengagement by *de-intensifying* continuity into a series of static tableaux.[13]

It is interesting to note that, despite this *under* rather than overstated pattern of presentation, some smart films rely on stylistic ironies that are themselves direct exaggerations of the four aspects of melodrama that Willemen sees magnified in Sirk. The 'meaningful' set décor that Sconce draws attention to sometimes appears overly symbolic, particularly in the case of Anderson, who conveys entire histories by way of carefully chosen details: something the titled prologues of *Rushmore* and *The Royal Tenenbaums* make overt.[14] As described in Chapter 1, one of Hal Hartley's signature effects is to freeze the action with a sudden dance sequence. Blankly performed and unabsorbed by the narrative, these sequences simultaneously celebrate and ironise the use of choreography as an expression of character: in Geoff Andrew's description, they are a 'modest but affecting variation on a stylistic convention familiar from classical Hollywood escapism' (1999: 293). The baroque colour schemes characteristic of Sirk's films are also apparent in the elaborate sets of Anderson's, most notably in the Tenenbaum house with its deep pink and pale blue walls, and its red, zebra-patterned wallpaper. The striking use of colour in costuming and environment in *Punch Drunk Love* has also been interpreted to play a typically Sirkian codified role, with colours used as 'key indicators of Barry's psychological battle' (C. King 2005).

Beyond the use of colour in the smart film, the technique that most consistently recalls Sirk's own stylistic ironies is the tableau presentation. The static camera and characters, long and mid-shots and straight-on, level framing overtly describe the space of the action as the 'echo-chamber' Willemen sees in Sirk's spaces. In the case of *Safe* and *The Royal Tenenbaums*, the patterns of framing and editing also perform the same narrative function as they do in *Imitation of Life*: emphasising both the spaciousness and the confinement of the décor (Willemen 1991a: 269). This stylistic repetition, though, is qualified by the historicisation of the smart film. As suggested, this sensibility addresses an audience whose taste for irony is radically different to that of Sirk's 1950s audience. Where stylistic devices relating to symbols, colour and space could embody a covert critique in the 1950s, they rely on effects of excess, overstatement and incongruity that have become familiar to later audiences (Babington and Evans 1990: 48). As such, the use of these stylistic devices is always at least partially self-conscious, and creates a distance from the spectacle for both director and audience in a way that often has a comic effect. This creates a new perspective on the closeness of stylisation and parody attended to by Willemen in relation to Sirk, insofar as the mere occurrence of such techniques appears 'strongly marked', and thereby somewhat parodic (1991a: 271). As suggested, the achievement of tone in the smart film, and particularly in Anderson's work, is to create a measure of affect within this self-conscious distanciation.

Paul Gormley is one writer who has directly addressed the tensions between self-conscious cultural knowledge and affect in contemporary American cinema. By way of an interest in what he describes as the 'new-brutality film' – a cycle including *Reservoir Dogs* (Quentin Tarantino, 1991), *Falling Down* (Joel Schumacher, 1992), *Strange Days* (Kathryn Bigelow, 1995) and *Se7en* (David Fincher, 1995) – Gormley asks a broad question regarding the kind of affect produced in Hollywood cinema of the 1990s. Specifically, he is interested in the cultural knowledge these films assume, and to what extent the viewer's response to their self-reflexive display of knowledge can be labelled affective (2005: 12). For Gormley, the 'body-first' approach of the films attempts to reanimate the immediacy of the cinematic experience by causing an assault that encourages the viewer to mimic the actions of the bodies on screen. While this experience subordinates knowledge outside the image to the affect of its impact, the reaction is complicated by the way the films simultaneously invite the viewer to laugh at their pop culture references: for example, the use of Stealers Wheel's 'Stuck in the Middle with You' in the torture scene in *Reservoir Dogs*. This secondary reaction relies on a system of knowledge that does extend beyond the image, thereby unbalancing its purely affective quality.

In a broad way, Gormley is postulating for the new-brutality film a modulated model of response recalling that suggested by Babington and Evans for Sirk's melodramas, and that being suggested for the smart film here: in all instances, a reliance on cultural knowledge means that neither a purely critical nor purely affective response can be experienced. As Gormley writes, 'it is not easy to discern clear-cut divisions between images that have a bodily affect and those that operate through referencing structures of cinematic knowledge' (2005: 12). The new-brutality film undercuts its affective assault by referencing pop culture systems that sit incongruously with the realist depiction of violence in the image. Similarly, the smart film relies upon techniques of excess and incongruity recognisable from the ironic melodramas of the 1950s to distance its own affecting stories of failure and anxiety.

It is the differing systems of knowledge appealed to by the new-brutality and smart cycles, though, and the way this appeal is made, that distinguishes their critical-affective trajectories. Gormley describes how the new-brutality film also relies upon past systems of knowledge to *create* affect, and cites the long takes and tracking shots of *Reservoir Dogs* as techniques associated with the realist depiction of violence in the films of Martin Scorsese and Sam Peckinpah. By contrast, when Sconce alludes to Tarantino, it is to link *Pulp Fiction* (1994) with *Your Friends and Neighbors* and *Night on Earth* (Jim Jarmusch, 1991) as evidence of the distanciating effect created when coincidence and synchronicity are mobilised as a principle of narrative organisation (2002: 363). As another school of popular 1990s American cinema, the affective objectives of the new-brutality film situate it as a *counterpoint* to the smart film.

Although the dampened sense of affect in the smart film also relies upon long takes and tracking shots, these techniques are couched in a system of stylisation that is antithetical to the realist objectives of the new-brutality film. The smart film's 'blank' cinematography is augmented by keen anti-naturalistic tendencies at the levels of narrative, performance, dialogue, *mise-en-scène* and music. Of all the films that can be included in the cycle, Anderson's demonstrate these tendencies best by way of their overwhelming formality. The stories are all overtly signalled as 'make-believe': from Dignan's caper-style 'escape' from the institution he is freely released from at the beginning of *Bottle Rocket*, to Team Zissou's 'adventures', which are packaged and preserved in episodic films. *Rushmore* and *The Royal Tenenbaums* are clearest in this way, with their narratives visually framed as, respectively, a play and a novel. With its action divided into chapters, the latter film magnifies the approach: befitting the anti-classical style of narration that was outlined in Chapter 2, each chapter functions as a formal and discrete unit. As described there, this narrative style positions the story as a continuous serial that extends beyond the script. The 'closure' signalled by *The Royal Tenenbaums'* titled epilogue is undermined by the hyperbole of the scene's presentation, and the 'functionally dysfunctional' way the family has been depicted; it is implied that the 'adventures' of the Tenenbaums, like those of Team Zissou in *The Life Aquatic*, will continue.

This last point indicates how, at every step, Anderson's formality actually exceeds itself, describing not a sparse, deadened world (something presented in other smart films, such as LaBute's *Your Friends and Neighbors*) but one that is teeming with life. Emotion may be stamped out at the level of presentation itself, but the shape of it lingers in *what* is presented. This is something that is perhaps most adequately demonstrated at the level of performance. The actors' understated, and even deadpan, delivery of the lucid dialogue does initially appear to flatten them into caricatured types. This impression is set up by the expository 'cast of characters' sequence, where each character is described in terms of a finite set of details captured in one shot – precisely, as figures in a book.[15] Throughout the film, as already noted, the impression is sustained by the characters staying in their respective 'uniforms': Royal's formal suits – which interchange easily with his actual Lindbergh Palace uniform when, near the film's end, he gains a job there – Pagoda's pink trousers, Etheline's pastel suits, Henry's shirt, blazer and bow tie, Eli's urban cowboy outfit and Dudley's

Figure 10   Ben Stiller, Danny Glover, Gwyneth Paltrow and Anjelica Huston in *The Royal Tenenbaums* (Wes Anderson, 2001). Courtesy Touchstone Pictures / The Kobal Collection / James Hamilton.

shorts and hat. As Jones has noted, too, these characterisations are ultimately based upon an extraordinary attunement to the private traits of the actors: 'Gene Hackman's penchant for bobbing and weaving with his scene partners . . . Bill Murray's wistful, sad-sack withdrawal and real-life disenchantment; Gwyneth Paltrow's tendency to singularize her characters and hone things down to a set of finite gestures; Ben Stiller's exaggeratedly physical, high-key comic attack' (2001: 25). The caricatures function as a façade within which something real and often delicate lurks.

The effect is also visible in Anderson's idiosyncratic tableau presentation. As in Haynes' *Safe*, Anderson draws on this technique to isolate his characters in symmetrically constructed space with a static camera and straight-on, level framing. Again, *The Royal Tenenbaums'* cast of characters sequence serves as the most precise example, where the 'meaningful' décor of each character's shot takes on a metonymic function that subtends his/her blank expression. Anderson emphasises the technique even further as the film progresses by setting up tableau shots that the action advances into: cabs pull into a static frame, characters walk in or out (for example, when Royal first confronts Etheline and she can't decide whether to walk towards or away from him, or in the final shot when all the characters leave the film). He also sets up shot reverse-shot tableaux that provide mirror reflections of character perspectives. The two most obvious examples of this technique frame discussions between Royal and his three children: once when he tells them, as children, that Etheline has asked him to leave; and later when he returns to them under the false premise of stomach cancer. In the first instance – the film's second scene – Royal is positioned at one end of the vast dining table, and the three children at the other. In line with their exchanges, the perspective shifts 180 degrees back and forth eleven times before lingering on Royal as Pagoda brings him a cocktail. In the second instance, the space is more intimately described, and Royal sits on a chair opposite a couch containing Richie and Margot, close together. Here, the perspective switches only four times before skewing to Chas, who stands to the side. In each instance, the presentation is clearly used to sketch character alliances: the covertly ironic camera-positioning that keeps Cary Scott separate from her two children in *All That Heaven Allows* is here presented explicitly (Willemen 1991b: 275).

The distance between *Safe* as analysed by Sconce and these scenes from *The Royal Tenenbaums* exemplifies the diverse manner in which tableau presentation is drawn upon by the smart film. Sconce describes the technique as a means of fostering a sense of clinical observation that imparts a sense of 'impassiveness, inevitability and resignation' (Sconce 2002: 360). Anderson's tableaux, though formally impeccable, confuse this clinical tone; largely by way of the warmth and detail of their *mise-en-scène*, and the humour and/or pathos evoked by the hapless characters' exchanges. As Jones writes, the formality of *The Royal Tenenbaums* is empathically connected to the depressed characters (2001: 25), whose 'depression' is worn as a type of caricatured shell. Accordingly, the moments captured in tableau presentation are often 'impossibly fragile'. In one of Richie and Margot's visits to the rooftop of the Tenenbaum house, Margot retrieves two ten-year-old cigarettes from under a brick in the chimney and, after lighting them and giving one to Richie, shyly places her hand on his shoulder as though posing for a family photograph as the two gaze off into the distance. The moment is statically framed but heavy with the weight of their long secret and its revelation, and also with nostalgic detail: Margot's teenage hiding place for her cigarettes; her ever-present fur coat, and Mordecai – the pet eagle that Richie released upon returning home but who returned with his feathers mysteriously whiter. Margot's stance strongly recalls the way she appears in one of Richie's portraits and, as they calmly contemplate their world in this newly confident pose, the image feels positively iconic.[16]

The more emphatic tableau scenes with Royal function similarly in the way that the formal presentation and blank performances capture two delicate moments in which a father is forced to confront the distance between himself and his children. In each instance, the highly stylised *mise-en-scène* of the Tenenbaum house – the pink walls, heavy furniture, chandeliers and framed portraits – augments this sense of critical pathos. As Mottram has observed, the film's densely detailed universe *distances* the audience from its 'very sad tale about a family shattered by failure' (2006: 346) but, via the mechanisation of nostalgia, it also brings us closer.

The grave beauty that the sense of nostalgia imparts to *The Royal Tenenbaums* depends significantly upon the film's creation of an archaic world, seemingly untouched by any post-1960s developments. Although contemporary dates are given (the lifespan on Royal's headstone is 1932–2001), and at least one contemporary song is used (Elliott Smith's 'Needle in the Hay'), the Tenenbaums' environment appears not to have changed since Chas, Margot and Richie's childhood. New York City is rendered as an extension of the museum-like Tenenbaum house, with the miniature and outmoded details inside of it (Margot's tiny television set strapped to the bathroom radiator, the record player that she and Richie listen to The Rolling Stones on) reflected and complemented by the broad details beyond it (the historic buildings and streetscapes, the battered cabs and buses). This anti-technology stance is replicated in Anderson's approach to filmmaking: on the Criterion Collection DVD commentary for *The Royal Tenenbaums* he describes his taste for built tracks and dolly shots over Steadicam, and for straight cuts over dissolves or fades: 'anything that keeps the film out of a lab'.

At a broader level, the archaic impression is supported by a lack of dependence upon popular culture as a system of knowledge. Where Tarantino alludes to Elvis, Madonna, pop tunes of the seventies, McDonalds and gangster and samurai films, Anderson recalls Proust, Orson Welles, Powell and Pressburger, Charlie Brown and *The New Yorker*. Across the board, the references in *The Royal Tenenbaums* are more veiled, and to a wholly different tenor of knowledge: the cast of characters sequence is inspired by *Death Takes a Holiday* (Mitchell Leisen, 1934); Richie's line 'I'm going to kill myself tomorrow' is from *Le Feu Follet* (Louis Malle, 1963), and Royal's 'I know you, asshole' is from *Witness* (Peter Weir, 1985); Henry's ascension of the stairs to expose Royal's fake illness is based on Cary Grant in *Suspicion* (Alfred Hitchcock, 1941) and the idea of Richie and Margot running away to live in the City Public Archives is from 'From the Mixed Up Files of Mrs Basil E. Frankenweiler' (Anderson 2002).

As was discussed in relation to Whit Stillman and Hal Hartley in Chapter 1, the sensibility of smart cinema relies on a system of intertextuality that is distinct from that of other 1990s American films. While the smart films necessarily vary in terms of their allusions and inspirations – and especially in their music, as will be discussed in the next chapter – an engagement with pop culture is generally avoided. As is evident from the examples described above,

Anderson's practice of allusionism produces moments of resonance rather than removal: it is another formally distanciating strategy that provokes an affective response. In conclusion, Anderson's creation of critical pathos can perhaps be described in terms of a regime of knowledge that reaches further back again to inform the peculiar aristocracy of *The Royal Tenenbaums'* revised family melodrama.

SHOWING AND TELLING

In a 1995 article titled 'Regimes of Subjectivity and Looking' Paul Willemen questions the assumption made by contemporary theories of vision that Cartesian perspectivalism definitively replaced the scopic regimes that preceded it. Specifically, Willemen wants to question this assumption in relation to the 'alleged in-built perspectival modernity of the cinematic apparatus', and put forward the converse hypothesis that films operate with more than one regime simultaneously (1995: 101). The regime that Willemen is opposing to Cartesian perspectivalism here is what he loosely calls pre-capitalist or feudal looking. If the Cartesian system locates the subject at the apex of a triangle and understands perspective to emanate from the individual's point of view, the feudal system that Willemen is proposing necessarily suggests a pre-individualist mode of subjectivity. He acknowledges that there are likely to be as many scopic regimes as there are social-historical forms of subjectivity, but uses the feudal mode as a means of suggesting that all discourses and cultural practices consist of discursive currents. Willemen is referring here not to the codes of content by which directors 'quote' historical movements – for example, Godard referring to Rembrandt or Goya – but to codes of expression: 'the alignment between regimes of looking and regimes of subjectivity as they affect cinematic discourse itself' (106).

Despite the multiple regimes that he perceives within filmic expression, Willemen notes that it is still rare for film studies to discern a variety of ideologies and discourses at work simultaneously in a film. He outlines two areas in which the foundations for this work have been laid: in Ashish Rajadhyaksha's work on the issue of 'frontality' in early Indian films, and in Tom Gunning and André Gaudréault's work on early film as a 'cinema of attractions'. Willemen details how Rajadhyaksha refers to a practice of representation in popular painting that flourished around the turn of the twentieth century, where a characteristic frontal view of Srinathji could be adorned with devotees' own photographs. Taken in profile and stuck on both sides of the god in the positions where priests and devotees were usually painted in the traditional mode, the photograph says not 'I was here', but 'I have been seen by the god'. Contrary to Cartesian perspectivalism, it is not the act of looking that affirms the subject's subjectivity but the process of being looked at by the authority, as when a subject is received in audience by an official dignitary (a king or pope) symbolising 'the order of things'. Rajadhyaksha draws on this ritual of representation as a way of explaining the organisation of gazes in films by Dadasaheb Phalke.

For Willemen, the notion of the 'cinema of attractions' is also instructive in conveying something about the medium of cinema as a composite form involving multiple regimes of perspective and subjectivity. Gunning and Gaudréault both emphasise early cinema's tendency to show or display the technical possibilities of the new medium rather than focus on character or narrative. The tableau was autonomous, with the objective of presenting 'the totality of an action unfolding in a homogeneous space' (Gaudréault in Willemen 1995: 113). Gunning describes the transition to narrative cinema as a shift in spatial coherence whereby the autonomous tableau gave way to a synthetic space constructed out of discrete shots. Rather than being bound to a pro-filmic scene, attention now shifted to issues of succession and causality, where the significance of the shot became dependent on those that preceded and followed it. For Gunning, this represents an uneven shift in the interplay between presentation and representation, spectacle and narrative, and showing and telling. Willemen also refers to Elsaesser, who sees spectatorship transformed here from a collective audience experiencing a performative space to isolated spectators each bound up with imaginary representations; the development of narrative structure implying a mode of address that encouraged Cartesian subjects.

While not wanting to overstate the relevance of these two scopic regimes to Anderson's contemporary, narrative-bound filmmaking, it does seem that the qualities of each system can be perceived in the formal structure and presentation of *The Royal Tenenbaums*, and can perhaps cast some light on the peculiar model of response the film provokes. Anderson's reliance on a frontal, tableau style of presentation that simultaneously keeps the spectator remote and draws them in via pathos does rely on a certain regal dialectic operating through both distance and devotion. In the frontal cast of characters sequence there is a strong impression that the apex of perspective does not lie with the viewer but with the figures who, gazing directly into the camera, return our stare. In setting up the imagined royalty of the Tenenbaums, the sequence wryly positions the family members as dignitaries into whose field of vision the audience is received. The grandiose set-up recalls the power of the family in the aristocratic family melodrama, whose influence does extend over the enclosed world that, for its residents, constitutes 'the order of things'. Behind the blank façade that initially appears to symbolise disengagement, these shots can in this way be read as making a profound connection.

Anderson's book motif overtly frames *The Royal Tenenbaums* as a story – a *narrative*. This strategy also tends to disrupt the film's causal flow, though: in practice, the titled chapters freeze the story into eight distinct 'scenes'. Each is obviously not restricted to one space, or even strictly to one time frame, but the impression is nonetheless given of a 'totality of action' whereby each character's contemporaneous activities are detailed before moving on to what they all do next. As an extension of the Tenenbaum universe, New York does appear as a homogeneous space – 'a big, faded magic playhouse' (Jones 2001: 26) in whose 'rooms' family members occupy themselves.[17] The sensation of an autonomous tableau is further emphasised by the dense detail of this universe, where information is overwhelmingly contained in small, unreferenced cues. When Etheline's former suitors are silently introduced as an explorer, an architect and a director in three two-second shots, the presentational aspect of cinema is foremost, equating camera and spectator. As Willemen writes, the 'showing' dimension remains distinct, even though it is inextricably entangled with the 'telling' dimension that it illustrates.

The perception of these regimes in *The Royal Tenenbaums* goes some way toward explaining the critical pathos that this film evokes. Over and above Anderson's specific references, these alternative scopic regimes mobilise cultural knowledge in a manner that is fundamentally different to other contemporary American filmmaking. Rather than functioning as codes of content that distance the spectator (as Gormley argues Tarantino's cultural references do), these regimes function as codes of expression that *bind* the spectator to the film. The smart and new-brutality cycles present two models of affect in 1990s American cinema, and two models of critical pathos as 'qualified empathy'. In the new-brutality film, the initial affective impact is qualified, and distanced, by cultural knowledge. In the smart film, as a revision of the narrative formula and stylistic approach of the family melodrama, the initial distanciated impact is qualified by emotional affect. *The Royal Tenenbaums* may evoke its codes of content and expression wryly but, in a manner that crystallises the smart cinema cycle as a whole, this works to pluralise their force.

NOTES

1. Sconce signals the connection himself when he uses the term 'cold melodrama' to distinguish *The Ice Storm*, *The Sweet Hereafter* and *Safe* in the overall smart taxonomy (2002: 350).
2. The most comprehensive account of this 1970s work and its key articles can be found in Gledhill, ed., *Home is Where the Heart Is* (1987).
3. Lynn Spigel has addressed in detail how the emergence of television at this time was another factor that worked to construct – and re-construct – the notion of the family. See *Make Room for TV: Television and the Family Ideal in Postwar America* (1992).
4. As Schatz notes, the most popular and 'optimistic' melodramas from this decade – *Meet Me in St Louis* (1944); *It's a Wonderful Life* (1946) – already relied for their impact on the gradual erosion of cultural confidence in the nuclear family. Despite the obvious aims to reaffirm traditional family and community values, the

conflict in these films is animated by 'nightmare' sequences that momentarily point to doubts about the stability that the surface stories and generic codes enact (Schatz 1981: 227).

5. See, for instance, Tania Modleski's *The Women Who Knew Too Much: Hitchcock and Feminist Theory* (1988) and Chuck Kleinhans' 'Notes on Melodrama and the Family under Capitalism' in Gledhill, ed. (1987).

6. The cycle can be likened in this sense to the era of 1980s television sitcoms where, after acknowledging 'alternative' family forms throughout the 1970s – *The Mary Tyler Moore Show* (1970–7), *One Day at a Time* (1975–84), *Three's Company* (1977–84) – this form reverted to overwhelmingly nuclear representations – *Family Ties* (1982–9), *The Cosby Show* (1984–92), *Roseanne* (1988–97) – in an era when social evidence of this form was in decline. See Muriel Cantor, 'The American Family on Television: From Molly Goldberg to Bill Cosby' (1991).

7. For two detailed accounts of Haynes' revision see Sharon Willis' 'The Politics of Disappointment: Todd Haynes Rewrites Douglas Sirk' (2003) and Salomé Aguilera Skvirsky's 'The Price of Heaven: Remaking Politics in *All that Heaven Allows, Ali: Fear Eats the Soul*, and *Far From Heaven*' (2008).

8. The frontal portrait of the Tenenbaums is the cover image for Murray Pomerance's edited collection *A Family Affair: Cinema Calls Home* (2008), and the film is attended to in Andrew Horton's chapter 'Is it a Wonderful Life?: Families and Laughter in American Film Comedies'.

9. One interpretation of Anderson's work sees the motif of uniforms as evidence of a certain fascist aesthetic that remains latent in the first three films but becomes patent in *The Life Aquatic*. See Nordstrum 2006.

10. The distinction of the three children by way of differing sports brands: Fila (Richie), Lacoste (Margot) and Adidas (Chas) is one of Anderson's few references to contemporary consumer culture, along with the inclusion of the Zissou-branded Adidas trainer in *The Life Aquatic*.

11. There is a strong impression of serialisation between Etheline, Eleanor in *The Life Aquatic* and Patricia Whitman in *The Darjeeling Limited* – all played by Angelica Huston. When Steve muses after Ned's death that this is the only time he's ever seen Eleanor cry in the entire time he's known her (except for once when she got her arm caught in a deck wench) he could be describing Etheline or Patricia. This serial characterisation supports the smart film's general tendency toward serialisation that was discussed in Chapter 1.

12. Babington and Evans acknowledge that this is largely the position formulated by Elsaesser in 'Tales of Sound and Fury: Observations on the Family Melodrama', and also agreed with by Gledhill in 'The Melodramatic Field: An Investigation', when she notes 'Pathos, unlike pity, is a cognitive as well as an affective construct' (Gledhill 1987: 30).

13. David Bordwell has suggested that Hal Hartley's preference for this style of presentation, and particularly for longer shot lengths, is not a rejection of intensified continuity but represents a 'prudent' assimilation. See 'Up Close and Impersonal: Hal Hartley and the Persistence of Tradition' (2005).

14. In his commentary on the Criterion Collection DVD of *The Royal Tenenbaums*, Anderson describes how entire sets were built for one line in the script.

15. In his predominantly psychoanalytic interpretation of Anderson's films, 'Making A Go of It: Paternity and Prohibition in the Films of Wes Anderson', Joshua Gooch reads the cast of characters sequence through the logic of the time-image. He argues that 'these impacted narrative images are grouped and juxtaposed to generate a subjectivity of prohibition expressed through mediation. As subjects that can find their expression only through image, characterization begins on the surface as a

self-conscious image bound up in narrative recursion. Thus in Anderson, the time-image is given over wholly to narrative, and its presentation of time is bound to the narrative as the presentation of diegetic time, not of time itself' (Gooch 2007: 30–1).
16. The general impression of icons in Anderson's films is emphasised upon seeing the Criterion Collection DVD releases, where Eric Anderson's hand-drawn images of moments both internal and external to the narratives decorate the menus and liner notes, freezing them into portraits.
17. The literal extension of this presentational style can be seen in the flat and open sets of Lars von Trier's *Dogville* and *Manderlay*. Anderson takes the idea further himself in the cross-section shots of the Belafonte in *The Life Aquatic*.

4. MUSIC: *SIMPLE MEN, MAGNOLIA, GHOST WORLD*

The sequence comprising one of the most palpable 'music moments' in the smart cycle occurs early in the film addressed in the previous chapter – *The Royal Tenenbaums*. Once Chas and Margot Tenenbaum have returned to the family home, the story turns to Richie Tenenbaum who, upon hearing of his father's alleged illness, halts his two-year excursion on the ocean liner *Côte d'Ivoire* to return home as well. Alec Baldwin's terse voiceover fills in the details on Richie's trip back to New York, concluding with the information that he had made a request for his 'usual escort' to meet him at the pier by way of the Green Line bus, and that, as always, she was late. There is a cut from a long shot of Richie lounging on his luggage before the terminal to a reverse long shot from his perspective, in which a bus pulls up and people begin to disembark. As Margot appears in the bus door in medium shot, the scene shifts into slow motion and, as she climbs down and pauses for a moment, her eyes fixed on Richie, Nico's 'These Days' begins in the newly stilled and silent scene. As the first guitar notes play, there is a cut to a close-up of Richie contemplating her from behind his sunglasses and beard, then a cut back to Margot as she approaches him, still in slow motion, a half smile playing upon her face. The song is still the only sound audible as the lyrics begin: *I've been out walking . . . I don't do too much talking these days, these days. These days I seem to think a lot about the things that I forgot to do.* As Margot draws to within a few metres of Richie the film returns to normal pace, the background noise is mixed back in and the music is faded down to allow for the words that mark the reunion of this brother and sister who will soon admit that they are in love with one another. J. Hoberman has suggested that the entire film might have been conceived to provide a frame for this song (Hoberman 2001).

The moment is typical of Anderson's approach to filmmaking as it was discussed in Chapter 3: it is at once understated and wrought with detail; detached and full of pathos. In a broader way, the moment expresses the centrality of music and musicality to the smart cycle as a whole. The original scores for *Rushmore*, *The Royal Tenenbaums* and *The Life Aquatic* were composed by ex-Devo member Mark Mothersbaugh, who has described the transition from music as a natural progression, claiming that Devo were always inspired by films (Reay 2004: 80). In conjunction with the Mothersbaugh scores, these soundtracks also feature an eclectic mix of material compiled by music supervisor Randall Poster, including The Clash, Ravel and Portuguese renditions of David Bowie songs. Paul Thomas Anderson has also demonstrated a particular concern with music across all of his films: *Boogie Nights* is structured by 1970s pop songs, he describes *Magnolia* as an 'adaptation' of Aimee Mann songs, and both *Punch Drunk Love* and *There Will Be Blood* demonstrate interesting collaborations with, respectively, experimental composer Jon Brion and Radiohead guitarist Jonny Greenwood. Hal Hartley composed for many of his 1990s films under the pseudonym Ned Rifle, and demonstrates some of the most pure examples of compiled music moments, Todd Solondz relies upon the awkward diegetic rendition of songs by untalented performers in his particular dystopian visions, and Terry Zwigoff's *Ghost World* – adapted for the screen by Daniel Clowes from his graphic novel – presents a director and characters that are similarly music-obsessed (Gross 2002: 16).

The general significance of music in the cycle distinguishes the smart film as a type where music supervision is more than an administrative role.[1] For the directors of the films mentioned, music functions as part of the filmmaking process itself, with specific songs and music written into the screenplay. Anderson has claimed he always has the music in mind first for key scenes such as the Richie and Margot meeting and in some instances for the film altogether: in a *Film Comment* interview he explains how he began *The Royal Tenenbaums* with the idea of the Nico song and of Ravel's string quartet in F major, which would accompany a group of characters statically facing the camera (Smith 2001: 28). He describes how music inspires specific ideas in his scripts, but also suggests the tenor of the films themselves. With a focus on this latter idea, this chapter is concerned with grasping the peculiar 'musicality' of the smart film. It will examine the way that music in this cycle both affirms and transforms the classical roles of music in film to create a type of 'music-image' that can be approached by way of ideas including cinephilia and figuration. In this way, the music-image can be understood as another dimension of the smart film's critical aesthetics.

POPULAR MUSIC IN FILM

As every writer on music in film tends to note, it is only recently that the audibility of film music has been critically recognised, and audiences still, on the whole, pay only limited attention to music in relation to the other dimensions of the soundtrack: dialogue and sound effects. In the most substantial study of this phenomenon, Annahid Kassabian outlines an 'Attention Continuum' in her 2001 book *Hearing Film: Tracking Identifications in Contemporary Hollywood Film Music*. Examining how music interacts with other aspects of the scene, Kassabian puts forward a scale ranging from instances that focus audience attention on the music – theme songs and scenes with only music on the soundtrack – through to scenes where music is used as background to dialogue, and commands the least attention. In between are scenes where other sounds have a low profile in comparison to the music, and scenes where there is a lot of visual action with sound effects and music but little or no dialogue (2001: 52–4). In more recent work, Kassabian has revised this approach by examining how the distinctions between noise, sound and music cannot be clearly drawn in films that make a 'textural use of sound' (2003: 143). Examples she alludes to include *Apocalypse Now* (Francis Ford Coppola, 1979) and *The Cell* (Tarsem Singh, 2000), but a similar argument could be made for *Punch Drunk Love*, where the percussive soundtrack blurs the line between sound and music, and confuses Kassabian's original continuum by often being mixed at the same level as dialogue.

Claudia Gorbman's 1987 book *Unheard Melodies* plays an influential role in the study of music in film, and her discussion of signification in classical film scoring is often used as a benchmark against which to compare and contrast the textual functions of popular film music.[2] Later writers frequently engage with the principle of 'inaudibility' that she expounds. Gorbman identifies seven principles of classical film scoring, including that which states 'music is not meant to be heard consciously. As such it should subordinate itself to dialogue, to visuals, that is, to the primary vehicles of narrative' (1987: 73). Other principles regarding the composition, mixing and editing of music in classical film outlined by Gorbman include that the technical apparatus of nondiegetic music must be *invisible*, that soundtrack music is first and foremost a *signifier of emotion*, that music provide *narrative cueing* by way of both referential cues supplying formal information on setting and character, and connotative cues by which music interprets and illustrates narrative events, and that music provide *continuity* by filling gaps between shots and scenes and *unity* via the repetition and variation of instrumentation.

As a dedicated study of popular film music, Jeff Smith's *The Sounds of Commerce: Marketing Popular Film Music* (1998) traces the forms, commercial functions and textual operations of the pop score as distinct from the classical score, and of the compilation score – or pop soundtrack – as distinct from both these types. For Smith, the pop score is defined according to two criteria: it must be composed or compiled in one or more popular musical styles, and it must be formally accessible to the average moviegoer. Smith outlines the distinctions between the classical score and those of popular composers such as Henry Mancini, John Barry and Ennio Morricone in terms of the more general differences between the pop idiom and the Romantic idiom, whose stylistic parameters dominated the classical tradition. These distinctions include a greater reliance on song forms, the decline of the variable *leitmotif* in favour of the more standardised riff or hook, a freer approach to rhythmic inflection, and an emphasis on timbre as the dimension constituting a particular musician's distinctive performance style (1998: 4–9).

In 1949, composer Aaron Copland suggested five narrative functions of music in film that provided a useful summary of the specific roles of popular film music as it was to emerge in the following decade. Smith describes how, for Copland, music works to: 1) convey a convincing atmosphere of time and place, 2) underline the unspoken feelings or psychological states of characters, 3) serve as a kind of neutral background filler to the action, 4) give a sense of continuity to the editing, and 5) accentuate the theatrical buildup of a scene and round it off with a feeling of finality (6). As Smith notes, for composers such as those mentioned above, the score was not an afterthought grafted onto the film in postproduction, but 'a calculated element in the film's larger schemes of production and marketing' (1998: 154). The 'logical extension' of their multi-theme scores for films such as *Breakfast at Tiffany's* (Blake Edwards, 1961), *Goldfinger* (Guy Hamilton, 1964) and *The Good, the Bad and the Ugly* (Sergio Leone, 1966) – where songs specifically composed for the films were combined with conventional scoring devices emphasising visual actions and character reactions – was the compilation score. While serving some of Copland's narrative functions, this type necessarily challenged others.

Emerging as a component of the New Hollywood period discussed in Chapter 2, the compilation scores to films including *Easy Rider* (Dennis Hopper, 1969) and *The Last Picture Show* (Peter Bogdanovich, 1971) 'presented a series of self-contained musical numbers, usually prerecorded songs, which were substituted for the repeated and varied occurrences of a score's theme' (Smith 1998: 155). In its purest form, pop and rock tunes were included as the only form of music, and the scoring process became a matter of song selection and placement – or 'spotting' – rather than original music composition. In 'hybrid' compilation scores, such as those for *The Graduate, Midnight Cowboy* (John Schlesinger, 1969) and *Zabriskie Point* (Michelangelo Antonioni, 1970), pre-existing songs were combined with music written directly for the moods, actions and editing patterns of the films. The general consensus reached by Smith and other writers on the compilation score is that, while demonstrating a distinctly more self-conscious use of music, it is a type that is still firmly ensconced within the boundaries of classical narration, with songs spotted in such a way as to perform any or all of the classical score's traditional functions. In this way, much of the work on pure and hybrid compilation scores remains within the parameters of the functions developed by Copland, and even the principles outlined by Gorbman. After a brief examination of these classical functions of the compilation score, and a consideration of their work in the various soundtracks of the smart cycle, the chapter will turn to some approaches that move decisively beyond these parameters to illuminate the particular musicality of the smart film.

FUNCTIONS OF THE COMPILATION SCORE

The classical principle most obviously contested by the compilation soundtrack is that of inaudibility. In her book *Settling the Score*, Kathryn Kalinak suggests that the compilation soundtrack ignores three fundamental principles of the classical score, including the use of music to illustrate narrative content, the use of music to provide structural unity, and the use of music as an inaudible component of narrative signification (1992: 186–7). Smith proposes that the expressive qualities of the compilation score derive less from its musical qualities than from the system of extra-musical allusion activated by the score's referentiality (1998: 155), a statement that clearly relies upon the audibility of the score. Pauline Reay observes how Smith's overarching consideration of film music within its economic context raises a number of significant theoretical questions with regard to the notion of inaudibility, referring back to Smith's comment in an earlier article that, 'far from being "inaudible", film music has frequently been both noticeable and memorable, often because of the various demands placed upon it to function in ancillary markets' (Smith in Reay 2004: 25). Further, Steve Lannin and Matthew Caley introduce their book *Pop Fiction: The Song in Cinema* by describing how the audibility of popular music in film can transcend the image: for them, a song's 'on-screen action . . . has multifarious abilities to extend the screen through affective and subjective dimensions, with limitless transcendence of the image' (2005: 10).

For all these writers, the audibility of popular music in film is related to the referentiality opened up by a song's lyrics. In their arguments, though, a number of broader functions are also evoked. Smith notes that the historical specificity of popular music makes it an effective means of denoting both time and place. While a genre of music can be drawn upon generally to signify a time period – for example, disco and the seventies – specific performers and styles can also evoke a more localised culture: Smith refers to the use of Hank Williams and Tony Bennett in *The Last Picture Show* to induce 'the atmosphere of a dying Texas town in the mid-fifties' (1998: 165). When music is used diegetically this periodising effect is obviously strongest: another of Smith's examples is *Nothing But a Man* (Michael Roemer, 1964), where Motown hits figure as the background noise of the film's contemporary Southern locales.

Another well-recognised function of the compilation score is the use of popular songs to inflect the emotional import of film. This function overtly relates the compilation score back to the classical Hollywood film which, as Gorbman has also noted, *is* melodrama – a drama where music marks the entrances of characters, provides interludes and gives emotional colouring to rapid and climactic scenes (1987: 34). In the specific genre of melodrama, music is a central component of excess insofar as it expresses the emotion that cannot be accommodated within the action: as Geoffrey Nowell-Smith has observed, along with the *mise-en-scène*, music *substitutes* for the action, rather than merely heightening it (1987: 73). In an article addressing how theories concerning the emotional functions of the classical score carry over to the compilation score, Murray Smith distinguishes the two types on account of the latter's dimensions of lyrics and performance. Drawing on Michel Chion's distinction between 'theatrical' and 'emanation' speech in film, Smith describes two ways in which song lyrics can express the emotion of characters and scenes, and elicit and arouse emotion in spectators: 'literary' songs by performers such as Bob Dylan and Aimee Mann rely on the meaning of utterances, where in other songs the vocals are less articulate and lower in the mix, functioning to 'evoke sequences of loosely related vivid images' that register a human presence, but not through language. Smith also makes a distinction between the classical and compilation score on account of the anonymity of the performance in the former, arguing that in the latter it is the features of a particular musician's performative style that is vital to, or even constitutive of, the expressive and emotional qualities of the music (Smith 2006).

The functions of periodisation and emotional expression have already alluded to the most obvious, and specific, function of the compilation score, which is to let the referential dimension of song titles and/or lyrics speak for characters or comment on a film's action. A key prejudice against the compilation score has related to the perceived interference of associational baggage carried by pre-existing songs when used in a film (Smith 1998: 164). Smith, however, describes how this effect is specifically mobilised by certain practitioners of the compilation score in order to enable a two-tiered system of communication; likening the use of popular songs in *Easy Rider*, *The Graduate* and *Mean Streets* (Martin Scorsese, 1973) to the cinematic allusionism also practiced in these films.[3] For Smith, the power of the compilation score as demonstrated by films like these derives from its *manipulation* of pre-existing associations attached to a particular song, performer or musical style. He argues that the associations of songs such as 'Born to be Wild', 'The Sounds of Silence' and 'Pledging My Love' are used to dramatic and/or ironic effect in the films above in highlighting themes of generational disaffection, independence and identity and, further, speak for the unmotivated protagonists whose stories are not told in the film's visuals (169–71). As with the practice of allusionism, the second tier of communication – where an informed viewer recognises the song's title, lyrics or performer and applies this knowledge to the dramatic context onscreen – doesn't negate the first tier, where a general audience will hear a song as background music.

THE SMART SCORE

The scores for the smart films discussed in this study all fall into Smith's 'hybrid' category, where pre-existing popular songs are combined with music composed specifically for the films. The scores enact their own two-tiered system of communication in that the songs can easily be interpreted in terms of the functions outlined above, but the signature self-consciousness of the cycle charges their occurrence with a certain excess that defies a literal understanding.

At the first tier, periodisation is one of the most obvious textual functions of music in smart cinema. The evocation of the past in *The Last Days of Disco*, *Donnie Darko* and *The Squid and the Whale* is significantly sustained through the use of music by (respectively) Blondie and Diana Ross; Echo and the Bunnymen and Joy Division; and Pink Floyd. Further, in all of these examples, and in many of the non-period films of the cycle that are set in an undifferentiated present of the 1990s or early 2000s, music is drawn upon as a harbinger of taste signalling certain subcultures within the broad period. Hence the protagonists of *The Last Days of Disco* are distinguished by their taste for disco music as a mode that signifies, in one character's words, 'the return of clubs, cocktails, dancing, conversation, the exchange of points of view, dressing up, and manners'. In *Ghost World*, Enid (Thora Birch) and Seymour's (Steve Buscemi) outcast status is most clearly expressed through their taste in music: Enid is introduced in the opening titles dancing wildly to a musical number in a Bollywood film, and seeks out other 'authentic' personas in punk and, most fulfillingly, the blues music that Seymour collects.

Existing critical work on music in the films that are here included in the smart cycle tends to favour the function of authorial commentary where, as Smith claims for the New Hollywood films, the titles and lyrics of songs speak for characters whose motivation is not made explicit by their action. In *Music in Film: Soundtracks and Synergy*, Reay includes a case study on *Magnolia* as a demonstration of the centrality of popular music to the filmmaking process of contemporary American directors. *Magnolia* provides a unique example of a compilation score in that it includes pre-existing Aimee Mann songs that inspired Paul Thomas Anderson in writing the film, as well as original songs

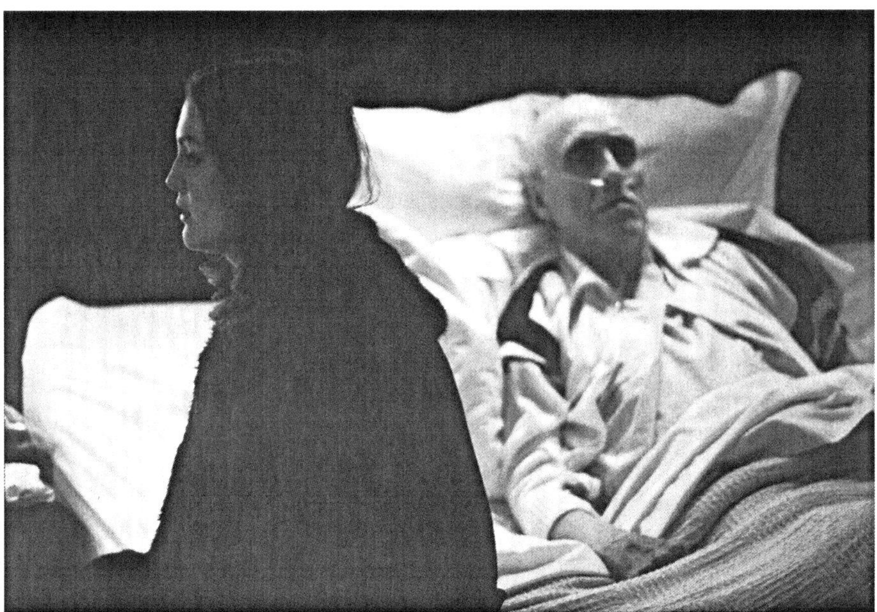

Figure 11   Julianne Moore and Jason Robards in *Magnolia* (Paul Thomas Anderson, 1999). Courtesy New Line / The Kobal Collection / Peter Sorel.

composed by Mann as the script developed (2004: 60–1). In this sense, it is not surprising to find direct links between the lyrics of the songs and the themes of loneliness, pessimism and romantic disappointment that run through the film. In the montage sequence set to the pre-existing song 'Wise Up', Reay describes how specific lines express individual characters' points of view as well as commenting on their personal crises from an authorial perspective. While signifying emotion in a classical manner, the audibility of the song challenges a classical interpretation: rather than being subordinated to dialogue, Mann's vocals function *as* dialogue. More interesting, though, are the comments on Mann's music as a function of structural unity: *Magnolia* is similar to *The Graduate* and *McCabe and Mrs Miller* (Robert Altman, 1971), suggests Reay, in the way that the songs of one artist are used to anchor several storylines.[4] The 'Wise Up' sequence – where nine of the main characters individually sing along with Mann's vocals – demonstrates this function most clearly, fulfilling Anderson's desire for one moment that would unite *Magnolia's* disparate plots and unrelated characters. For Reay, Mann's music provides a dimension of continuity as well as unity, for she understands the plot to be advanced by the strong narrative drive of each song (61–5).

In another example, Carole Lyn Piechota suggests that the most sophisticated articulation of Richie and Margot's grief and longing in *The Royal*

Tenenbaums is expressed through the lyrical content and instrumentation of the songs by Nico, Elliott Smith and Nick Drake. In the context of 'obtuse' dialogue and unreliable communication, the music works, for Piechota, as 'both catalyst and translator of the siblings' emotions' (Piechota 2006). She proposes that the intimate, melancholy tone of 'These Days' binds the song's confessional message to Margot and her past while, simultaneously, the lively tempo suggests a desire to move forward, and imparts Margot with the courage to approach Richie. Similarly, Piechota interprets the 'bare, doubled vocals' of 'Needle in the Hay' as Richie's confession that he is going to kill himself, making links between the song's subject of heroin addiction and Richie's obsession with Margot, as well as between Richie and performer Elliott Smith, who committed suicide in 2004. By identifying music as something that supplants other elements of *mise-en-scène* in the expression of intense emotion, Piechota's understanding of these songs again directly links *The Royal Tenenbaums* to the genre of melodrama.

THE MUSIC-IMAGE

If interpretations such as Piechota's account for the first tier of expression in the music of films like Anderson's, the second tier is enabled by a move away from a film-music paradigm that is bound by principles of classical narration. In the approaches to the compilation score taken by writers including Kent Jones, Royal Brown and Howard Hampton this second tier is constituted by an understanding of the song/image juxtaposition as something that can be broadly described as the *music-image*. While music may still be understood as an element that establishes mood and constructs formal unity, it can be avoided as one directly communicating details of context or character. The approaches taken by the writers above all rely to some extent on the notion of cinematic excess as a reading strategy that also attempts to move beyond an explanation of the narratively functional aspects of a film. Following work done by Roland Barthes and Stephen Heath, Kristin Thompson describes 'excess' as the material aspects of a work that are not contained by its unifying forces: '[a] film depends on materiality for its existence; out of image and sound it creates its structures, but it can never make all the physical elements of the film part of its set of smooth perceptual cues' (1986: 131). Thompson draws on Barthes to argue that as soon as a viewer begins to notice style for its own sake, excess comes forward and must affect narrative meaning by making the reading 'skid' away from a direct progression through an economical structure. From a structuralist perspective, the key function of excess is the barrier it presents to an understanding of the causal structure of the narrative as 'some sort of inevitable, true, or natural set of events' (141). Thompson specifically notes that music is one material aspect of the film that can exceed motivation by calling attention to its own formal qualities apart from its immediate function in relation to the image track.

From this perspective, the sheer prominence of much of the music in the smart cycle means it can be approached as an aspect that unbalances rather than unifies narrative meaning. In the Wes Anderson and Paul Thomas Anderson films cited, the duration of the song excerpts, the specific form of the accompaniment (other sound blocked out, stylisation of the associated image via montage or slow motion) and the repetition of the sequences throughout the films align with three of the ways that Thompson suggests the material of the film can exceed motivation. Specifically, the *form* of the music selected by Wes Anderson – the British Invasion tracks present across all of his scores – works not to unify the worlds of the films but to historically abstract them, by including songs by The Kinks, The Rolling Stones, The Clash, Devo and David Bowie over apparently contemporary settings. In Anderson, and especially in *The Darjeeling Limited*, where the bulk of the score is made up of songs quoted from Satyajit Ray films, music works in conjunction with the production design as a highly stylised element creating anti-realistic and nostalgic worlds. Elena Gorfinkel has explored this idea by describing the song choices in Anderson's films as one dimension of his fascination with anachronistic detail, arguing that those filmic elements that reference the past (the British Invasion songs, Richie's 1970s headband, the 1960s style Bauhaus-style typeface of the titles) create a dual effect. While, on one hand, the viewer strives to discern the location of the object in its original place in the past, the sheer extent and variety of signs and objects accumulated in the films simultaneously effect a break with historical specificity, making the text 'a fully fledged plastic space of fantasy, placed outside of time because it is irreconcilable with any one moment or period' (Gorfinkel 2005: 165). In Anderson, music is a key dimension in releasing the viewer from a perception of the narrative as a natural set of events.

Within the smart cycle, one of the first directors to draw on pop music in the construction of such a plastic space was Hal Hartley. One of the purest examples of a 'music moment' in the entire cycle occurs in *Simple Men*, Hartley's story of brothers Bill (Robert Burke) and Dennis (Bill Sage) who, in search of their fugitive father, meet two women – Kate (Karen Sillas), a diner owner, and Elina (Elina Löwensohn). Mid-way through the film, a typically morose and unpredictable Martin Donovan, here playing Kate's ex-husband, drives down a dirt road in the rural Long Island setting where her diner is located. As he comes to a sudden halt, jumps out of the car and screams 'I can't stand the quiet!' the first guitar riff of Sonic Youth's 'Kool Thing' starts up in the background. The scene cuts to the inside of the cleared diner, where the song now blocks out all other noise, and the five main characters begin dancing to the apparently non-diegetic beat – Martin and Dennis awkwardly following

Elina's smooth, choreographed movements, and Bill and Kate swaying together a little apart. After around three minutes, the song and sequence are abruptly cut off by an edit to the next, music-free scene, where the five characters, still in the diner, are in the middle of a conversation about Madonna and popular music. Although contemporaneous with the early 1990s setting of *Simple Men*, the use of 'Kool Thing' here engenders a space outside of time rather than periodising the film. The visual image is precisely reconcilable with the song as 'object', insofar as the two are matched at the level of a rhythm that becomes the subject of the sequence. Indeed, the scene is most striking for this autonomy: by blocking out all other noise on the soundtrack, playing the song nearly in full, and deferring narrative action for its duration, it stages the dimensions of performance and music supervision rather than any obvious content or theme, despite the links that can be made between Kim Gordon's satirical vocals ('Hey Kool Thing . . . are you gonna liberate us girls from male, white, corporate oppression?') and the anti-naturalistic argument that follows regarding Madonna's exploitation of her sexuality 'on her own terms'.

The type of excess that characterises this sequence brings to mind the music video form, insofar as the narrative appears to cede to the spectacle of an isolated sequence. Smith attends to the notion of music video in relation to the Beatles' films *A Hard Day's Night* (Richard Lester, 1964) and *Help!* (Richard Lester, 1965), and those sequences that anticipated the MTV era by very loosely organising footage of the band around songs including 'Can't Buy Me Love' and 'Ticket to Ride'. Although agreeing that these films are notable precursors of music video, Smith argues that the sequences had more immediate consequences for film scoring in proving that rock music could be used as an underscore for filmed action: the lyrics could be immaterial to the narrative as long as the music was '[treated] as an element equal to the image' (1998: 159–60).[5] Smith's comments here recall an argument made more definitively a few years earlier by Royal S. Brown in his book *Overtones and Undertones: Reading Film Music*. For Brown, film music since the 1960s is most interesting and indicative not for the evolution of its styles and sounds but for the redefining and resiting of the very role of music in the imaged universe of the cinema. Brown suggests that the excerpts of classical music that replace an original score in films such as Godard's *Une Femme Mariée* (1964) and Stanley Kubrick's *2001: A Space Odyssey* (1969) 'no longer function purely as backing for key emotional situations, but rather exist as a kind of parallel emotional/ aesthetic universe' (1994: 239). Rather than being transferred onto a diegetic situation to which it is subordinated, affect remains within the music itself, as a fragment evoking in a different medium what the film expresses in visual and narrative terms. In this way, music achieves equality by rejecting its classical role: by becoming *visible* it stands as an image in its own right. Like the structuralist understanding of excess, Brown identifies that this shift is central to the ontology of cinema itself for, as he writes, it '[helps] the audience read the film's other images as such rather than as a replacement for or imitation of objective reality' (240). Crucially, though, Brown perceives the material aspect of music not as a blunting or obscuring of meaning, but as the *crystallisation* of meaning: as the film itself, expressed in a different medium.[6]

In this sense, the 'autonomy' of the *Simple Men* sequence, which, as mentioned in Chapter 1, has been interpreted as Hartley's homage to the dance sequence in *Bande à Part*, is perhaps better described in terms of an *equality* between music and image. Music is used as an underscore to filmed action is a manner that, although spectacular, forms a highly expressive part of the anti-naturalistic narrative. In addition to sketching the character alliances and power plays through bodily movement (the elusive Elina initiating the mysterious performance; the infatuated Dennis the first to copy her; Kate and Bill in an intimate yet suspicious tryst to the side), the pure rhythm of the sequence succinctly articulates the film's overriding concern with style and artifice. Further, the particular self-consciousness that the sequence evokes in the viewer externalises something of the reflexivity that typifies Hartley's work. The narrative doesn't cede to the moment but *is* the moment: unbounded by the story, it channels the film as a whole into an abbreviated, parallel expression.

One of the obvious explanations for this impression in *Simple Men* is that for the whole dance sequence the music appears to be something the characters can hear – a part of the filmic world. Although, as is typical of Hartley, the distinction between diegetic and non-diegetic sound is actually blurred here, the diegetic illusion can point up another significant characteristic of music in the smart cycle, in that there is an unusually high instance of characters themselves listening to or performing music. In *The Squid and the Whale*, Walt is seen playing the film's signature song – Pink Floyd's 'Hey You' – on three separate occasions, either alone or to an audience. In *The Sweet Hereafter*, the first indication of the ambiguous bond between Nicole (Sarah Polley) and her father (Tom McCamus) comes as he watches her perform on the elaborate fairground stage that he has built for her. The inverse connotations of *Happiness'* title are most succinctly summed up as Joy zealously sings the song 'Happiness' to herself in her childhood bedroom. And, after Richie checks himself out of hospital following his suicide attempt in *The Royal Tenenbaums*, he and Margot together listen to The Rolling Stones in the makeshift tent he has set up in the Tenenbaum ballroom. Upon this film's release, Jonathan Romney noted that 'this may be the only film I have ever seen in which characters actually listen to two consecutive tracks from the same LP (whether or not they actually appear in this sequence on any extant edition of *Between the Buttons*)' (2002: 15).

In many of these moments, the song is used as a bridge that commingles diegetic and extra-diegetic worlds: it plays or is performed in the space of the film and recurs later in a clearly distinguished recording on the soundtrack.

This confusion of filmic space by way of music is a strategy most commonly associated with the musical, and the super-diegetic situation in which songs are part of a narratively motivated performance (Smith 1998: 158). As Kelly Ritter has discussed in relation to *Boogie Nights*, though, the identification practices characteristic of the classical musical are dismantled by the specific pop song/image juxtapositions of the smart film. In her extrapolation of 'the new American musical', Ritter argues that Paul Thomas Anderson exploits the possibilities of the 'aural spectator' by making *Boogie Nights'* popular songs the sole point of spectator engagement in a narrative whose flashy visual subject – the 1970s porn industry – most viewers would have trouble identifying with (2000: 167–8). However, the effect of diegetically played songs such as 'Boogie Shoes', 'Best of My Love' and 'Brand New Key' only 'bait' the audience toward the utopian, empathetic participation of the classical musical, where spectators fantasise that they are part of the diegesis. Rather, for Ritter, the songs '[challenge] us to form new, countercultural associations with the pop songs in our collective memory, *against* the on-screen characters, who are part of the visually defined subcultures appropriating this music for their own non-visual pleasures' (171). In other words, the familiar songs actually highlight the spectator distance from the distinctly on-screen community of the porn industry. It can be argued that *Magnolia* similarly baits the audience toward a false utopian identification. Gorfinkel describes how, as in the musical, the rendition of 'Wise Up' intentionally ruptures filmic space when the characters start to sing along with the diegetic soundtrack (2005: 162). This 'anomalous moment' provides only the *illusion* of community though: by directing character attention to the extra-diegetic and disrupting the film's realism, Anderson once more uses music to highlight spectatorial distance. In both these films, the music again becomes 'visible' not to comment on the film's action but to emphasise the plasticity of the image.

Another film that plays with the diegetic situation in its construction of a type of music-image is *Ghost World*, a work that is *about* music more so than any other example in the smart cycle. Further, it showcases one aspect of the smart sensibility with particular clarity. As 'overly bright, undermotivated smart-asses disheartened by the world and the compromising options it offers' (Olsen 2001: 31), Enid and Becky (Scarlett Johansson) are the clearest manifestations of the Generation-X 'slacker' attitude. Against the backdrop of their bland, suburban environment, the girls' taste for kitsch objects, activities, clothing and music plays out as an ironic engagement that equates exactly to Douglas Coupland's category of cultural 'slumming': from their visits to the 1950s-style diner Wowsville to Enid's initial fascination with the obsessive Seymour himself (Coupland 1991). In a further distillation of the smart sensibility, though, Clowes and Zwigoff frame such 'slumming' as a form of posturing that only thinly veils acute nostalgia. Describing how nostalgia, 'and

Figure 12   Scarlett Johansson and Thora Birch in *Ghost World* (Terry Zwigoff, 2001). Courtesy ITV Global / The Kobal Collection / Tracy Bennett.

the conflicting impulses to hold onto it tightly or let it go' is one of the major themes of Clowes' work, Mark Olsen identifies the resonance of the film's title as 'everything that has come before and that lingers on in some way, hidden just out of sight' (2001: 32). On Zwigoff, Howard Hampton writes that he is 'more of a throwback – an unfashionable, anti-hip mixture of cynic, curmudgeon, and ramshackle closet humanist – than the mock-abject, "go ahead and kill me" posturing in his films suggests' (2006: 30–1). Together, these comments describe the sceptical anti-heroes – Enid, Becky and Seymour – with a tone of 'gentle grace' that, as one dimension of the smart film's debt to the teen film, ultimately expresses an adolescent desire for things to remain fixed and unchanging.

In addition to sketching the parameters of Enid and Seymour's contempt for their surrounds – clearest in Enid's dismissal of the student rap performed at her high school graduation and the pub band 'Alien Autopsy', and in Seymour's outrage at 'Blueshammer' being billed above Lionel Belasco – music has a key function in *Ghost World* in expressing this idiosyncratic grace. This function can be isolated in two purely diegetic moments of listening. In the first, Enid, after trying out a 'punk' persona and being mistaken for emulating Cyndi Lauper, returns home in a rage at people who are too stupid to 'get' her. She listens to a few seconds of The Buzzcocks, before switching the tape off in frustration and looking around her bedroom, searching for a new persona. Her gaze falls on the Skip James LP she bought from Seymour at a garage sale in an earlier scene. She puts the record on and, as she dyes her hair from green back to black, it plays in the background of the scene. When the song 'Devil Got My Woman' starts after a temporal ellipsis, though, she stops drying her hair and listens, instantly absorbed. After another ellipsis, bridged by the continuous song, she is seen stretched out on a lounge with her eyes closed, listening to the dying seconds of the song. When it finishes, she starts it again and returns to her trance. The song here works as a plot device, prompting Enid to return to Seymour's sale and kindle the friendship that becomes the focus of the narrative. Before this happens, though, the brief moment of listening itself expresses the transformation in Enid that the friendship, and the film, goes on to embody: a level of self-awareness outside of pastiche. Hampton's captivating commentary on the sequence in *The Believer* describes its measurement of the 'seismic impact' of the song in 'a one-way passage from genesis to revelation':

> Call 'Devil Got My Woman' the embodiment of negative pantheism or a love letter from hell, but either way it proffers the lure of the open void . . . James's song evokes a world made of loss, doubt, and despondency, which seems to give Enid hope even as it crystallises her incipient sense of amputation. The music is like the memory of a limb she never realised was missing, an absence that haunts her every dismayed step as she stubbornly trudges the streets, a stalker searching for signs of a life which has so far eluded her. (Hampton 2003)

The plastic space engendered by the equality of music and image in this sequence channels the film into a ninety second expression. In its oblique summation of Enid's conflicted awareness, the sequence is answered by the second moment of listening, late in the film. Here, Enid is again in her bedroom, packing up to move in with Becky. She finds an old record from her childhood and, in a direct echo of the earlier moment, places it on her tiny, portable record player as she continues to pack. Again, the moment is drained of action to become a pure expression of *listening*, and Enid slumps on her bed as the tinny strains of a childish voice singing 'Ribbon in My Hair' draw to a close. This moment embodies a more direct epiphany than the previous one: Enid's listening, as Olsen describes, is accompanied by 'the process of her decision quietly playing itself out across her face' (2001: 32). After making amends with Seymour and Becky, Enid boards a bus on a mysterious, cancelled line and, in the film's last shot, is framed in its back window travelling off down a deserted highway.

Privileged Moments

Where *Ghost World* foregrounds music in terms of direct narrative epiphanies, Brown's description of the music-image as a 'universe' that channels the film itself can illuminate the way that all the moments mentioned here function in terms of revelation. It is in this sense that a discussion of the music-image necessarily engages the discourse(s) of cinephilia. A forum that brings both areas together is the round table conversation initiated by Jonathan Rosenbaum in 1997 as a series of letters between, in his description, four 'professional cinephiles' based around the world: Adrian Martin (in Melbourne), Kent Jones (in New York), Alexander Horwath (in Vienna) and Nicole Brenez (in Paris) (Rosenbaum and Martin 2003: vi). Later collected in Rosenbaum and Martin's edited collection *Movie Mutations: The Changing Face of World Cinephilia*, Rosenbaum's goal with the round table letters was to explore a certain unconscious global simultaneity of critical interest, existing in both the tastes of these cinephiles and in the style and themes of certain directors. His idea was to elucidate this particular 'brand' of cinephilia as an attitude directly opposing the dominant critical position advanced by critics including Susan Sontag and David Denby, who routinely claim that cinephilia is dying. In the letters, Rosenbaum was interested to discover the experiences that gave rise to the attitudes and tastes that make up this 'new' cinephilia as 'rebellion against the amnesia regarding both film and criticism that affects nearly everyone else' (2). Jones is the first to indicate how one dimension of this 'sensibility' is an abiding interest in the structuring role of popular music in contemporary film-making. From a discussion of the relationship between video and film culture, Jones suggests how his own enthusiasm for certain contemporary filmmakers is something at least partially embedded in music:

> One of the key experiences for American teenagers of my generation was driving with the radio on and feeling the intoxicating effect produced by the marriage of rock music and the passing landscape ... A secretly manufactured form of virtual reality, producing mysterious epiphanies when the blur from the car window was mixed with the sounds of whatever was coming from the airwaves, the music/movement experience was soon refined by the appearance of the tape deck, thus allowing the music to be chosen and to fit either the exterior or interior landscape (they had a way of mixing together), and henceforth become an actual soundtrack ... I think that the feeling of being 'mixed up' with the music (since under supposedly ideal circumstances it should sound like it's coming from the middle of your head) ... the simultaneous feeling of driving and being driven, has given birth to a new strain of narrative film-making which risks weightlessness in order to build from this new

> genre of modern experience. It's present in Edward Yang's last two (very unpopular) films, *A Confucian Confusion* (1994) and *Mahjong* (1996); in Wong Kar-Wai's *Chungking Express* (1995), *Fallen Angels* (1996) and *Happy Together* (1997); in *Irma Vep*, and in all of Atom Egoyan's movies. In many ways, its most extreme manifestation can be found in *Breaking the Waves* (1996), a film that strikes me as a perfect realisation of the music/landscape fusion in Lars von Trier's head, which he guarded preciously from his teenage years through adulthood. (Rosenbaum and Martin 2003: 9)

Jones' comments here can be linked to the historical discourse of cinephilia in the way that the 'music/movement experience' he describes resonates with the mode of 'panoramic perception' outlined by Wolfgang Schivelbusch in *The Railway Journey*. There, Schivelbusch discusses how the increased speed in travel facilitated by the railway forced people to acquire a new mode of perception: where pre-rail travel allowed full visual and sensory experience of a landscape, rail travel disconnected the traveller from the passing landscape. In contrast to traditional perception, panoramic perception 'no longer belongs to the same space as the perceived objects: the traveller sees the objects, landscapes, etc. *through* the apparatus which moves him through the world' (1986: 66). 'Panoramic' here describes how the traveller fixes on a discrete object or detail in the tableau for the brief moment it is in their field of vision. Given that, under different circumstances, the object or detail would have gone unnoticed, rail travel enables a mode of watching that yields a 'productive look'. Jones describes a productive look that is also enabled by technology and is also multi-sensory: here the speed of the car creates a 'blur' which – mixed with the added dimension of sound – produces a form of 'virtual reality'.

As Christian Keathley notes in his book *Cinephilia and History, or The Wind in the Trees*, numerous film theorists have likened Schivelbusch's description of panoramic perception to the experience of viewing films. In work by Mary Ann Doane, Tom Gunning and Anne Friedberg, the analogy is couched in terms of the convergence of two different technologies of modernity and the effects they produce.[7] Jones also frames his idea this way, linking the music-image in the work of the directors he mentions to the genres of modern experience allowed by the radio and tape deck (and later the Walkman). For Keathley, such general analogies, although suggestive, overlook the defining feature of panoramic perception, namely that it fixes on 'marginalia' in the landscape or, by extension, the images on the screen (2006: 44). In the context of Keathley's project, panoramic perception is productive because it consists of 'the tendency to see the discrete indiscriminately' (Schivelbusch 1986: 61). It is interesting not for its description of the perceptual habits of the ordinary film viewer but for those of the cinephile who, in addition to 'reading' the action of the film, scans the image for those moments or details that 'lie outside of, exceed, or are marginal to the "given-to-be-seen" of the film at hand'.[8] It is the type of perception described by Schivelbusch that, for Keathley, *enables* what Noel King describes as the cinephile's 'fetishising of a particular moment, the isolating of a crystallisingly expressive detail' (quoted in Willemen 1994: 231).

In a related way, it is the particular perception enabled by the experience of driving with the radio on that, for Jones, gives rise to the music-image as another type of privileged moment – a 'mysterious' epiphany. The analogy is not completely precise, though, in that panoramic perception engenders not a mode of viewing but a mode of *practice*: Jones hypothesises that the music/movement experience is a felt category of revelation that 'gives birth to' a new mode of filmmaking. In this way, the revelatory experience is *mediated* for the viewer. If, as Keathley suggests, the panoramic perception described by Schivelbusch and echoed by Jones can be likened to the viewing practice of the cinephile, the mode of filmmaking that Jones sees embodied in Assayas, Von Trier and Egoyan can in turn be understood as an expression of that viewing practice.

Jones' proposition can best be understood in the terms offered by Horwath in his own contribution to the round-table series of letters, as a 'precise genealogy of the relationship between pop music, image and movement in America' (Rosenbaum and Martin 2003: 17). It is a reflection on the genesis of the 'coreless sense of perpetual motion' that is portrayed in a group of films that, for Jones, 'represent the end of the lovely moment in film culture that began with the *nouvelle vague*'. In his response, Horwath is more explicit on the musical qualities of the films: he includes a quote from an earlier letter to Jones where he described his impression, upon seeing *Cold Water* (Olivier Assayas, 1994) and *Exotica* (Atom Egoyan, 1994), that Assayas and Egoyan 'act/move/think in musical and filmic terms *at the same time*. They produce sensations by pushing both together, they do not illustrate, prostitute one for the other; they cannot but feel on in the other' (16). Horwath's own conception of the music-image (a term he specifically uses) extends to his perception that entire scenes are 'authored' by non-diegetic music in 'strange places' such as *Nothing to Lose* (Steve Oedekerk, 1997), and that 'oceanic narratives' such as *Lost Highway* are modelled after strategies in electronic music. While suggesting that the music-image has become one of the most 'thrilling' aspects of auteur cinema, Horwath also acknowledges how it has strongly changed the mainstream since the early to mid-1980s.[9]

Some of the directors alluded to by Jones and Horwath are included in the trend of the 'international art film' that was linked to the smart cycle in Chapter 1. Along with an interest in film references, and a general concern with issues of repetition and serialisation, the music-image is another aesthetic approach that characterises this trans-national mode as a particularly cinephiliac style of filmmaking. Rather than specific texts, though, this approach 'quotes' the practice of viewing that makes a secret connection with a film by seeing it crystallised in a place or moment that lies outside of the action. In the music-image, this connection is located in the virtual link between music and image: the music is, as Jones suggests, the audible dimension of a 'fusion' in the director's head. In the 'California Dreaming' moment(s) in *Chungking Express*, the 'Tunic: Song for Karen' moment in *Irma Vep* and the 'Hot Love' moment in *Breaking the Waves*, the image, drained of story action, frames the cinephile experience of drift in the specific terms of music.

These sequences resonate with the discourse of cinephilia that is concerned with 'privileged' moments in that they exist outside of, or *alongside*, the movement of the plot. Clearly, though, the overt stylisation of the moments presents a challenge to the logic of this discourse: they may be mysterious, but they are far from accidental. As suggested, the experience of cinephilia as understood by N. King, Willemen and Keathley is here restricted to the historical experience of the auteur, and *expressed* for the viewer, who is more likely to experience these moments in terms of excess. The examples from the smart cycle make the discrete nature of this experience especially clear. Insofar as the films by Wes Anderson, Paul Thomas Anderson, Hartley and Zwigoff are less marked by a total pattern of narrative drift than those by Wong, Assayas or von Trier, the sequences here likened to the notion of the music-image do appear as bounded, excessive moments. In the context of the type of self-reflexive authorship that characterises the smart film, it is tempting to read these sequences as 'planted' cinephiliac moments that, in quoting the revelatory experience of cinephilia, internalise the practice as a strategy of auteur theory. In this interpretation, the music-image can be read as an aesthetic tactic akin to the knowing approach to serialisation that is taken by some of these directors: it announces and dissimulates their own authorship.

As was suggested for the strategies of serialisation in Chapter 1, though, a certain revelatory quality can itself be perceived in this dissimulative approach. Hampton's writing on *Ghost World* clearly betrays such an encounter, and Jones suggests something similar in relation to *The Royal Tenenbaums* when he writes that, '[t]he word epiphany gets thrown around a lot, but it should be reserved for moments such as the flight of Richie's falcon across the New York skyline, representing the lost glory of the Tenenbaums[10] [or] Margot's slow-motion approach to Richie to the tune of Nico's evanescent "These Days"' (Jones 2001: 27). Jones gives the best clue on how to approach such incarnations of the music-image when he suggests 'you get both the current of feeling between Margot and Richie and the absurdity of their damaged personae as well'. As with other aesthetic characteristics of the smart cycle, the music-image animates a register where affect is qualified but fully felt. Unlike the historical process of cinephilia, where the revelation is located in the viewer's subjective encounter with the text, this experience comes out of the materiality of the image itself. For this reason, the music-image is perhaps most adequately approached in terms of the 'new' cinephilia of the *Movie Mutations* group, and considered in terms of its *figuration*.

Figuring Music

As part of an introduction to the work of Nicole Brenez hosted by the Australian journal *Screening the Past* in 1997, Adrian Martin describes figural analysis as a 'practical activity of French film theorising' (Martin 1997). For Martin, Brenez' innovation is to internalise the 'epistemological rupture' created by the structuralist and poststructuralist turns of the 1960s and 1970s; to take for granted the 'radical degree of the break between aesthetic, formal works and the "real" to which they refer'. A theory of figuration opens a breach in film studies by directly confronting assumptions on the analogical quality of the cinematic image: 'the cinema leaves behind its last vestiges of mimesis, copying, or resemblance to the real: the cinema traces, figures, weaves *ex nihilo* its fully imaginary, endlessly renewed repertoire of spaces, places, movements, gestures, worlds and bodies' (Martin 1997).

Martin links Brenez' approach to Deleuze's work on painting and cinema, and Deleuze's insistence that, in both media, lines, colours and bodies are not givens to be reproduced but are *created*: 'movies create bodies from nothing, just as they are created from nothing in other visual arts like drawing and painting. Dynamically, in the process of being rendered from shot to shot and scene to scene, they proceed from a line to a shape to a volume to a character, and at any point they can be abstracted, enhanced or obliterated' (Martin 2000).[11] The theory of figuration has a particular interest in human figures, but Martin stresses its broad value as a way of grasping the art of cinema as the *composition* of an entire material and virtual world. Resting upon a rejection of *mise-en-scène* analysis and its attention to the pro-filmic reality of bodies moving in space, Martin describes the figural approach as one that is 'granular', concerned less with shots and scenes than with the arrangement of screen particles in ensembles: 'slices of text and texture that demonstrate the economy and logic of a film's ceaseless transformation of its elements' (Martin 2000).

This figural approach resonates with much of what has been discussed in terms of the music-image and its occurrence in both the 'international art' and smart cycles. The music-image can be understood as a figural model for the way that it represents a distinctly plastic space: the 'parallel emotional/ aesthetic universe' described by Brown is, precisely, a virtual, material world. Brown also anticipates Martin's description of a figural approach as that which internalises the rupture of structuralism when he suggests that the music-image helps the audience read the film's other images in non-analogical terms (1994: 240). Further to this, Jones seems to ground the approach itself in musical conditions:

> I must return to audio technology to get to the core of *our* cinephilia. Ours was a generation for whom *listening* to music was a central and obsessive experience . . . And we listened to the same songs over and over, our ears became attuned to each of them as unique sonic events. In other words, it was not the song but the recording which was the thing . . . Music was not simply the melody or the structure but the timbre of the voice, the colouring of the instrumentation, the texture of the sound, the slightest idiosyncrasy in the performance, well beyond the boundaries of the term 'phrasing' . . . The 'cinematic' organization of rock music and our obsessive adolescent relationship with that music created a paradigm which now reflects back on film-making, reaching a fetishistic extreme with *Breaking the Waves* (where the grain of the image is exaggerated by correction on video, and endless infinitesimal jump-cuts as well as a relentless hand-held camera become an aesthetic evocation of a common idiosyncrasy in documentary film-making of the 70s). (Rosenbaum and Martin 2003: 10–11)

By linking 'his' cinephilia to a granular relationship with music, Jones here suggests a peculiarly *sonic* engagement with film that resonates with Brenez' approach. Demonstrating Rosenbaum's perception that this type of broad critical interest exists in both the tastes of professional cinephilia and the style of certain trans-national directors, Jones understands this obsessive relationship to reflect back on filmmaking in the form of figural models such as *Breaking the Waves*. Like the experience of driving with the radio on, a highly personal mode of *listening* is internalised.

The polished images that make up the sequences from *The Royal Tenenbaums*, *Magnolia*, *Simple Men* and *Ghost World* differ markedly from von Trier's aesthetic, but can similarly be understood in terms of their obsessive relationships with music and specific songs. By extension, the sequences present their own kind of figural models, which, as described, are concerned less with narrative action than with rhythm, materiality and movement. In line with the figural approach, these qualities often relate directly to *bodies*. The high incidence of diegetic music in the autonomous sequences focuses attention directly on the impact of music on bodies: hence the *Magnolia* sequence is a moment of 'song', the *Ghost World* sequence a moment of 'listening', and the *Simple Men* sequence a moment of 'dance'. In each, the characters these human forms embody slip for a moment: they are seen less in terms of their story function and more as composed bodies in mobile arrangements. Elsewhere in the cycle, in sequences where the music is non-diegetic, something of this impact on the body remains, for it is still gestures and movements that are most compelling: in Margot's half smile as she approaches Richie, in the small, measured movements of Max in *Rushmore's* opening extra-curricular montage (set to 'Making Time' performed by Creation), in the fluid sweep that Donnie makes through his suburb at the beginning of *Donnie Darko*, borne along on his racing bike by Echo and the Bunnymen's 'The Killing Moon', and in the frenzied, hustled movements of Barry Egan in *Punch Drunk Love* as he moves toward Hawaii to the sound of Shelly Duvall singing 'He Needs Me'. In each sequence, the music-image momentarily *transforms* the body, and foregrounds its cinematic figuration.

Of the Refrain

As described, Martin emphasises that a figural approach is interested in the composition of an entire material world. To understand the music-image as a figural model, then, prompts the question of how music itself is figured in the image. This approach identifies music not as a given thing selected *for* the image, but as something composed – or *re*-composed – *by* the image. In this sense, *music* is also transformed by the music-image. With this in mind, one last way of grasping the peculiar musicality of the smart music-image is to pick up on the connection that Martin makes between Brenez and Deleuze, and refer to the work on music in *A Thousand Plateaus*. 'Of the Refrain' outlines how music, like the other arts, is comprised of elements that are *created*, not given. In significant ways, the mobility of this process is easier to grasp in reference to music on account of the increased intangibility of the medium. For Deleuze and Guattari, the creation or composition of music is constituted by the double movement of territorialisation and deterritorialisation. In this schema, 'the *refrain* is properly musical content, the block of content proper to music' (2003: 300). The refrain is essentially territorial: its operation is typified for Deleuze and Guattari in bird song, when a bird sings to mark its territory. It is also present when a child sings or repeats a phrase to comfort itself: 'the song is like a rough sketch of a . . . calm and stable center in the heart of chaos'. Music, by contrast, is the 'creative, active operation that consists in deterritorializing the refrain': by submitting the refrain to the treatment of the diagonal or transversal, music takes up the refrain in order to take it somewhere else, to uproot it from its territoriality. Music exists because the refrain exists also, but the refrain is itself *anti*-musical: it is 'a means of preventing music, warding it off, or forgoing it' (300). It is only when music lays hold of the refrain that it reterritorialises upon itself *as* music.

Although Deleuze and Guattari refer only to classical musicians in their chapter, commentators have drawn upon this schema to discuss jazz, heavy metal, electronic and pop music. For Ian Buchanan, the type of popular music mostly favoured by the smart cycle *is* a refrain, for its prerequisite is the inclusion of the refrain as 'a tune that sticks in your head and can be easily whistled or hummed' (2000: 184). In a chapter titled 'Is Pop Music?' Greg Hainge takes up Buchanan's comments on pop to argue that certain incarnations *can* become-musical. As Hainge outlines, pop music is determined not by its content but by its relation to the market: it is born of a desire to become populist. In this way, the mode according to which it operates is not one in which it is desirable to perform the deterritorialisation of the refrain that is intrinsic to a proper musical expression (2004: 42). Pop as an expression necessarily takes as its model those forms already existing within the milieu that constitutes the popular, rather than deterritorialising or reterritorialising those forms – or refrains – as music. As such, artists – such as Tricky and Björk – whose expressions are, for Hainge, properly musical are included in the category of pop, but don't entertain the same relationship to its commercial plane. In Hainge's description, these artists dismantle the punctual organisation of pop by way of their deterritorialisations of the English language, and through the singularity of their musical vocalisations, whose harmonic patterns cannot be objectively grasped. Hainge analyses how, in the Tricky song 'Makes me wanna die', the vocal and guitar lines don't consolidate the organisation of the rhythm section but warp and bend the regular, ordered metre of the pulsed beat (2004: 44). By enunciating recurrent rhythms that never recur at the same time, Tricky, for Hainge, denies the confluence of instrumental and vocal melodies that typify pop, and thus deterritorialises its prerequisite refrain.

Insofar as the 'international art' and smart cycles are comparable to the musical sector that Tricky and Björk belong to, Hainge's argument can be drawn upon to illuminate the music-images of the films attended to here. The textual functions and synergistic processes that characterise a populist use of music in film can be linked to Deleuze and Guattari's concept of the refrain in that they mobilise those refrains internal to popular music in a highly ordered and purposeful way designed to both impose meaning, and construct a marketable narrative image. These operations are consistent with the territorial action of the refrain in that they effectively construct stable platforms upon the open system of the film. The refusal by directors such as Wes Anderson, Paul Thomas Anderson, Hal Hartley and Terry Zwigoff to stick to the classical or synergistic functions of music in film is evidence of how their work is not born of a strict desire to become populist. By arranging music according to a personal and invisible soundtrack, these directors produce a music-image that refuses the punctual structures that music in film typically adopts. If these *structures* are understood as a refrain, it can be said that these directors perform a certain deterritorialisation by distorting the traditional functions of music: by abstracting the period of the narrative in drawing on music from a range of eras, by selecting songs that often have no clear reference to the image, by using music to fragment rather than consolidate formal unity, and by mobilising music to create the cycle's signature contradictory tone of detached pathos. Beyond this, though, it can also be suggested that the music-image deterritorialises the refrain internal to the selected songs themselves by denying them the individuation that is central to pop.

The term 'pop' is here used to broadly describe the typically punctual structures of the variously inflected songs drawn upon in the smart cycle.[12] It has been suggested in this chapter that, by refusing the classical principles that subordinate music to image, these songs *become visible* in the films in the construction of a type of music-image. By approaching this phenomenon in terms of figuration, this visibility is being grasped in a non-metaphorical way. Martin explains the point by reference to the image at the end of Robert Aldrich's *The Legend of Lylah Clare* (1968), which focuses on a pack of snarling dogs in a TV commercial. The image is clearly designed to equate the characters of the film to the animals but, taken as a figural model, there is a more literal sense to this equation than a metaphorical comparison claiming the characters are *like* dogs: rather, 'these people *are* dogs, they've been transformed into dogs, substituted for dogs. This is not poetic licence on my part. There is a physical transmutation – of human into non-human – which films often suggest or explore, sometimes across the space of a mere cut' (Martin 2000). Understanding the music-image as a similarly material ensemble allows for the perception of such a transmutation across the disparate categories of music and image, as the song *becomes* image. Hearing a song such as 'Kool Thing' or 'These Days' in the context of one of these sequences is a different experience to hearing it in isolation, where the refrain does tend to dominate. This could perhaps explain why the compiled soundtracks to these films often sound somewhat hollow and disengaged: an eclectic collection of songs designed not so that each song fits with every other but rather so as to fit with an absent image.[13] The music-image does not express itself in line with the punctual organisation of these popular songs but 'forms a block' with each individually and takes it somewhere else. The song is not reproduced as something given but is recomposed in an ensemble whose elements are, as Martin describes, in 'ceaseless transformation'. The music-image denies a popular song its internal individuation by opening it up to this movement and, in this sense, is properly musical: by becoming visible the pop song is reterritorialised upon itself as music.

As already observed, Horwath's reflections on music and film rely on the term 'music-image' as a way of describing contemporary auteur cinema, but also to describe the transformation that the networking of the music and film industries has had on the mainstream sector (Rosenbaum and Martin 2003: 16). Jones also acknowledges the commercial aspect of this aesthetic phenomenon: the 'weightlessness' that he claims the music-image risks refers to the disposability of the music video, the 'intuitive outgrowth' of the car radio experience (Rosenbaum and Martin 2003: 9). Although occurring contemporaneously, the music-image in the work of the directors discussed here is finally most adequately characterised by its *distance* from the technique of synergy, where music and image are synchronised to promote one another. One of the obvious qualities of the smart cycle, as part of the broader 'international art' sector, is that its films can experiment in ways that those of the strictly commercial sector cannot, and the use of music in each is one of the clearest examples of this. The music-image in the smart cycle has a 'musicality' that is eluded by both the cool practice of synergy and by a classical approach to the role of music in film: here the function is not synchronisation – the illustration of one term *by* the other – but figuration – the illustration of one *in* the other. As the song becomes image, the image simultaneously becomes music, and the fragmentary aesthetic universe that arises is not reducible to either component.

NOTES

1. For a discussion of the role of the music supervisor see Smith's *The Sounds of Commerce: Marketing Popular Film Music* (1998): 209–14.
2. For such engagements with Gorbman see, for example, Brown (1994), Smith (1998), Reay (2004) and Lannin and Caley (2005).
3. For a discussion of the practice of allusionism in the New Hollywood see Carroll, 'The Future of Allusion' (1982).
4. This is one of two musical motifs that signal the connection that exists at both a thematic and collaborative level between Anderson and Altman. The other, more explicit, link is made through the inclusion of Shelley Duvall's performance of 'He Needs Me' in *Punch Drunk Love* – a song which she originally sang in Altman's *Popeye* (1980).
5. Howard Hampton supports this celebration of Lester's film by describing it as 'the first movie to capture, and then sustain, the energy of the music itself . . .' (Hampton 1997: 39).
6. In this way, Brown's understanding comes closer to Barthes' reflection on excess in photography in terms of the *punctum*. See Barthes, *Camera Lucida* (1981).
7. Keathley cites Doane, '. . . when the direction of the force acting on the body is changed' (1985), Gunning, 'An Aesthetic of Astonishment: Early Film and the (In) Credulous Spectator' (1989) and Friedberg, *Window Shopping: Cinema and the Postmodern* (1993).
8. Keathley is here citing Silverman's *Threshold of the Visible World* 1995: 181.
9. Horwath here appears to be including the synergistic practice of music marketing within his conception of the 'music-image'. For a description of the rise of this practice through the 1970s and 1980s as a way of sustaining high concept films in the market, see Wyatt, 'Marketing the Image: High Concept and the Development of Marketing' in *High Concept: Movies and Marketing in Hollywood* (1994).
10. This dialogue-free moment forms the climax of the film's expository set-up, and is accompanied by the chorus of The Beatles' 'Hey Jude' as it swells in volume.
11. While noting certain resonances between Brenez's theory of figuration and aspects of Deleuze's work on aesthetics, Martin specifies that Brenez deliberately doesn't align her work with other understandings of figurality in art historical and film theory. In particular, he notes that her formal and aesthetic figural model 'bears little similarity to the understanding of figurality proposed in English-language film

theory by D.N. Rodowick . . . Brenez owes more to Lyotard's work on the plastic arts . . . than to the more situationally and socially centered model that Rodowick derives from Foucault and Deleuze' (Martin 1997). The connections between Brenez and Deleuze that Martin makes in his article 'The Body Has No Head' can be felt in – among other places – Deleuze's work on Francis Bacon: 'Never (except perhaps in the case of Michelangelo) has anyone broken with figuration by elevating the Figure to such prominence. It is the confrontation of the Figure and the field, their solitary wrestling in a *shallow depth*, that rips the painting away from all narrative but also from all symbolization. When narrative or symbolic, figuration obtains only the bogus violence of the represented or the signified; it expresses nothing of the violence of sensation – in other words, of the act of painting' (Deleuze 2003: xiv–xv).

12. The music that clearly stands out from this schema is the original blues recordings in *Ghost World*. As a distinct example of the genre, this music – like Hainge's evaluation of music by Tricky and Björk – performs an internal deterritorialisation of its own.

13. The soundtracks to all of Wes Anderson's films are striking in this way, as is another 'adjunct' smart example – Jim Jarmusch's *Broken Flowers*.

5. SUBURBIA AND UTOPIA: *HAPPINESS, YOUR FRIENDS AND NEIGHBORS, THE CHUMSCRUBBER, DONNIE DARKO*[1]

In February 1998, *Sight and Sound* reached the letter 'U' in its 'A–Z of Cinema' series and set out a catalogue of various cinematic 'utopias'. While the figure of utopia is historically based in works of political philosophy – most notably Thomas More's *Utopia* (1516) – attention to the topics of utopianism and anti-utopianism in cinema studies has primarily followed on from work done in contemporary literary and cultural studies and focused on the genre of science fiction.[2] Accordingly, Philip Kemp includes the futuristic 'split-level utopia' in his *Sight and Sound* series, citing *Metropolis* (Fritz Lang, 1927), *Blade Runner* (Ridley Scott, 1982) and *Gattaca* (Andrew Niccol, 1997) as much-examined instances of a 'pampered overclass [disporting] itself in luxury while the despised masses toil in subterranean squalor' (1998: 24). Other cinematic utopias included are the 'shining city on a hill' (*The Wizard of Oz*, Victor Fleming, 1939), the communal 'village Eden' set against the corrupt, Westernised materialism of the city (*Samba Traore*, Idrissa Ouedraogo, 1993), the 'socialist utopia' (Ealing's *They Came to a City*, Basil Dearden, 1945) and the 'nostalgically lyrical version of childhood' (*The Blue Lagoon*, Frank Launder, 1949 / Randal Kleiser, 1980).

Although including 'smalltown America' as one location for the settled values of the 'mini-utopia' that neutralises, expels or absorbs potentially disruptive forces – citing *Doc Hollywood* (Michael Caton-Jones, 1991) as a representative example – Kemp avoids the specifically suburban utopia which, at the time of his article, had been recently animated by films including *Blue Velvet* (David Lynch, 1986), *The Unbelievable Truth* (Hal Hartley, 1989), and

SubUrbia (Richard Linklater, 1996). To date there remains limited sustained work done on the dialectics of the suburban cinematic utopia and dystopia.[3] This is despite the fact that the issue, which has been of interest to Hollywood since the 1940s (*It's a Wonderful Life*, Frank Capra, 1946; *The Graduate*, Mike Nichols, 1967; *The Swimmer*, Frank Perry, 1968; *The Stepford Wives*, Bryan Forbes, 1975) exploded during the 1990s to become a staple of contemporary Hollywood (*The Truman Show*, Peter Weir, 1998; *Pleasantville*, Gary Ross, 1998; *American Beauty*, Sam Mendes, 1999; *The Stepford Wives*, Frank Oz, 2004) and, especially, popular television (*Six Feet Under* 2001–5; *Desperate Housewives* 2004–; *Weeds* 2005–).

A common critical response to works such as these is to lament the way that popular culture continues to peddle an overdetermined image of suburbia inherited from 1950s sitcoms such as *Leave it to Beaver* (1957–63) and *The Donna Reed Show* (1958–66). For critics like Robert Beuka, films such as Weir's and Mendes' rely only on inverting the harmonious model depicted in these shows, and perpetuate a dysfunctional vision of community as a cliché of suburban life (2004: 10). This chapter is concerned with how smart cinema fits into and challenges this representational system. As a narrow tendency within the popular field characterised by films such as *Pleasantville*, it can be argued that the entire cycle of commercial/independent films that are here identified as smart are defined by the image of suburbia. Within this cycle, though, the *suburban* smart film can be understood as a distinct entity, with a consistent narrative structure and a characteristic set of thematic concerns. A key group of films that together perpetuate this impression and will be focused upon here are *Happiness, Your Friends and Neighbors, Magnolia, The Safety of Objects, Donnie Darko* and *The Chumscrubber*.[4] In these films, the family and the suburb are parallel models of 'planned environments' that limit and control the action and identities of the characters. By focusing not on one family – as smart films by Wes Anderson, Noah Baumbach and Hal Hartley do – but on several, interconnected milieus, the foundation of anti-utopianism in this suburban sub-cycle lies in the way the characters are rendered as both psychically and physically interchangeable. After discussing the extrapolation of this broad anti-utopian vision in the films, the chapter will draw on some of the utopian elements in the philosophy of Deleuze and Guattari, and in particular the concept of *becoming-democratic*, as a way of singling *Donnie Darko* out as a properly utopian smart vision.

The Suburban Smart Film

While demonstrating similar formal qualities, and the same broad interest in issues of family and relationships as the six suburban films listed above, the features of Anderson, Baumbach, Hartley and Stillman typify what may be understood as the 'urban smart film'. In keeping with cinematic traditions of urban representation, the cities of the urban smart films are 'ruthlessly particularised and lovingly evoked, often almost characters themselves' (Felperin 1997: 15). This is evident in Anderson's minute, fantasy New York in *The Royal Tenenbaums* and Stillman's aristocratic versions in *Metropolitan* and *The Last Days of Disco*, in Baumbach's literary and well-worn Brooklyn in *The Squid and the Whale*, and in Hartley's carefully described trio of New York, Berlin and Tokyo in *Flirt*, where the local differences carry the very idea of the film. The suburban smart films are most obviously differentiated by an equally stylised but conversely shallow rendering of locale. These films are united most immediately by their representation of suburbia as a landscape carved up into blankly drawn and forgettable spaces: carparks, schools, kitchens, bedrooms, parks, backyards, car interiors. Even after several viewings, it is difficult to recall with any certainty a kitchen or backyard from one of the films as distinct from that in another. To varying degrees, the landscapes are all rendered flat and bright: Solondz chooses ugly, lurid shades of green, purple and yellow for his New Jersey interiors; Troche pulls away in the last shot of *The Safety of Objects* to an aerial view that flattens the pictured backyard and those surrounding it into a map of lawns and pools, and the streetscape of *The Chumscrubber* flickers into view in the film's opening as a graphic match on a video game's own version of suburbia. The stylised sameness of these depictions is a motif of suburban representation as the projection of a 'no-place', a world devoid of local, realistic detail. As Leslie Felperin has written on *SubUrbia*, the opening montage that sets its fictional suburb up as 'slightly eerie [and] a little dull' implies that '*all* suburbs are a little like this bleak, sunny place: all highways lead to a Burnfield' (1997: 15).

The homogeneous depiction of the suburban landscape in the smart cycle is in keeping with both the physical design of the post-war suburbs and the literary, cinematic and televisual imagery that has described them since the 1950s. Hinting at the exclusionary principles and rigid control of the landscape that would almost immediately emerge as a negative inflection in its representation, the key characteristic of suburban design was the elimination of any visual evidence of difference between residents. The effect, as Beuka writes, was to '[position] new suburbanites as interchangeable elements of a planned environment rather than as individuals active in the shaping of their own space and identities' (2004: 110). As was examined in Chapters 2 and 3, the narrative trajectory of the smart film is founded upon characters' inability to permanently modify the forces of their family milieu. In the suburban smart film, this model of the family is mapped onto the physical environment of suburbia, where the theme of entrapment is made explicit in the motifs of fences, gates and doors, and in the crushing patterns of routine that recur as common sequences across the films: the tense family meals and awkward coupling shots, interior scenes in cars or buses driving to and from work or school, shopping, watching television and preparing food. Further, the continuous nature of the typical smart narrative (S'AS' . . .), where character struggles manifest as dramatic episodes that are ultimately folded back into their lives, is exaggerated in the suburban films by a reliance on the ensemble narrative.

Arguing for the 'emergent genre' of the Los Angeles ensemble film, Hsuan L. Hsu has discussed this form as a narrative tracking the daily lives and interactions of a large cast of seemingly unrelated characters. Although the representation of the suburban smart film environment as a 'no-place' often precludes a specific geographic location, and some visions – notably Solondz's and Hartley's – are fiercely *east* coast, many of the qualities Hsu identifies can also be observed in this cycle. In *Magnolia*, one of Hsu's own examples, the setting of the San Fernando Valley expresses a specifically LA-based suburbia. In the other films, suburbia stands in for LA as an expressive geographical setting that gives rise to common themes and formal strategies. As a direct effect of metropolitan sprawl, the more confined suburban settings ensure the characters are not as obviously unrelated: they form a matrix of 'friends and neighbours' who, expressing the ethos of the contemporary suburb, are spatially proximate but only superficially known to one another. These characters share the characteristic psychological malady of those in the LA ensemble film as a 'blasé outlook' that devalues 'the entire objective world': they have formed *sub*-urban egos that function as a similarly alienating, protective shell safeguarding the self from contact with others (2006: 136).

As well as sharing the interpersonal, sexual and psychological themes identified by Hsu, the suburban smart film as ensemble narrative demonstrates many of the formal strategies he sees in *Grand Canyon* (Lawrence Kasdan, 1991), *Short Cuts* and *Crash* (Paul Haggis, 2005). These include: the time frame of a few days; the rapid crosscutting that produces 'short cuts' of each narrative thread, often graphically matched; the propensity for montage and scenes choreographed to music; and the irony produced through a juxtaposition of story threads – accessible only from the viewer's omniscient point of view. Even the natural 'disasters' that book-end the LA films' narratives (the Medfly spraying and earthquake in *Short Cuts*, the city snowfall in *Crash*) can be paralleled by the 'apocalyptic' events that bring the characters and narrative threads of the suburban smart film together, as will be discussed below. Hsu concludes that the LA ensemble film deploys its external, geographical setting to demonstrate how dozens of connections exist in spite of felt loneliness. While some of the suburban smart films hint at this kind of retribution (*Magnolia, The Safety of Objects, The Chumscrubber*), others invert the schema: demonstrating that, in spite of the felt connections of the suburb, loneliness and disconnection triumph (*Happiness, Your Friends and Neighbors, Donnie Darko*).

In addition to its flatly rendered environment and ensemble narrative, the suburban smart film is also distinguished by – and perhaps most recognisable for – its 'taboo' themes. The key films in this chapter address issues of paedophilia, rape, serial adultery, misogyny, kidnapping and murder. Other suburban smart films that can be considered peripheral to these six narratively-defined films cover similarly divisive areas: abortion (*Palindromes*), suicide (*The Virgin Suicides*), incest (*The Sweet Hereafter*), online child molestation (*Me and You and Everyone We Know*) and student-teacher relations (*Election*). When Sconce begins his smart film article with a quote from film reviewer Manohla Dargis deploring *Happiness* and *Your Friends and Neighbors* as films that encourage our 'sadism and scorn toward other human beings' (Dargis 1998), he is demonstrating a certain moral reaction to Solondz and LaBute's distinctively flat representations of these types of issues. Dargis' disaffection with the films is based on a perceived failure on the part of the directors to create characters that are 'recognisably human': the most successful of the films, for Dargis, are those that do humanise their characters by displaying some evidence of 'self-awareness' beneath their 'malaise, disaffection and petty cruelties'. Dargis frames the concept of the human here as something *beneath* the way we act and represent ourselves. As this chapter continues, it will consider how the suburban smart film's animation of utopian dialectics may understand that it is only *through* such action and representation that any concept of the human can emerge.

For the moment, though, it is sufficient to observe that the suburban smart film couches its critique of contemporary America in its environment, which it represents as a prime site of 'therapy culture': a breeding ground for loneliness, anger, hatred, anxiety, violence and jealousy. The six films addressed here all demonstrate clear representational differences toward their respective issues. Solondz and LaBute's unflinching portraits are countered by Posin's open parody, and by the pathos that Troche and Paul Thomas Anderson arouse for their characters in (hyperbolic) moments of community. In no film, though, is the nostalgia that was discussed in Chapters 3 and 4 especially apparent. Beuka argues that the nostalgic mode is a characteristic gesture in suburban fiction, citing John Updike, F. Scott Fitzgerald, John Cheever and Anne Beattie as writers who all invoke 'the resonance of "eulogized spaces" from the past to suggest the flatness of experience in the contemporary suburban landscape' (2004: 120). While *Donnie Darko*, like *The Squid and the Whale* and *The Last Days of Disco*, describes its 1980s setting in terms of fondly evoked details, this type of periodisation is quite distinct from the nostalgic universes created by Baumbach and Stillman, or by Wes Anderson and Zwigoff, where the present itself appears as a type of 'eulogized space' made up of artefacts from the past.

The flat and generic *mise-en-scène* of the suburban smart film opposes the wistful tone of Anderson or Zwigoff with a perspective that, while highly stylised, belongs to a more obviously realist tradition that focuses attention on the often controversial subject matter. The blank presentation that is the smart film's signature is here less clearly subtended by pathos. Critical assessment of this approach again tends to fall into binary responses: on the one hand are moral reactions that perceive an anti-humanist tone or, less judgementally, a simple inversion of utopian suburban ideals; on the other are responses that read strategically, and understand the films' aesthetic as something that in fact overcomes the representation of suburbia as utopian *or* dystopian. Commenting on films by Hal Hartley and Stacy Cochran, Richard Porton suggest that the minimalist style shrinks from injecting moral outrage or political commentary: 'the suburban milieu is merely the topos for an exploration of the quotidian; pursuits as different as homicide and housework are treated with the same deadpan equanimity' (1993: 14).

Suburban Utopia; Suburban Anti-utopia

In their introduction to *The Utopia Reader*, Gregory Claeys and Lyman Tower Sargent identify the utopian genre as a form invented with More's *Utopia* in 1516. From this point on, they describe four main historical stages in the evolution of the tradition that expresses 'the need to dream of a better life': the egalitarian schemes of the sixteenth and seventeenth centuries linked to Spartan ideals and Christian monasticism that eventually gave rise to socialism in the nineteenth century; the debates over the virtues and vices of primitive peoples and their relation to the pagan and Christian traditions of an original age of innocence that emerged as a result of the sixteenth century's voyages of discovery; the promise of the human species' indefinite progress toward a longer and healthier life and the domination of nature borne out by scientific discovery and technological innovation from the seventeenth century on; and the aspirations for a society of greater virtue, equality and social justice that emerged in the late eighteenth-century revolutionary movements of North American and France and in the transformation of socialism after 1848 (Claeys and Sargent 1999: 2–4). On the basis of these four stages, utopian thought is cast as the envisioning of a different form of society as an ideal-type or its negative inversion. As a specific literary – and cinematic – tradition, the utopian genre refers to 'works that describe an imaginary society in some detail'. In this imaginative expression, the utopian impulse amounts to a political project insofar as it draws attention to issues in human social existence by way of a reflection on alternate systems. This reflection can take any number of forms – from travel writing to magical realism to ecotopias – but all will link broadly back to one of the four traditions outlined. As the mode of reflection most fully articulating the third tradition, twentieth-century science fiction is, for Claeys and Sargent, the characteristic genre expressing the hopes and doubts of our own era.

Fredric Jameson's book *Archaeologies of the Future: The Desire Called*

Utopia and Other Science Fictions is an important work that consolidates this connection. Jameson's conception of science fiction as a characterisation of utopian imagination stems from Darko Suvin's own understanding of utopia as 'the socio-political subgenre of science fiction' (Suvin 1979: 45). Jameson describes utopian form as 'a representational meditation . . . on the systemic nature of the social totality, to the point where one cannot imagine any fundamental change in our social existence which has not first thrown off Utopian visions like so many sparks from a comet' (2005: xii). This description emphasises two critical dimensions of Jameson's thinking on utopia: first that, as the imagination of a system radically different from this one, the fundamental dynamic of any utopian thinking will always lie in the dialectic of Identity and Difference; and second that, as a 'meditation', utopia must be grasped not as sheer representation – 'a "realised" vision of a society or social ideal' – but as *process* (1988: 80–1). The theoretical fantasy of utopia has been conceptualised in many ways. As 'a plan of society by and for the School', Michèle Le Doeuff describes utopia as a category that, having been formed over the course of history, is necessarily 'fuzzy'. Working through an historical review of the 'overloaded notion', Le Doeuff suggests that utopian texts – both dreams and nightmares – cannot be looked upon as mere objects: 'Dreams or nightmares, it makes little difference, texts of our desires or our hatreds, it is all one: for if we are bound as a social group to this form, if it interests us, positively or negatively, it is understandable that we have not mastered it' (1982: 446).

In the fields of both cultural studies and urban planning, the notion of suburbia as an attempt to master a utopian form has been thoroughly examined. Practically all commentators on suburbia refer to the example of Levittown, New York – the American 'ur-suburb', and describe architectural firm Levitt and Sons' 1947 production of 17,000 four-room 'Cape Cod' style houses on identical plots of land as an attempt to embody the American Dream of both home ownership and domestic life itself (Cuff 2005). Built to standards specified by local and federal agencies, Levittown projected a post-war fantasy of individual living that directly opposed the overcrowded and collectivised existence of the 1930s and 40s. The utopian ideals of suburbia flowed from an ideological dream of the perfect society: meticulous, efficient land use and architecture offered its residents privacy but also visual evidence of their similarity to their neighbours, evoking the communal values central to any idea of utopia (Beuka 2004: 5). In this way, Dana Cuff argues that Levittown, the first embodiment of American suburbia, didn't so much reflect as *construct* the American dream. It positioned the phenomenon of the suburb as what another urban theorist, Dolores Hayden, refers to as 'a landscape of the imagination where Americans situate ambitions for upward mobility and economic security, ideals about freedom and private property, and longings for social harmony and spiritual uplift' (2003: 4).

Of course, the standardised nature of this dream was immediately vulnerable to castigation. Cuff refers to the documentary *Wonderland* (John O'Hagan, 1997), where early residents of Levittown describe the uniform landscape as a veil for wife-swapping, racism, alcoholism and general malaise. Such exposure began almost immediately, with many sociologically critical works emerging at the very height of suburban expansion and positioning the suburb as a breeding-ground for emasculation, disaffection and misogyny.[5] The prominence of the themes of gender, culture, power and sexuality in the suburban smart films make them clear descendants of these earlier attitudes, as well as obviously politicised examples within the smart cycle as a whole. Given these considerations, the concept of utopia is a lens through which these films' commentaries can usefully be approached. If the positive expression of suburbia was immediately coupled with its discursive consideration as an *anti-utopia*, the visions of the suburban smart film can be understood in an inverted way: their broadly anti-utopian visions indirectly envision what utopia would be. They are, as Peter Ruppert has written, negations that don't reconstruct (1989: 103). The parameters of this vision can be traced in those aspects of the suburban smart film that align it with the anti-utopian 'genre'.

Representations of utopia are concerned to induce a critical attitude toward an existing social situation by creating a tension between what is and what is possible. This dialectical orientation typically plays out in the imagined or realised utopian situations themselves in such a way that the 'moment of possibility' is annihilated in the very process of being enunciated (Kumar and Bann 1993: 1). As both Le Doeuff and Foucault have examined, the construction of utopia as a 'planned society' of its own – a society for the School – necessarily sits uneasily with ideas of possibility.[6] Hence the idea of utopia in the popular imagination almost always holds negative connotations. As Jameson notes, during the Cold War, utopia became a synonym for Stalinism, and came 'to designate a program which neglected human frailty and original sin, and betrayed a will to uniformity and the ideal purity of a perfect system that always had to be imposed by force on its imperfect and reluctant subjects' (2005: xi). The majority of the classical science-fiction films laid out at the beginning of this chapter depict utopianism as this forcefully imposed system, with the totalitarian motifs made explicit in *Metropolis*, *Blade Runner* and *Gattaca* by way of their clearly articulated overclasses. In the suburban smart film, a similar shift has occurred in that the motifs of material success that were initially imbued with utopian promise (spacious houses, gardens, pools) have, through the cycles of popular culture, come to be perceived as evidence of the failure of the suburban dream. As Beuka writes in relation to Updike's *Rabbit* series and Nichols' *The Graduate*, 'material success becomes odious . . . evidence of capitulation to an unreflective consumer society' (2004: 137). The utopian ideals of suburbia have, by the 1990s, been well and truly annihilated

Figure 13   Amy Brenneman and Aaron Eckhart in *Your Friends and Neighbors* (Neil LaBute, 1998). Courtesy Gramercy Pictures / The Kobal Collection / Bruce Birmelin.

by materialistic victory: if, as Beuka suggests, the utopian vision of inclusion and togetherness that informed the post-war suburban migration had, by 1967, given way to a popular image of 'disjointed development neighbourhoods characterised by a form of crass materialism readily observable on the landscape itself ', then this image has become a fully-fledged, anti-utopian cliché in the smart film.

By inverting ideal utopian solutions into nightmare possibilities, such visions are frequently cast as discrediting the possibility and desirability of social change, and therefore as being politically reactionary (Ruppert 1986: 102). The continuous narrative structure of the suburban smart film is again relevant here, in terms of the protagonists' typical failure to modify the anti-utopian situation that is presented at the outset. By remaining unambiguously within their nightmare scenarios, the films by Solondz and LaBute would, in this sense, be perceived as the most conservative in the cycle. The semantic features of anti-utopianism are clear in all the films, though. The parodic characteristic of the genre is obvious: in their blank and unflattering depictions of proximate living, material success and family dynamics, each of the six films satirises the original values of suburbia, exposing the false assumptions of this specific brand of utopianism. In *Happiness*, Trish Maplewood's smug claim to 'have it all' is subtended by the viewer having just seen her psychiatrist-husband masturbating to a pre-teen magazine in a crowded mall carpark, and recount-ing a dream of himself as a serial killer to his own psychiatrist. In *The Safety of Objects*, Jim Train mentally ticks off his attributes (smart wife, healthy kids) while commuting to his job as a lawyer before being enlightened by a piece of bus graffiti – 'a man needs a purpose' – and abandoning his job and family to pursue a mall competition to win a car. And, in *Your Friends and Neighbors*, Barry (Aaron Eckhart) describes his suburban house as 'heaven' to his dinner guests, before, in the next scene, his wife consents to an affair with the male guest (Ben Stiller).

In each film, the suburb is rendered as a veritable totalitarian state that denies individuality and represses freedom through its institutions of work, school and family. Limited detail is given on the particulars of any character's job: all are sketched in broad, cartoonish terms of boredom and surveillance. Bill is seen working only once, near the beginning of *Happiness*, where he fights the drowsiness induced by his client (Philip Seymour Hoffman) recount-ing his violent sex fantasies by compiling a mental list of tasks to do after work. In *Donnie Darko*, the two sympathetic teachers – Kenneth Monnitoff (Noah Wyle) and Karen Pomeroy (Drew Barrymore) – both lose their jobs after exposing students to texts that are regarded as inappropriate – *The Philosophy of Time Travel* and Graham Greene's *The Destructors*. The com-fortable, educated life that suburban-utopianism imagined is represented as stultifying and destructive, leading only to violence, unhappiness and abuse. Ruppert describes how the literary anti-utopia centres on the incompatibility of contentment and freedom: the paradigm of utopian happiness overwhelms the values of choice, individuality and change. In this way, the state is main-tained under the 'benign yoke' of a 'benefactor' whose concern lies with the well-being of the citizens. As Ruppert identifies, the anti-utopia is concerned not just with the projection of a brutal future but also with the question of human happiness (1986: 106). In some of the suburban smart films, the 'ben-efactor' figure, or order, is clearly distinguished from the anti-hero(es) who recognise that self-realisation is possible only through breaking away from the deforming social order.

When apparent, this differentiation is typically drawn along generational lines: the adults, subscribing to the utopian values of suburbia much as Ben Braddock's parents do in *The Graduate*, are cast in the 'benefactor' role, while their teenage children have discovered the paradox upon which these ideals are based, and esteem the values of individuality and freedom. It is in this way that the suburban smart film articulates the cycle's broad concern with the reversal of parent/child roles that was discussed in Chapter 3, as well as demonstrates the smart cycle's most obvious links to the teen film. The 'benign yoke' of the parents' authority is made clear in the confrontation scenes typical of the anti-utopian genre. In *Donnie Darko*, Donnie – the anti-hero – is pitted directly against an overtly utopian guide to happiness created by life coach Jim Cunningham (Patrick Swayze) and taught in Donnie's polished suburban school. In a typical classroom sequence, Donnie exposes the false assumptions of the model. When asked to complete a lifeline exercise based on the premise that 'fear' equates to negative energy and 'love' equates to positive energy, he confronts his teacher with an anti-reductionist argument, describing how the model ignores the spectrum of human emotion. A similar confrontation scene occurs early in *The Chumscrubber*, when Dean Stiffle's (Jamie Bell) pop-psychologist father Bill (William Fichtner) attempts to test his own wellbeing-model on his reticent son, probing Dean on how he 'feels' about his best friend Troy's suicide. Although insisting that the two are 'just talking . . . man to man', Bill takes notes on his son's response, prompting Dean to maintain that if his father writes about him in another one of his stupid books, he'll kill him. In both films, the adults are caricatured 'benefactors'; their concern with the question of their teenagers' happiness is reduced to naive terms that the younger people refuse to subscribe to.

SUBURBAN SMART SCIENCE FICTION

Donnie Darko and *The Chumscrubber* can be singled out in a discussion of the smart film's suburban utopianism as they are two of the only films in the entire smart cycle to contain clear science fiction elements. In her overview of American science fiction cinema, Christine Cornea follows Suvin and Jameson in emphasising the connection between science fiction and utopia: she draws on Judith Merril's understanding of science fiction as 'speculative fiction' in order to link the genre with the earlier tradition of utopian fiction exemplified by Edward Bellamy's *Looking Backwards: 2000–1887* (1888) and William Morris's *News from Nowhere* (1890) (2007: 2–3). By understanding utopia as the inherent theme of the genre, this critical position situates science fiction texts as those that prompt reflection on one's own situation. The perspective brings out the comparative dimension of the utopian discourse emphasised by Raymond Williams, for whom utopia and dystopia are not finite visions but deal, respectively, with 'a happier life' and 'a more wretched kind of life' (1973: 196).

In a *Cinéaste* article, Ruppert describes how it was the latter vision that dominated the cinematic science-fiction imagination in the twentieth century: films such as *Alien* (Ridley Scott, 1979) and *Blade Runner* bear testament to the significant changes in social values and attitudes that the corruption of utopia entails, and demonstrate how 'we have difficulty imagining our future other than in terms of some kind of catastrophe' (1989: 8). As Ruppert acknowledges, these classical science fiction films differ ideologically from both earlier and more recent examples in their unambiguous representation of the social conditions of late consumer capitalism: they depict worlds of mass advertisement and mass consumerism where technological corporate capital has commodified nature and human relationships. The overstated and fantastic images of *Blade Runner* are understood to evoke its period's anxieties about the amorality and aggression of the post-industrial era; it imagines scenarios of waste, decay and despair that locate hope only in the possibility of escape, which, as the ending demonstrates, is itself inevitably ironic and ambiguous. In their own work on science fiction cinema, Cornea and Vivian Sobchack also identify *Blade Runner* in dystopian terms. For Cornea the 'retrofitted dystopian cityscape' works as a backdrop against which 'emerging questions of human subjectivity within a postmodern, post-industrial environment' are dealt with (2007: 154). For Sobchack, the 'excess scenography' works as more than background by itself expressing the film's dystopian attitude toward commodification: she emphasises how *Blade Runner's mise-en-scène* fetishises material culture as 'sensuous clutter': 'the space mapped here is valued for its acquisitive power, its expansive capacity to accumulate, consume and hold on to "things"' (1987: 262).

Sobchack's description of *Blade Runner* demonstrates Jameson's understanding of science fiction as a perspective by which the present can be apprehended as history (Milner et al. 2006: 331). Discussions of cinematic utopias and dystopias have no doubt focused on science-fiction films because their overtly futuristic imagery displays this strategic method most unambiguously. The particular stylisation of the suburban nightmare film can also be understood to enable this apprehension, though, and to project alternate worlds as a critical exposition of social fact. As with the anti-utopias of classical science-fiction, the suburban smart film is overtly concerned with the concrete representation of late capitalist culture: all the films in this cycle present their anti-utopian visions as the extrapolation of a society where commodity culture is negatively linked to social values, life patterns and personal relationships (Ruppert 1989: 8). The projected worlds of the suburban smart film may not be as visibly futuristic as the anti-utopias of classical science-fiction, but their conspicuous and parodic stylisation clearly distinguishes them from a more realist suburban paradigm.[7]

In his discussion of urban dystopias, Andrew Milner draws on Williams' suggestion that science-fiction represents four characteristic types of utopia and dystopia: 'the paradise or hell, the positively or negatively externally-altered world, the positive or negative willed transformation and the positive or negative technological transformation' (2004: 263). Where the popular suburban nightmare films articulate their scenarios in terms of technological transformation – *The Stepford Wives, The Truman Show, Pleasantville* – the broadly realistic tone of the suburban smart films tends to preclude their articulation of the second and fourth types. Their visions, though, can clearly be understood as negatively willed transformations. Suspended in the past or located in an indistinct present unmarked by culture or history, these worlds are, as suggested, the extrapolation of materialistic will. Their satirically blank scenography depicts the suburb as a degraded social sphere where self-interest, greed, mass production and mass consumption have inverted the utopian ideals of community and sub-urban nature. In idiosyncratic renderings of broadly flat and bright scenes, each film projects this vision slightly differently.

Happiness and *Your Friends and Neighbors* encode their depersonalised nightmares in their rigid and unlovely form. Solondz favours unsightly and vivid settings, unflattering costuming, flat and unsympathetic performances, objectionable music and plain cinematography to present a distinctly robotic middle-class world that in no substantial way differs from Bill's – supposedly heightened – dream of mass murder. As a playwright and theatrical director, LaBute's naturally static style presents highly unnatural filmic worlds that appear hermetic and stunted. The rigid frames and long takes of *Your Friends and Neighbors* exemplify the blankest style of any smart film: here Solondz' plainness is exaggerated into a rigid window onto bland settings and inane conversations that demonstrate the self-obsession, lack of imagination and cruelty of the upwardly mobile characters. Outside of the obviously fantastic dimension of *Donnie Darko* that will be considered below, Kelly's world is already unreal in its heightened evocation of a privileged but socially degraded 1980s (the Smurfs, Stephen King, Michael Dukakis, *Married with Children*) and its polished scenography, which, captured in Steadicam, appears as fluid and heightened as LaBute's is rigid and flat. *The Safety of Objects* and *Magnolia* both present worlds whose details are for the most part rounded and life-like, but whose reality is burst by stylistic flourishes and hyperbolic moments: in Troche's seamlessly incorporated talking dolls, and Anderson's rain of frogs and ensemble sing-a-long. In each example, suburbia is presented as an unnatural space: as in science-fiction, it is a present that is bracketed off and able to be apprehended.

Of all the films in the suburban cycle, *The Chumscrubber* is the most unequivocal in this regard. In *A Cinema of Loneliness*, Robert Kolker suggests that the decline of the *film noir* cycle is most adequately indicated by the self-consciousness of late films such as *Kiss Me Deadly* (Robert Aldrich, 1955) and *Touch of Evil* (Orson Welles, 1958). The worlds of these films are, for Kolker, brutal and exaggerated: 'their characters are bizarre to the point of madness and realize to an extraordinary pitch the hysteria inherent in most inhabitants of the noir universe' (1980: 23). In this way, Kolker suggests, these films are the climax of the genre, 'or perhaps its coda'. Due in part to its specific science-fiction dimension, *The Chumscrubber* can be approached as a similar marker in the trajectory of smart cinema: the film raises the cycle's satire of suburbia to an hysterical pitch, and subsequently realises the other anti-utopian motifs in a highly self-conscious manner.

Posin's film traces the experiences of a group of interconnected families living in Hillside, a glossy Southern Californian suburb marked out into subdivisions such as the 'Ocean Crest Development' and 'Sunnycrest'. At the beginning of the film, teen protagonist Dean discovers his best friend Troy (Josh Janowicz) has hanged himself in his bedroom. As Troy was drug-dealer to the local high school, the introverted Dean soon finds himself threatened by the violent and unpredictable Billy (Justin Chatwin) and sidekick Lee (Lou Taylor Pucci), who demand he hand over Troy's stash. When Dean ignores their threats, the two, along with Billy's girlfriend Crystal (Camilla Belle) kidnap a younger boy, Charlie (Thomas Curtis), who they believe is Dean's brother. The film proceeds as a series of 'short cuts' tracking Billy, Lee and Crystal as they drift between their family homes with Charlie in tow. These sequences also address the conflicts and addictions of the teenagers' parents: vitamin saleswoman Allie Stiffle (Allison Janney) and husband Bill; Troy's emotionally fragile mother Carrie Johnson (Glenn Close); Crystal's attractive mother Jerri (Carrie-Anne Moss); Billy's lonely father (Jason Isaacs) and the kidnapped Charlie's father, local police officer Lou Bratley (John Heard), who jealously stalks his ex-partner Terri and bullies her fiancée with parking tickets.

Critical responses to Posin's film were mixed, with many commentators making negative comparisons to *Donnie Darko* and complaining about the iteration of the by now too-familiar themes of disaffected teen life in suburbia.[8] What is witnessed here, argues one reviewer, is 'the commoditization of teen trauma' in the shape of a new subgenre: 'the post-*Donnie Darko* metaphysical teen-angst picture' (Schneider 2005). Cast in this way, Posin's film is undeniably overplayed, with characters, themes and symbols from earlier suburban smart films flattened into one-dimensional types. As in *Your Friends and Neighbors*, the interchangeability of the characters is signalled in their syntactically similar names: Terri, Jerri, Carrie, Allie. Suburbia's utopian iconography is meticulously reproduced in glossy, landscaped gardens and pools, neat backyard settings, sunny kitchens, expensively fitted-out teen bedrooms and ever-present blue skies and palm trees. At least three of the families live in the same cul-de-sac – that most distinctive form of the suburban street which, as Cuff notes, implies a small, closed web of neighbours. The impression is furthered by one of the protagonists being Hillside's mayor – a figure with clear community associations. The dreams of success traditionally located in suburbia are evoked in the aspirations of many of the adults – Allie's zeal for selling vitamins, Bill's absorption in his pseudo-celebrity, Terri's identification with her interior design job and the concern Lee's parents have that he work hard to avoid getting into a second-tier school and sub-standard job. The perfecting of mind and body is an explicit priority that is signalled in Allie and Bill's jobs,

Figure 14   Jamie Bell and Richard Gleason in *The Chumscrubber* (Arie Posin, 2005). Courtesy El Camino Pictures / The Kobal Collection.

in Jerri's obsession with her age and weight, in Lou Bratley's concern over his son Charlie's small size, and in Michael's utopian realisation – derived directly from Bill's book 'The Happy Accident' – that nothing is random and that it *is* possible for us 'to actually conjure magic'.

Relations between the adults in the narrative are depicted with an exaggerated tone of benevolence: the 'community' of Hillside is emphasised in the webs of endless cul-de-sacs, the neighbourliness of pool parties and casual drop-ins and, most emphatically, Carrie's manic insistence on how 'unbelievably nice' everyone has been in the wake of Troy's suicide. As in *Brave New World*, the question of happiness is here reduced to an undifferentiated, chemically induced feeling that is initially subscribed to by both adults and teenagers (Ruppert 1986: 106). The opening monologue that describes 'the best of all possible worlds' is explicitly linked to the circulation of drugs throughout the school by Troy. This habit stamps out all individuality between the teenagers: Dean, the tormented outsider from the outset, swallows the same pills that Billy and Lou are so desperate to get hold of after Troy's death. The more obviously buoyant attitudes of the adults are also held in place by stimulants like Allie's 'Vegi-force' – 'an entirely new life-system' – and alcohol. The anesthetised facades slip only briefly: in Carrie's silent scream as she hides behind the front door where Allie stands bearing a casserole; in Terri's similarly masked plea that Michael not leave her after she attacks him and insists he 'pull himself together'; and in a monologue from Allie to Dean: in the garden over a glass of wine she openly wonders to him what it would be like if he were the adult and she the child.

The parodically sanitised and unreal environment can be attributed to Posin's self-described concern to strip away any evidence of real-life popular culture (Posin 2005). Instead, he builds his own singular example from the ground up in 'The Chumscrubber' video game, which, played by the teenagers throughout, functions as the most unambiguous motif in the film's vision of a denaturalised anti-utopia. The protagonist of this game is The Chumscrubber himself, who explains his existence like this:

> I live in the city, in an apartment above the cloud left by the blast. I'm one of the lucky ones. One morning I awoke to discover that my head was no longer attached to my body. I'm not dead, but who could call this a life? So I did what I had to do, in a world of freaks and sub-human creatures. I became the Chumscrubber.

Depicted on television screens throughout the film wandering a dark and fiery animated landscape of suburban houses, head held aloft, the Chumscrubber is a clear science fiction element: he embodies an alternate, post-apocalyptic suburbia.

The animated suburb here fulfils the role that the city plays in typical anti-utopian visions, as the dystopian novum. In *Metropolis* and *Blade Runner*, Milner describes the cityscape as 'a synecdoche for the wider catastrophe that has overcome their respective populations' (2004: 267). The catastrophe of The Chumscrubber video game – 'the blast' – is not explained, but its shape is similarly encoded within the game's scorched suburban landscape and has refracted such that The Chumscrubber is the last human – or post-human – on earth. The game motif is Posin's most hyperbolic smart gesture: it sketches a literal flip-side to the satirical suburban community. The digital nightmare vision makes explicit the fears that are reflected in the excessive scenography of the surface world: its scenario of violence and isolation is suggested as the negatively transformed result of the selfish and alienated attitudes apparent in the characters of Hillside. As narrator of both game and film, The Chumscrubber is the individual mediating consciousness that anchors the game's anti-utopia: his wry attitude suggests an understanding of this transformation, and thereby of the paradox upon which the utopian happiness of the surface world is based. It is in their blinkered engagement with the game and its merchandise that the film situates the teenagers' own understanding of this paradox, and thereby, in the terms of the anti-utopian genre, identifies them as the 'anti-heroes' and the adults as the naïve 'benefactors' of this imposed suburban world.

It is as this figure that The Chumscrubber also anchors the film's take on the utopian type of the Apocalyptic myth, and can throw into relief the other suburban smart films' own interpretations. Throughout the course of the narrative, the juxtaposition of the game with the surface world enables Posin's articulation of some of the key characteristics of this paradigm: most obviously, its bipolar internal structure of positive and negative elements, which includes Light vs. Dark, Death vs. Rebirth, Terror vs. Hope and Regeneration (Fortunati 1993: 83). The game also organises the film in terms of the three basic elements of apocalyptic writing: Destruction, Judgement and Regeneration. As narrator, the rhetoric of this organisation belongs to the enlightened animated figure: he, as Viva Fortunati writes in reference to this myth, 'exudes awareness of his superiority, his worthiness to be spokesman for the elect, the chosen heir to the apocalyptic vision'. The nuance that the 'end' takes on by way of the game and its knowing perspective can be understood to characterise the anti-utopian visions of all the suburban smart films discussed here. The end or 'catastrophe' of *The Chumscrubber* is most obviously encoded within the game, in the undescribed blast that resulted in The Chumscrubber's isolated existence. In his narration of his own story, the three dimensions of destruction, judgement and regeneration make up his 'becoming' The Chumscrubber. As suggested, though, this 'regenerated' life – nomadic, fragmented – is unambiguously posited as a flip-side to the satirically utopian surface world: its destroyed society functions as a judgement on the corrupt attitudes and values that transformed it as such.

In this way, the collective will of the suburban community is posited as catastrophe *and* regeneration: it functions as both the cause of the fantastic fall that created the game, and the state of being that continues as the object of its metaphor. The 'catastrophe' internal to the surface narrative – when all the story threads come together in the cul-de-sac and Billy is hit by a car – supports this interpretation, insofar as it is followed by an explicitly regenerative montage sequence that details how the 'utopian' order is restored. This circular orientation indicates how the anti-utopianism of *The Chumscrubber,* and the other suburban smart films, can be approached as an annihilative take on the Apocalyptic myth. The other films don't sketch their 'catastrophes' quite so literally, but in all there is a violent or disjunctive event that triggers a type of regeneration: in *Happiness,* Bill is arrested after molesting his son's friends; in *The Safety of Objects,* Esther (Glenn Close) murders her comatose son; in *Your Friends and Neighbors* the character of Cary (Jason Patric) delivers a lengthy monologue detailing his part in a gang rape as a teenager. These examples all suggest how the suburban smart film tends to feed upon disaster and *yearn* for Apocalypse. As such, the myth is emptied of its cathartic powers and the possibility of true regeneration is discredited: the final scenarios are described in terms of satire, hyperbole, ambiguity or emptiness.

In many, including *The Chumscrubber*, *Your Friends and Neighbors* and *Happiness*, the characters' lack of consciousness is highlighted by the straightforward restoration of the prevailing anti-utopian order. *The Safety of Objects* evokes the mock-transcendent ending of much science-fiction by abruptly shifting from critical exposition to utopian fantasy (Ruppert 1989: 8), with all the damaged families of the film gathered over a meal in a suburban backyard listening to a teenage girl sing a song written by the dead boy – her brother. The ending here is not as openly parodic as Posin's in *The Chumscrubber* or as emotionally nihilistic as Solondz' or LaBute's in *Happiness* or *Your Friends and Neighbors*, but its animation of the utopian dialectic – its glimpse of a better world – is highly ambiguous, and does little to counter the apocalyptic logic advanced by all the films, namely that 'the end of our civilisation is . . . inevitable because of qualities inherent in human nature' (Fortunati 1993: 88).

In the logic of utopianism, the ostensibly inflammatory sub-cycle of suburban smart cinema can be cast as reactionary and nostalgic. By appearing to discredit the potential for transformation in human existence, these films align with the anti-utopian genre as a negative discourse that doesn't reconstruct. Further, the emphatic violence and cruelty of their scenarios posits the modulated family as a personally and socially discontented form. By juxtaposing this form with a traditional nuclear set-up, the films indirectly project a utopian scenario as the imagination of the ideal suburban settings that encapsulate them. The film that offers the most significant challenge to both the negative discourse and its indirect utopian vision is *Donnie Darko*. Due in part to its own science-fiction orientation, Kelly's film offers an alternate and more radical take on the concept of transformation. By examining this transformation in terms of the Deleuzean discourse of becoming, the film can be understood to animate a dialectic that is properly utopian.

BECOMING-DEMOCRATIC; BECOMING-ANIMAL

In an article in the journal *Deleuze Studies*, Paul Patton casts Deleuze and Guattari's way of 'doing philosophy' as a political project in which the aim is overtly utopian (Patton 2007). Deleuze and Guattari understand philosophy as the creation of concepts, where these philosophical concepts are open-ended and a-systematic multiplicities. In *What is Philosophy?*, the utopianism of this project is made clear when they stipulate that 'the creation of concepts in itself calls for a future form, for a new earth and people that do not yet exist' (1994: 108). Patton's concern in his article is with the shift in orientation between Deleuze and Guattari's early work – particularly in *Anti-Oedipus* and *A Thousand Plateaus* – and the later *What is Philosophy?*, as well as Deleuze's solo thought in works such as *Negotiations* and *Essays Critical and Clinical*. Patton's suggestion is that the later works imply an awareness of normative political issues that is less prominent in the earlier books: as he describes, *Anti-Oedipus* and *A Thousand Plateaus* 'do not set out to provide normative standards for the justification or critique of political institutions and processes. Instead, they outline a political ontology that enables us to conceptualise and describe transformative or creative forces and movements' (Patton 2007: 42). Nonetheless, there is a normative dimension to this ontology in the systematic priority of 'minoritarian becomings' over 'majoritarian being', to 'lines of flight' over 'forms of capture', and to 'planes of consistency' over 'planes of organisation'. When Deleuze does later engage with the political values and concepts that inform basic liberal democracy, it is the normativity that founds these earlier concepts – and particularly the concept of *becoming* – that enables Deleuze's suggestion that philosophy can respond to the present.

This normative reference is best exemplified in the phrases that Patton focuses on: 'becoming-revolutionary' and 'becoming-democratic'. In the context of *What is Philosophy?*, the concept of becoming-revolutionary implies 'forms of individual and collective self-transformation in response to what is intolerable or shameful in the present' (Patton 2007: 47). The concept is defined not in terms of these forms themselves, but in terms of the transformation that remains irreducible to its historical manifestations. Here, as Patton describes, becoming is a pure event: 'an 'unhistorical element' that is necessary in order for new forms of life to emerge. As the normative dimension of the transformative process, the concept of becoming means that the political vocation of becoming-revolutionary is focused on the forces and processes that produce or inhibit changes to the character of individual or social life. Patton reads the concept as utopian because it doesn't simply posit an ideal future or a blueprint for new social arrangements. Instead, it aims to connect up with those forces that are present in – but stifled by – the present milieu. Deleuze and Guattari suggest that utopia stands for absolute deterritorialisation, 'but always at the critical point at which it is connected with the present relative milieu' (1994: 99). The concept of becoming-democratic expresses the potential for extending processes of *relative* deterritorialisation that already exist in a social milieu – so, resistant political forces and the ideals or opinions that motivate them – to the limits of what is possible under present conditions. It 'points to ways of criticising the workings of actually existing democracies in the name of the egalitarian principles that are supposed to inform their institutions and political practices' (Patton 2007: 50).

As has been suggested, the anti-utopian visions of the suburban smart films all embody their own critiques of liberal democratic culture: in these films the suburb replaces the city of classical dystopian science-fiction as a site magnifying the commodification of social values and human relationships. The films focused on so far principally achieve this critique in terms of satire. Although Kelly has suggested that, first and foremost, *Donnie Darko* does function as a piece of social satire,[9] the terms in which this is elaborated can be understood in relation to the concept of becoming-democratic. In this way, *Donnie Darko* is utopian in a way that the other films are not. The narrative of the film is structured by an atypically literal deployment of Sconce's third smart characteristic: the formal and thematic interest in issues of coincidence and random fate (Sconce 2002: 358). At the beginning of the film, the teenage Donnie's (Jake Gyllenhaal) house is struck by a stray airliner engine. The accident is seen twice: once at the beginning and once at the end of the film. In the first version of events Donnie lives; in the second he is killed. The space between the two accidents is structured as a twenty-eight day countdown to the end of the world that is predicted by the vision that saves Donnie the first time: Frank (James Duval), the figure dressed in a rabbit suit with a demonic, skull-like mask. Over the twenty-eight days Donnie, diagnosed as a borderline schizophrenic, struggles to comprehend his visions of Frank and the awareness of the world they seem to impel in him. Increasingly disturbed by Frank's prophecy, Donnie turns to the philosophy of time travel as a means of understanding his situation.

Like the other suburban smart films, *Donnie Darko* can be linked to the anti-utopian genre by its depiction of the suburb as an environment repressed by the institutions of work, school and family. As in some of these films, *Donnie Darko's* critique of this culture is partially contained in a semantic device lifted from the teen-film, where the adults are cast as naïve and the teenagers as cynically enlightened. As described earlier, the motivational speaker Jim Cunningham and his staunchest supporter, the PE teacher Kitty Farmer, fill out the caricatured 'benefactor' roles most adequately. Kelly confuses the model, though, with other characters: both Donnie and some of the sympathetic adults (the science and English teachers, his parents) are depicted with an earnestness that is unusual for both the smart and teen mode. It is not either cycle's favourite constraint of family that emerges as Donnie's 'problem'; far more limiting are those other bureaucratic powers that operate behind and around the family: in Jim Cunningham's reduction of life to attitudes of either love or fear, and in Donnie's therapist twisting his fears and compulsions into a search for God. Against both powers, Kelly transforms the teen film by exaggerating the device of the 'wise' teenager: Donnie is the literally visionary youth who rejects his teachers and psychiatrist.

The real distinction of the film, though, can be located in the way that this rejection is enabled by the figure of Frank, whose presence anchors a narrative ambiguity that remains definitively open. Interpretations of *Donnie Darko* have relied on the paradigms of both science fiction and mental illness.[10] If the science fiction line is taken, Frank's appearance signals the point where the Tangent universe opens up and the film diverges from realism: thematically, Donnie becomes the super hero that his girlfriend Gretchen (Jena Malone) comments his name suggests – the 'Living Receiver' chosen to keep the Primary and Tangent universes separate. If the mental illness line is taken, Frank's appearance is the first of Donnie's paranoid schizophrenic hallucinations. In this interpretation, the narrative doesn't diverge from realism for Frank is simply understood as 'not real', and the film as a teen piece tapping directly into the contemporary therapeutic imagination. A third possibility is that the appearance of Frank – the man-animal – is understood as Donnie's act of what Deleuze and Guattari conceptualise as *becoming-animal*. In this possibility, Frank is neither a symbol nor a symptom but an active force forging Donnie's escape: he is the intensity that *disrupts* the film.

Becoming-animal is one example of the type of minoritarian becoming that Patton suggests can fill out the concept of becoming-democratic. For Deleuze and Guattari, becoming-animal is one way of overcoming the transcendental logic of being, and affirming an order of immanence from which being is organised. In practice, this manifests as an attempt to expand the concept of reality from the parameters of what *is* (what is actual) to what is also *becoming* (what is virtual). In this schema, any positive form is expanded by a plane of virtual tendencies. Deleuze and Guattari's project can be cast as a non-reductive ontology in that it contests those claims to primacy of any pre-given positivity that directs and controls these tendencies (Urpeth 2004: 102). This project does not claim that there is no actuality, but that there is always *more than* the actual. Fixed identities of form or function are always expanded by a virtual plane of potential which *subtracts* from them the unique or the characteristic. Animality, for Deleuze and Guattari, is aligned with this virtual, subtractive force: the mode they privilege is not that of the individuated, domestic pet but of the roaming, anonymous pack. They refer throughout their work to rats, fleas and wolves as types that consist not of identities and representations but of *intensities*. Animality expresses the composite of virtual tendencies at the heart of any actual perception, as a real multiplicity without uniqueness. Becoming-animal describes the attempt to perceive this order of pure difference as an *escape*; it is an attempt at not-*being*: at not being-animal, but also at not being-human. One does not imitate or represent the animal, but creates a new molecular mode of individuation. Instances of becoming-animal identified by Deleuze and Guattari include those in Kafka's 'The Metamorphosis' and Melville's *Moby Dick*. In these stories, they write, 'the animal is the object *par excellence* of the story: [it is] to try to find a way out, to trace a line of escape' (1986: 34).

Understanding Frank as symptomatic of a virtual mode of individuation in this way goes against the dominant readings of *Donnie Darko*, where the disruption of Frank is absorbed into the register of theme: he is the 'Manipulated Dead' in the elaborate time travel schema or that standard mental illness icon, the vision compelling Donnie to destroy. In either instance he is identified as

Figure 15   Jake Gyllenhaal and Jena Malone in *Donnie Darko* (Richard Kelly, 2001). Courtesy Flower Films/Gaylord/Adam Fields Prod / The Kobal Collection / Dale Robinette.

representational. But, against the exaggerated anti-utopian suburb, Frank's emergence can also be taken more literally. In opposition to the institutions of falsely utopian happiness, Frank transpires as Donnie's *act* of becoming-animal – he is an active alternative, a refusal, and a means of transforming these institutions: 'I can do whatever I want', Frank explains to Donnie, 'and so can you'. In this way, Frank is the form Donnie's self-transformation takes in response to what he finds intolerable in the present: he signals Donnie's perception of difference beyond the actualised forms of his suburban, middle-class life. Critically, as an 'imaginary' friend, Frank indicates Donnie's becoming-animal as a state *escaping* those binaries representing the limitations around him: love/fear, truth/falsity, god/chaos, real/imaginary. 'Imaginary' is here a third term, not a second. This orientation aligns the film as a whole, where the satirical bent relies upon an implicit questioning of binaries. By throwing into relief respectively overstated attitudes on topics from *The Destructors* to emotional dysfunction, the film questions, in classic teen-film style, the affirmation of one over the other.

The figure of animality fills out this mode of questioning, for it is deployed practically: as a means of challenging the literal. When Frank first appears and starts the countdown to the end of the world it seems like a linear timeline set out by a mysterious, visionary being. After the twenty-eight days, though, the film abruptly diverts back to its starting point: October 2, 1988. Frank's vision is not actualised into a real, apocalyptic event but dissolves into another take on an earlier event. One jet engine accident is virtual but it's not clear which. The timeline doesn't indicate a beginning and end point but suggests infinite 'middleness' as the ceaseless movement of forms in time and space. Donnie's becoming-animal animates a utopian dialectic in *Donnie Darko* by framing *this* vision as a glimpse of a genuinely transcendent world. The vision directly opposes the utopian order of happiness that is satirised in the surface world of this film and of the other suburban smart films discussed: Donnie's transformation amounts to an awareness of himself not as a unique origin for a perceived world (as the adults see themselves) but as one more form itself becoming-different. For Donnie, this is not a positive recognition that fleshes out an existing system of understanding but is the subtraction of everything that he does 'know'. The relative forces and processes of deterritorialisation that the narrative connects up with here can be interpreted as the symptoms of schizophrenia, but also as the more ordinary emotional confusion of being a teenager. These conditions are rendered as 'desirable' insofar as they prompt the deterritorialisation of an actual world: Donnie's 'insights' amount to a virtual awareness of the immanence of life that may or may not destroy him. The ambiguity that *Donnie Darko* leaves suspended is whether this recognition of life does propose a greater self-awareness or not. The utopianism of its action lies in the *possibility* of resistance and transformation: a possibility that it locates, like the other films, in the figure of the teenager.

In his book *Deleuze, Cinema and National Identity: Narrative Time in National Contexts*, David Martin-Jones draws on Deleuze's philosophy to describe how a recent group of films manipulate narrative time to construct national identity. For Martin-Jones, *Run Lola Run*, *Memento* (Christopher Nolan, 2000) and *Eternal Sunshine of the Spotless Mind* are 'hybrid' films because they employ a non-linear or labyrinthine model of time that evokes the time-image within a more broadly classical, linear, movement-image structure (2006: 2). In attending to films that have been linked to the smart cycle elsewhere in this project, Martin-Jones' argument can also illuminate the sensibility at work in *Donnie Darko*. This chapter has drawn upon some Deleuzean concepts that can be understood in utopian terms – becoming-democratic, becoming-animal – as a way of exploring Kelly's film in a manner that disrupts a linear genre interpretation: as an encounter between a movement-image model of suburban anti-utopianism and a time-image model of transformation. To understand this film as either a time travel story *or* a portrait of schizophrenia reduces the film to the binary logic it satirises, making the story reliant upon the explanatory oppositions of *The Philosophy of Time Travel* or the fundamental opposition of sane/mad.

The logic of becoming-animal is a third way of approaching the film because it is a refusal of binary reason on two fronts. Internally, Frank forges Donnie's line of escape from its oppressive structures. Externally, Donnie's becoming-animal is the becoming-molecular of the dominant, molar forms of interpretation because it overwhelms their own dyad of 'real' (science fiction) or 'not real' (schizophrenia). The sub-cycle of the suburban smart film is hereby opened up as a form that *questions*: How should we live? Must our lives, as Kitty Farmer insists, be simply righteous? Should we be more 'like' Donnie, in the sense that he is 'like' Frank and strive to perceive beyond our actual conditions, or will this realisation overwhelm us? This ambiguity signals how the utopianism of the suburban smart film is ultimately embedded not in the paradigm of science-fiction but in the liminal terms of the teen film: it connects up with that tense, overwrought moment *between*: the moment 'between yesterday and tomorrow, between childhood and adulthood, between being a nobody and a somebody, when everything is in question, and anything is possible' (Martin 1994: 68).

NOTES

1. A version of this chapter was originally published as 'Becoming-democratic: *Donnie Darko* and other recent suburban utopias', by Claire Perkins, in *Rhizomes* 16 (2008).
2. Key cultural studies works emphasising the connection between science fiction and utopia include Raymond Williams' essay 'Utopia and Science Fiction', Darko Suvin's *Metamorphoses of Science Fiction*, Tom Moylan's *Demand the Impossible: Science Fiction and the Utopian Imagination*, and Fredric Jameson's *Archaeologies of the Future: The Desire Called Utopia and Other Science Fictions*.
3. This specific area of research is indicated but for the most part elided in two other broad areas: on the one hand in the work that relies on ideas of utopia and dystopia in addressing cinema and the city – see, for instance, various essays in Mark Shiel and Tony Fitzmaurice's *Cinema and the City: Film and Urban Societies in a Global Context* and *Screening the City* (2003) and David B. Clarke's *The Cinematic City* (1997) – and, on the other, in work that looks at urban and suburban spaces from an architectural perspective – Nan Ellin's *Architecture of Fear* (1997), Steven Harris and Deborah Berke's *Architecture of the Everyday* (1997) and Sallie Westwood and John Williams' *Imagining Cities: Scripts, Signs, Memory* (1997).
4. Other films mentioned by Sconce and/or elsewhere in this work that consolidate the idea of the suburban smart film include *Ghost World, The Virgin Suicides* (Sofia Coppola, 1999), *Election, I Heart Huckabees, Me and You and Everyone We Know, Safe, Palindromes, Boogie Nights* and *The Ice Storm*.
5. Beuka lists a number of texts that demonstrate this critique: David Riesman's *The Lonely Crowd* (1950), William H. Whyte's *The Organization Man* (1956), John Keats's *The Crack in the Picture Window* (1957), John McPartland's *No Down Payment* (1957), Paul Goodman's *Growing Up Absurd* (1960) and Betty Friedan's *The Feminine Mystique* (1963) (Beuka 2004: 6).
6. This dimension of Foucault's critique of utopianism is evident in his essay 'Panopticism', where he describes 'the plague-stricken town, traversed throughout with hierarchy, surveillance, observation, writing . . . immobilized by the

functioning of an extensive power that bears in a distinct way over all individual bodies' as 'the utopia of the perfectly governed city' (Foucault 1977: 198).

7. The stylised suburb of the smart film bears little resemblance, for instance, to the neutral representation of suburbia in the family dramas that emerged in the period between the decline of the first New Hollywood and the rise of the Sundance generation and the smart film (roughly 1975–89) – films such as *Ordinary People* (Robert Redford, 1980), *E.T.* (Steven Spielberg, 1982), *Gremlins* (Joe Dante, 1984) and *The 'burbs* (Joe Dante, 1989).

8. See, for instance, Steve Schneider and Scott Foundas's reviews of *The Chumscrubber*.

9. Kelly has commented in one interview, 'Maybe it's the story of Holden Caulfield, resurrected in 1988 by the spirit of Phillip K. Dick, who was always spinning yarns about *schizophrenia* and drug abuse breaking the barriers of space and time. Or it's a black comedy foreshadowing the impact of the 1988 presidential election, which is really the best way to explain it. But first and foremost, I wanted the film to be a piece of social satire that needs to be experienced and digested several times': http://www.electricshadows.com.au/film/2401883878

10. A typical summary of both positions is given on the Salon blog 'Everything you were afraid to ask about "Donnie Darko"': http://dir.salon.com/story/ent/movies/feature/2004/07/23/darko/index.html

CONCLUSION

In 2006, a revised version of Sconce's *Screen* article on the smart film appeared as the final chapter in Linda Ruth Williams and Michael Hammond's broad collection on post-1960 American cinema, *Contemporary American Cinema*. Following chapters on the contemporary blockbuster, DVD viewing and new black cinema in the book's 'The 1990s and Beyond' section, smart cinema is here positioned by Williams and Hammond as a transitional notion that bridges post-classical American cinema and its next stage. Sconce's revision supports this situation by foregrounding smart cinema as a generational struggle over culture, and suggesting that the influence of its moral and tonal qualities – as elements closely tied to age, history and generational experience – will necessarily dissipate as the next 'millennial' generation move into film-making. He also indicates that ongoing evidence of the smart sensibility – as a style defined in opposition to Hollywood – depends on how thoroughly it is incorporated by mainstream culture.

By describing a condition that is constructed by the perception of shareable elements in differing assemblages, this book has supported Sconce's conception of smart cinema as a shifting sensibility by indicating how its qualities can be felt beyond the parameters of a particular time and place. In tracing the connections between the smart sensibility and certain historical traditions and discourses, it has suggested how smart cinema reinvents these traditions while keeping their attitudes and ideologies in place. Conceiving of the sensibility in this way necessarily opens up the directions in which it can be perceived. As suggested in the Introduction, television is one place where the 'mainstreaming' of the sensibility discussed in this study is apparent. Specifically, the notion of 'quality' television has a clear resonance with Sconce's conceptualisation of smart cinema as an industrial, textual and audience category. Janet McCabe and Kim Akass highlight how the issue of taste connects the two categories when they observe that 'there is something inherently divisive about the term quality – its meaning, its use, which often finds colleagues compelled to apply quotation marks as qualifiers around the word' (2007: 2). In Robert Thompson's original evaluation, quality television predates smart cinema, and describes the critical perception in the 1980s of an emergent type of programming that was 'better, more sophisticated, and more artistic than the usual network fare' (1996: 12). As in Sconce's work, the emphasis on taste and discursive construction here is offset by Thompson's identification of a list of 'defining characteristics' that suggests a generic style. This list delineates quality television as something that will: hybridise genres, attract a 'blue chip' audience, struggle to be produced in the face of 'profit-mongering networks', have a large ensemble cast that allows for multiple plots, demonstrate 'literary' writing, be self-conscious in regard to both high and popular culture, and favour subject matter that tends toward the 'controversial' (13–15).

Writing in 1996, Thompson finds evidence of these characteristics in programs including *Hill Street Blues* (1981–7), *St Elsewhere* (1982–8), *Twin Peaks* (1990–1), *Northern Exposure* (1990–5) and *Picket Fences* (1992–6). Later work on the topic makes much of how, in the mid-1990s, cable networks such as Home Box Office (HBO) and Showtime began to produce a particular style of 'quality' programming where the consolidation of a subscription-only, niche audience allowed for the exaggeration of certain aspects of the 'genre'. Here, smart cinema's taste for controversy, allusion and self-reflexivity is recognisable in the sometimes contentious subjects and acute self-consciousness of programs like *True Blood* (2008–), *The L Word* (2004–9), *Californication* (2007–), *Entourage* (2004–) and *Deadwood* (2004–6). Within this broad band of programming, individual series including *The Sopranos* (1999–2007), *Six Feet Under* (2001–5), *Weeds* (2005–), *Big Love* (2006–) and *Breaking Bad* (2008–) demonstrate a further coincidence of smart qualities in their stylised suburban settings, their focus on idiosyncratic family dynamics, and their cultivation of a detached tone by way of incongruous juxtapositions and understated performances.

Within the format of the sequential serial, these programs are able to literally enact the smart film's narrative tendency toward a collection of episodic moments that are folded back into a continuing life. As a genre with a 'memory', quality programming has a particular interest in referring back to events and details as it tracks the change and development in characters over an extended period of time (Thompson 1996: 14). As part of this project, the programs above clearly exaggerate the 'functionally dysfunctional' premise of the television family drama – including portraits of families described in terms of the Mafia, polygamy and drug-dealing – but neither individual plots nor the series as a whole articulate this premise in terms of a populist recognition that it is this 'imperfection' that keeps them together. In a manner that resonates with smart cinema's revision of the attitudes of the historical family melodrama, the programs are committed to exploring the augmented relations that arise from their situations with a limited sense of nostalgia for an imagined ideal of 'functionality'.

In a similar way, Jason Reitman's *Juno* (2006) has found much popular success with its largely unassuming interpretation of broad smart concerns.[1] While magnifying key dimensions from both Wes Anderson and *Ghost World* in its musical orientation, its hand-drawn aesthetic and its semiotically literate teenagers, Reitman's film under-emphasises the dysfunctionality of its premise – whereby sixteen-year-old Juno (Ellen Page) becomes pregnant – by focusing on the new and specific dynamics that emerge between Juno and the adoptive parents she selects, and between Juno and her baby's father (Michael Cera). By contrast, the 'dysfunctional' qualities of each member of *Little Miss Sunshine's* ensemble family – drug-addicted grandfather, suicidal gay uncle, a son who's taken a Nietzschean vow of silence – are all exaggerated to the point of parody, as is the inherently 'functional' orientation that underpins all of this and sees them set out together on the 700 mile journey to the 'Little Miss Sunshine' beauty contest that seven-year-old Olive (Abigail Breslin) is desperate to compete in.

As a film *about* standards of normativity – tagline: 'everyone pretend to be normal' – *Little Miss Sunshine's* narrative is necessarily driven by an imagined ideal that is met neither by the initial, absurd Hoover milieu nor by the monstrous groups at the beauty contest. By bringing these two family standards together, though, the action of the plot ultimately *re*-inverts the Hoovers by consolidating their underlying solidarity into the ideal scenario represented in the ending, where the ensemble family are united in their frenzied escape from the beauty contest crowd after Olive's 'inappropriate' performance. Promotional material for Dayton and Faris' film also evoked the hyperbole – if not the conflict – of Anderson by freezing its group in single-file movement as, like the family groups at the end of *The Life Aquatic* and *The Darjeeling Limited*, they run for the vehicle that symbolises their unity.

The Savages

This study has focused on a group of films in which tonal continuity is achieved through differing configurations of the qualities of irony and dysfunctionality. By stressing the smart sensibility as an affect of tone, the preceding chapters have identified the condition as something in which films 'participate without belonging' (Derrida 1992: 230). This defining characteristic has been empha-sised in discussions of the various types of tonal detachment that are evident in smart cinema: from the formal distanciation of *Flirt* and the careful tableau presentation of *The Royal Tenenbaums*, to the semiotic awareness of *Ghost World* and the synchronous scenario of *Donnie Darko*. In each instance, it has been concluded that the strategy of detachment is drawn upon not as a means of excluding the film from what it 'says' but – in an opposite move – as an interrogation of its own utterance. Each film mobilises aesthetic detachment as the awareness of its own contingency, but simultaneously recognises that this aesthetic itself inscribes a speaking position that is host to a constellation of effects and relations. Some of the chapters have described the magnitude of this recognition by suggesting how it might resonate with certain Deleuzean modes of becoming.

Tamara Jenkins' *The Savages* is a recent commercial/independent American production in which the effect of this 'mark' can be fully felt. Both formally and thematically, *The Savages* is entirely in keeping with the qualities of smart cinema that have been discussed in this study. Outside of the film itself, in which two adult siblings' lives are disrupted by the onset of their estranged father's dementia, the personnel involved with the production also indicate this 'belonging'. Jenkins signalled certain smart preoccupations in her previous feature *The Slums of Beverly Hills* (1998), which focused on an ensemble family struggling to live together in a small apartment block. Additionally, Alexander Payne acts as executive producer on *The Savages*, alongside his regular produc-tion designer Jane Ann Stewart, and the music supervision is by Randall Poster, whose compilation of songs by The Kinks, The Velvet Underground and Peggy Lee distinctly recalls his work on Wes Anderson and Noah Baumbach's films.[2] The most palpable impression of the sensibility, though, comes from the pres-ence of Laura Linney and Philip Seymour Hoffman in the lead roles of Wendy and Jon Savage, where they exploit a type of smart 'stardom' constructed from the variously anxious, depressed, fretful and highly-strung performances they have contributed to films including *The Squid and the Whale, You Can Count On Me* (Kenneth Lonergan, 2000), *The Hottest State* (Ethan Hawke, 2006), *State and Main* (David Mamet, 2000), *Boogie Nights, Happiness, Magnolia, Punch Drunk Love* and *Synecdoche, New York*.

Elsewhere, *The Savages* signals its tonal participation in the smart cycle by demonstrating numerous strategies of detachment and awareness. The settings mirror a stylised, Arizonian suburbia ('Sun City') with a non-descript, wintry Buffalo. Wendy and her married boyfriend Larry (Peter Friedman) offer an archetypal example of the 'expressionless sex' shot early in the narrative and, as they're told they need to find a home for their father, Jon and Wendy are the 'awkward couple' captured primly on a couch in tableau shot, with Jon holding a helium balloon saying 'I Love You'. Wendy captures the neuroses of every

Figure 16   Laura Linney and Philip Seymour Hoffman in *The Savages* (Tamara Jenkins, 2007). Courtesy Fox Searchlight Pictures / The Kobal Collection.

smart character late in the film, when she anxiously asks Jon if he thinks her play dramatising their unhappy childhood is 'self-important and bourgeois'. Less tangibly, the oneiric strains of Stephen Trask's original score and the precise, *New Yorker*-style promotional images link the film to examples like *Ghost World*, *Happiness* and *Rushmore*, and evoke the critical pathos that has been identified there. The dramatic scenario in which all this occurs, though, emphasises the condition of smart cinema as a transposable sensibility, by moving away from the ensemble and nuclear family set-ups of other smart films to attend to the dynamics between adults and their own, ageing parents. Supporting the conception of smart cinema as a generational phenomenon, various reviews of *The Savages* have linked Jenkins' film to Sarah Polley's *Away From Her* (2006), and suggested that the focus on the issue of ageing and senility – evident also in *About Schmidt* and *Little Miss Sunshine* – reflects the real-life preoccupations of commercial/independent writers and directors born in the 1960s and 70s.[3]

Released from a specific association with the popularly imagined 'slacker' attitude of Generation X, the generational argument here is compelling. In *The Savages*, the suggested narrative preoccupation opens up new perspectives on the issues that are raised around the notion of the family in the smart films where adults of a similar age to Wendy and Jon deal with their own children and teenagers. Jenkins offers a precise enactment of the reversed roles that Chapter 3 suggested characterise the modulated families of smart cinema: here the adult siblings are cast in their *biological* role as children to a father who requires physical care. The force of this transposition is felt most fully at the level of Linney's performance, where the tightly-wound concern that she focuses on her sons as Joan in *The Squid and the Whale* is directed at her father. The guilt that Linney's character feels in both films for prioritising her own needs above those of her family is externalised and labelled by *The Savages* in its dramatisation of the process of choosing a nursing home, which, for Wendy and Jon, unambiguously acknowledges them as 'the guilty demographic'.

By using this process to explore the relationship between adults who have been affected by an (implicitly) abusive upbringing, *The Savages* demonstrates the recognisable smart technique in which sibling dynamics metonymically describe the core of family tension. As with the Tenenbaum children in *The Royal Tenenbaums*; Peter, Francis and Jack Whitman in *The Darjeeling Limited*; Bill and Dennis McCabe in *Simple Men*; Barry Egan and his five sisters in *Punch Drunk Love*; Charlie and Donald Kaufman in *Adaptation*; Helen, Joy and Trish in *Happiness* and *Life During Wartime*; Margot (Nicole Kidman) and Pauline (Jennifer Jason Leigh) in *Margot at the Wedding* and Roger and his travelling brother Phillip (Chris Messina) in *Greenberg*, Wendy and Jon's bickering and competitiveness provide much of the drama and humour in *The Savages*. Commentators have described how the film is 'not heavy on story', taking form instead as a 'study of human beings' in a family context, and commentators have also noted the typically smart narrative structure of the film, as the 'maximizing of individual moments' (McCarthy 2007) in 'a slender string of everyday episodes' (Stables 2008: 83).

The most compelling of these smart moments feature the two siblings interacting with acute defensiveness or quiet complicity as they unconsciously parent each other as well as their father through this last stage of his life. Some of the most loaded examples include: a tennis sequence, where – like the match that begins *The Squid and the Whale* – the game expresses the pair's diametrical positions, here on where their father should reside; a conversation where Jon, trapped in a chin sling after injuring his neck in the game, responds with envy and emotion to Wendy's lie that she's been awarded a Guggenheim grant to write a play about their childhood, and the later scene where Wendy finally admits that the grant she received was in fact from the Federal Emergency Management Agency as compensation for the lack of temp work available after 9/11; and an early hospital scene, where Wendy gallantly reminds her father that Jon is not *that* kind of doctor, and doesn't teach medicine but 'the theatre of social unrest'.

The Savages also distinguishes itself from other smart films that rely on the sibling dynamic as a metaphor for a troubled past. One way that this occurs is in the overwhelmingly physical presence of Lenny Savage (Philip Bosco) himself. Where, elsewhere in the cycle, members of this generation are most often symbolically absent and in need of finding or avenging – as in *Simple Men* and *The Darjeeling Limited* – or a type of live emblem of the distance they have always kept from their children – Royal Tenenbaum, Steve Zissou, Patricia Whitman – Jenkins focuses on Lenny as a tangible burden. The smart film's typical concern with particularised settings and props is here expressed as a preoccupation with physical space – with finding Lenny a place to live and with the difficult passage from his initial apartment and the hospital in Arizona to Buffalo and the 'Valley View' nursing home. Jenkins imagines this road trip as a series of physically emphasised moments in which the force of her father's dependency becomes clear to Wendy, who accompanies him. Once back in Buffalo, she directs her anxiety over the situation into Lenny's new living space itself. Troubled by the clinical starkness of the Valley View, she strives to have her father accepted by the 'very beautiful' Greenhill Manor – which, for Jon, 'sounds like an insane asylum'. When Lenny fails the mental capacity test for admission, Wendy turns her insistent concern to adorning the Valley View room with props that bewilder him – a red pillow from Urban Outfitters, a lava lamp, and – disastrously – her cat, Genghis. Jon tolerates her 'flailing, neurotic tenderness' (Stables 2008: 83) across these endeavours with his own divergent brand of pragmatic benevolence.

The tangibility with which these slight episodes unfold indicates the transposition that *The Savages* achieves in the smart sensibility. As one review of the film has noted, 'it's hard to imagine a more potent test of family solidarity than the decision-making process regarding what to do with a sick and help-less relative' (Taylor 2007). The ambiguous 'solidarity' that is typically evoked in smart cinema is rarely something that is tested. Instead, it is *conclusive* – brought out by the episodes of the narrative as the recognition of the impossibility of modifying or overcoming the 'dysfunctional' family milieu. As has been indicated throughout this study, the conflicted understanding that this recognition brings about is often expressed in highly aestheticised sequences that induce a type of critical pathos. In the films of Wes Anderson and Paul Thomas Anderson – and in those that resemble them – this affect emerges through the narrative as an awareness of both the unhappiness and the potentiality that the breakdown of traditional roles and identities gives rise to. In *The Savages*, this awareness operates not as the film's conclusion but as its premise. As in Baumbach's *Margot at the Wedding*, the conflicted dynamics of estrangement are not uncovered by deliberate narrative incidents but function as the very motivation for the action. In Baumbach's film this sees Margot travel to the wedding of the sister she's not speaking to – 'we're supporting her' she instructs her pubescent son; in Jenkins' it sees Wendy and Jon meet up to look after a father who was 'obsolete in the parenting department'.

This distinction indicates a significant distance from those films that dwell on the atypicality of their scenario. Formally, the continuous, episodic structure is magnified, in that *less* is proposed as the result of narrative action. Beginning and ending in the middle of action, these films register minimal change in the complicity of their erratic scenarios. As Baumbach and Jason Leigh have said in a discussion of their film, it is as though the audience is living with these people: they never get ahead of the film, and 'they're always slightly out of breath' (2007). Thematically, the change evoked here suggests the capacity of the smart sensibility to resonate with an outlook recalled by Adrian Martin in his chapter on the 'functional dysfunctional family', where he identifies Robert's (John Cassavetes) matter-of-fact declaration in *Love Streams* (John Cassavetes, 1984) that 'life is a series of suicides, promises broken, children smashed, whatever' as evidence that Cassavetes's films are 'among those very few works in the sphere of popular art that accept the breakdown of once-cherished values (such as the nuclear family) as a simple fact ...' (Martin 1994: 74). By never choreographing Wendy and Jon to broach the subject of their past with their gruff, ailing father or with each other, the collection of uneasy moments that these three share in *The Savages* demonstrates the potential for the smart film – as another example of popular art – to also accept this as given.

This book has attended to the smart sensibility as an affective force that manifests in some contemporary American commercial/independent filmmaking as an acknowledgment of the dual force of ironic speech. By examining the critical aesthetics of these films through the paradigms of authorship, narrative, genre, music and setting, the project has described how the varying strategies of tonal detachment function not only to question certain vocabularies, but as utterances in themselves. *The Savages* crysallises the 'mark' of the smart sensibility in its episodic structure and qualities of blankness and incongruity, which are mobilised not as quotation marks that frame the 'dysfunctionality' of the scenario as something that longs for an ideal of normativity, but as an expression of the reality of estrangement and the pragmatic relationships that this gives rise to. With a typically smart dramatic focus on the dynamics between three members of a family unit, Jenkins' film also demonstrates how the practice of 'quotation' in these films can be relevantly understood as a perceptible stance toward film history. Here, as in many of the films discussed in this project, the episodic narrative is a direct effect of the family milieu which – like those of the historical family melodrama – cannot be modified or overcome. The connection indicates how smart cinema's dual awareness of the contingency of its own terms can be expanded to an interpretation that sees it both repeat and reinvent the attitudes and structures of discourses including the European art cinema, the New Hollywood, the 'aristocratic' family melodrama, the 'cinephiliac moment', and the dystopian tradition. When contextualised this way, the tonal strategies of the smart film resonate with techniques of detachment and distanciation that are evident well beyond the parameters of a postmodern vocabulary. Where the majority of work on the commercial/independent cycle describes an industrial condition in which the latter type of filmmaking has 'triumphed' on the stage of the former, the notion of smart cinema allows for an interpretation that makes these films intelligible in less categorical ways. As a critical sensibility, smart cinema is a site of transformation, plurality and potential in contemporary American filmmaking.

NOTES

1. At the 2008 Academy Awards, *Juno* was nominated in the categories of Best Performance by An Actress in a Leading Role (Ellen Page), Best Motion Picture of the Year (Lianne Halfon, Mason Novick, Russell Smith), Best Achievement in Directing (Jason Reitman) and Best Writing, Screenplay Written Directly for the Screen (Diablo Cody). The film won the latter award, in addition to awards from many other societies. At the 2007 Academy Awards, *Little Miss Sunshine* was nominated in the categories of Best Performance by an Actress in a Supporting Role (Abigail Breslin), Best Motion Picture of the Year (David T. Friendly, Peter Saraf, Marc Turtletaub), Best Writing – Original Screenplay (Michael Arndt) and Best Performance by an Actor in a Supporting Role (Alan Arkin). The film won the latter two awards and, like Juno, many others (source: imdb.com).
2. *Juno* and *The Savages* both feature songs by The Kinks ('Well-Respected Man' and 'Sitting By the Riverside' respectively), and both incorporate The Velvet Underground's 'I'm Sticking With You'.
3. See, for instance, Kate Stables, David Edelstein and Todd McCarthy's reviews of *The Savages*.

BIBLIOGRAPHY

Allen, Don (1974), *François Truffaut*, London: Secker and Warburg.
Altman, Rick (1999), *Film/Genre*, London: BFI Publishing.
Anderson, Wes (2002), Director's Commentary, *The Royal Tenenbaums* (2001), DVD, The Criterion Collection.
Andrew, Geoff (1999), *Stranger than Paradise: Maverick Film-Makers in Recent American Cinema*, New York: Limelight.
Babington, Bruce and Peter Evans (1990), 'All that Heaven Allowed: Another Look at Sirkian Irony', *Movie* 34/35, pp. 48–58.
Balio, Tino (ed.) (1985), *The American Film Industry*, Madison: University of Wisconsin Press.
Barnes, Brooks (2008), 'To Reduce Costs, Warner Brothers Closing 2 Film Divisions', *The New York Times* (9 May), http://www.nytimes.com (last accessed 5 September 2008).
Barthes, Roland (1977), *Image, Music, Text*, Stephen Heath (trans.), New York: Hill and Wang.
—(1981), *Camera Lucida: Reflections on Photography*, Richard Howard (trans.), New York: Hill and Wang.
Baumbach, Noah (2008), 'A Conversation with Noah Baumbach and Jennifer Jason Leigh', *Margot at the Wedding* (2007), DVD, Paramount.
Beers, David (2001), 'Irony is dead! Long live irony!', *Salon* (25 September), http://www.salon.com/mwt/feature/2001/09/25/irony_lives (last accessed 8 June 2005).
Bellamy, Edward [1888] (1951), *Looking Backward: 2000–1887*, New York: Modern Library.
Beller, Jonathan L. (1994), 'Cinema, Capital of the Twentieth Century', *Postmodern Culture* 4.3, Project Muse, http://muse.jhu.edu.ezproxy.lib.monash.edu.au/journals/postmodern_culture/v004/4.3beller.html (last accessed 20 May 2005).
Ben-Ghiat, Ruth (2000), 'The Fascist War Trilogy', in David Forgacs, Sarah Lutton and Geoffrey Nowell-Smith (eds), *Roberto Rossellini: Magician of the Real*, London: BFI Publishing, pp. 20–36.

Berg, Charles Ramirez (2006), 'A Taxonomy of Alternative Plots in Recent Films: Classifying the "Tarantino Effect"', *Film Criticism* 31.1–2, pp. 5–61.
Bergman, Ingmar (1995), *Images – My Life in Film*, Marianne Ruuth (trans.), London: Faber and Faber.
Bernstein, Kate (2005), 'Palindromes', *Cineaste* 30.4, pp. 53–4.
Beuka, Robert (2004), *SuburbiaNation: Reading Suburban Landscape in Twentieth-Century American Fiction and Film*, New York: Palgrave Macmillan.
Biskind, Peter (2004), *Down and Dirty Pictures: Miramax, Sundance, and the Rise of Independent Film*, New York: Simon and Schuster.
Bjorkman, Stig (2004), 'Lars von Trier: The Defects of Humanism', *Sight and Sound* 14.3, pp. 25–7.
Boggs, Carl and Tom Pollard (2003), 'Postmodern Cinema and the Demise of the Family', *The Journal of American Culture* 26.4, pp. 445–63.
Bogue, Ronald (1993), 'Gilles Deleuze: The Aesthetics of Force', *Journal of the British Society for Phenomenology* 24.1, pp. 56–65.
—(2003a), *Deleuze on Cinema*, New York: Routledge.
—(2003b), *Deleuze on Music, Painting and the Arts*, New York: Routledge.
Bordwell, David (2002), 'Intensified Continuity: Visual Style in Contemporary American Film', *Film Quarterly* 55.3, pp. 16–28.
—(2005), 'Up Close and Impersonal: Hal Hartley and the Persistence of Tradition', *16:9* 3.12, http://www.16–9.dk/2005–06/side11_inenglish.htm (last accessed 5 July 2006).
Bourdieu, Pierre (1984), *Distinction: A Social Critique of the Judgement of Taste*, Richard Nice (trans.), Cambridge, MA: Harvard University Press.
Bowen, Peter (1994), Introduction to 'In Images We Trust: Hal Hartley Interviews Jean-Luc Godard', *Filmmaker* 3.1, pp. 14, 16–18, 55–6.
Bowman, James (2000), 'Whit Stillman: Poet of the Broken Branches', *Intercollegiate Review* 35.2, pp. 15–20.
Boyle, Kirk (2007), 'Reading the Dialectical Ontology of *The Life Aquatic with Steve Zissou* Against the Ontological Monism of *Adaptation*', *Film-Philosophy* 11.1, http://www.film-philosophy.com/2007v11n1/boyle.pdf (last accessed 15 November 2007).
Brabazon, Tara (2005), *From Revolution to Revelation: Generation X, Popular Memory and Cultural Studies*, Aldershot: Ashgate Publishing.
Brenez, Nicole (1997), 'The ultimate journey: remarks on contemporary theory', William Routt (trans.), *Screening the Past* 2, http://www.latrobe.edu.au/screeningthepast/rcruns/brcnez.html (last accessed 10 May 2008).
—(2007), *Abel Ferrara*, Adrian Martin (trans.), Urbana: University of Illinois Press.
Brown, Royal S. (1994), *Overtones and Undertones: Reading Film Music*, Berkeley: University of California Press.
Brunette, Peter (1987), *Roberto Rossellini*, New York: Oxford University Press.
Buchanan, Ian (2000), *Deleuzism: A Metacommentary*, Durham, NC: Duke University Press.
Buchanan, Ian and Marcel Swiboda (eds) (2004), *Deleuze and Music*, Edinburgh: Edinburgh University Press.
Buhler, Jim, Anahid Kassabian, David Neumeyer and Robynn Stilwell (2003), 'Panel Discussion on Film Sound/Film Music', *The Velvet Light Trap* 51, pp. 73–82.
Byrnes, Paul (2005), Review of *Thumbsucker*, *The Sydney Morning Herald* (23 November), http://www.smh.com.au/news/film-reviews/thumbsucker/2005/11/23/1132703250096.html (last accessed 5 July 2006).
Cameron, Ian and Robin Wood (1968), *Antonioni*, New York: Praeger.
Cantor, Muriel (1991), 'The American Family on Television: From Molly Goldberg to Bill Cosby', *Journal of Comparative Family Studies* 22.2, pp. 205–16.

Carroll, Noel (1982), 'The Future of Allusion', *October* 20, pp. 51–81.
Chang, Chris (1998), 'Cruel To Be Kind: A Brief History of Todd Solondz', *Film Comment* 34.5, pp. 72–5.
Chion, Michel (1994), *Audio-Vision: Sound on Screen*, Claudia Gorbman (trans.), New York: Columbia University Press.
Christensen, Bryce J. (1991), 'The Family in Utopia', *Renascence* 44.1, pp. 31–44.
Claeys, Gregory and Lyman Tower Sargent (eds) (1999), *The Utopia Reader*, New York: New York University Press.
Clarke, David B. (ed.) (1997), *The Cinematic City*, London: Routledge.
Colebrook, Claire (2002), *Gilles Deleuze*, London: Routledge.
—(2004), *Irony*, London: Routledge.
Collins, Jim (1993), 'Genericity in the Nineties: Eclectic Irony and the New Sincerity' in Collins et al., pp. 242–64.
Collins, Jim, Hilary Radner and Ava Preacher Collins (eds) (1993), *Film Theory Goes to the Movies*, New York: Routledge.
Combs, Richard (1973), Review of *Scarecrow*, *Monthly Film Bulletin* 40.468/479, p. 212.
Conn, Andrew Lewis (1999), 'The Bad Review *Happiness* Deserves or: The Tyranny of Critic-Proof Movies', *Film Comment* 35.1, pp. 70–2.
Corliss, Richard (2007), 'The Year of the 3quel', *Time* (4 January), http://www.time.com/time/magazine/article/0,9171,1574141,00.html (last accessed 6 June 2010).
Cornea, Christine (2007), *Science Fiction Cinema: Between Fantasy and Reality*, Edinburgh: Edinburgh University Press.
Corrigan, Timothy (1991), *A Cinema Without Walls: Movies and Culture After Vietnam*, New Brunswick, NJ: Rutgers University Press.
—(1998), 'Auteurs and the New Hollywood' in Lewis (ed.), pp. 38–63.
Coupland, Douglas (1991), *Generation X: Tales for an Accelerated Culture*, London: Abacus.
Cuff, Dana (2005), 'Enduring Proximity: The Figure of the Neighbour in Suburban America', *Postmodern Culture* 15:2, Project Muse, http://muse.jhu.edu.ezproxy.lib.monash.edu.au/journals/postmodern_culture/v015/15.2cuff.html (last accessed 9 February 2008).
Dalton, Stephen (2005), Review of *Last Days*, *Sight and Sound* 15.9, p. 66.
Dargis, Manohla (1998), 'Whatever: the new nihilism', *LA Weekly* (26 November), http://www.laweekly.com/ink/99/01/film-dargis.shtml (last accessed 26 July 2005).
Davies, Philip John and Paul Wells (2002), *American Film and Politics from Reagan to Bush Jr*, Manchester: Manchester University Press.
Deleuze, Gilles (1986), *Cinema 1: The Movement Image*, Hugh Tomlinson and Barbara Habberjam (trans.), London: The Athlone Press.
—(1989), *Cinema 2: The Time Image*, Hugh Tomlinson and Barbara Habberjam (trans.), London: The Athlone Press.
—(1992), 'Three Questions about *Six Fois Deux*' in *Jean-Luc Godard: Son + Image, 1974–1991*, Raymond Bellour and Mary Lea Bandy (eds), New York: Museum of Modern Art, pp. 35–41.
—(1995), 'Postscript on Control Societies' in *Negotiations: 1972–1990*, Martin Joughin (trans.), New York: Columbia University Press, pp. 177–82.
—(2003), *Francis Bacon*, Daniel W. Smith (trans.), London: Continuum.
—(2004), *Difference and Repetition*, Paul Patton (trans.), London: Continuum.
Deleuze, Gilles and Félix Guattari (1986), *Kafka: Toward a Minor Literature*, Dana Polan (trans.), Minneapolis: University of Minnesota Press.
—(1987), *A Thousand Plateaus: Capitalism and Schizophrenia*, Brian Massumi (trans.), London: Continuum.

—(1994), *What is Philosophy?*, Hugh Tomlinson and Graham Burchell (trans.), New York: Columbia University Press.

Denby, David (2005), 'Family Matters', *The New Yorker* (24 October), http://www.newyorker.com/archive/2005/10/24/051024crci_cinema (last accessed 20 September 2006).

Dermansky, Marcy (2006), Review of *The Squid and the Whale*, *World Film*, http://worldfilm.about.com/od/r/fr/squidandwhale.htm (last accessed 28 August 2006).

Derrida, Jacques (1992), 'The Law of Genre', Avital Ronell (trans.) in *Acts of Literature*, Derek Attridge (ed.), New York: Routledge, pp. 221–52.

Deutsch, Stephen (2007), 'Editorial', *The Soundtrack* 1.1, pp. 3–13.

Dillman, Joanne Clarke (2005), 'Twelve Characters in Search of a Televisual Text: *Magnolia* Masquerading as Soap Opera', *Journal of Popular Film and Television* 33.3, pp. 142–51.

Doane, Mary Ann (1985), '. . . when the direction of the force acting on the body is changed', *Wide Angle* 7.1–2, pp. 42–58.

Druxman, Michael B. (1975), *Make It Again, Sam: A Survey of Movie Remakes*, South Brunswick: A.S. Barnes.

Durgnat, Raymond (1988), 'Next Time You Say That – Smile: The Comedy of Manners', *Monthly Film Bulletin* 55.656, pp. 258–60.

Edelstein, David (2007), 'Savage Grace', *New York Magazine* (23 November), http://nymag.com/movies/reviews/41278/ (last accessed 5 September 2008).

Ellin, Nan (ed.) (1997), *Architecture of Fear*, New York: Princeton Architectural Press.

Elliott, Anthony (2004), 'Therapy Culture and its Discontents', *Meanjin* (1 December), pp. 47–52.

Elsaesser, Thomas (1987), 'Tales of Sound and Fury: Observations on the Family Melodrama' in Gledhill (ed.), pp. 43–70.

—(1994), 'Putting on a Show: The European Art Movie', *Sight and Sound* 4.4, pp. 22–7.

—(2004), 'The Pathos of Failure: American Films in the 1970s: Notes on the Unmotivated Hero' in Elsaesser et al., pp. 279–92.

—(2005), *European Cinema: Face to Face With Hollywood*, Amsterdam: Amsterdam University Press.

Elsaesser, Thomas, Alexander Horwath and Noel King (eds) (2004), *The Last Great American Picture Show: New Hollywood Cinema in the 1970s*, Amsterdam: Amsterdam University Press.

Erickson, Tamara (2010), *What's Next, Gen X?*, Boston: Harvard Business Press.

Felperin, Leslie (1997), 'Close to the Edge', *Sight and Sound* 7.10, pp. 15–18.

Ferncase, Richard (1996), *Outsider Features: American Independent Films of the 1980s*, New Haven: Greenwood Press.

Fischer, Lucy (ed.) (1991), *Imitation of Life: Douglas Sirk, director*, New Brunswick, NJ: Rutgers University Press.

Flaxman, Gregory (2000), *The Brain is the Screen: Deleuze and the Philosophy of Cinema*, Minneapolis: University of Minnesota Press.

Forrest, Jennifer and Leonard R. Koos (eds) (2002), *Dead Ringers: The Remake in Theory and Practice*, New York: SUNY Press.

Fortunati, Viva (1993), 'The Metamorphosis of the Apocalyptic Myth: From Utopia to Science Fiction' in Kumar and Bann (eds), pp. 81–95.

Foucault, Michel (1977), *Discipline and Punish: The Birth of the Prison*, Alan Sheridan (trans.), London: Allen Lane.

—(1986), 'Of Other Spaces', *Diacritics* 16, pp. 22–7.

Foundas, Scott (2005a), Review of *The Chumscrubber*, *Variety* 398.3, p. 45.

—(2005b), 'Walking and Talking', *LA Weekly* (13 October), http://www.laweekly.com/2005-10-13/news/walking-and-talking/1 (last accessed 28 August 2006).

Freedman, Carl (2000), *Critical Theory and Science Fiction*, Hanover: Wesleyan University Press.

Friedan, Betty (1963), *The Feminine Mystique*, London: Gollancz.

Friedberg, Anne (1993), *Window Shopping: Cinema and the Postmodern*, Berkeley: University of California Press.

Fuller, Graham (1994), Introduction to *Barcelona* and *Metropolitan: Tales of Two Cities* by Whit Stillman, Boston: Faber and Faber, pp. vii–x.

Furedi, Frank (2004), *Therapy Culture: Cultivating Vulnerability in an Uncertain Age*, London; New York: Routledge.

Gaudréault, André (1994), 'Temporality and Narrative in Early Cinema 1895–1908' in *Film Before Griffith*, John Fell (ed.), Berkeley: University of California Press, pp. 311–29.

Gerstner, David A. and Janet Staiger (eds) (2003), *Authorship and Film*, New York: Routledge.

Gilbey, Ryan (1998), 'Pulling the Pin on Hal Hartley', *Sight and Sound* 8.11, pp. 8–9.

Gledhill, Christine (ed.) (1987), *Home is Where the Heart Is: Studies in Melodrama and the Woman's Film*, London: British Film Institute.

Gledhill, Christine (1987), 'The Melodramatic Field: An Investigation' in Gledhill (ed.), pp. 5–39.

Gooch, Joshua (2007), 'Making A Go of It: Paternity and Prohibition in the Films of Wes Anderson', *Cinema Journal* 47.1, pp. 26–45.

Goodman, Paul (1960), *Growing Up Absurd: Problems of Youth in the Organized System*, New York: Random House.

Gorbman, Claudia (1987), *Unheard Melodies: Narrative Film Music*, Bloomington: Indiana University Press.

Gorfinkel, Elena (2005), 'The Future of Anachronism: Todd Haynes and the Magnificent Andersons' in *Cinephilia: Movies, Love and Memory*, Marijke De Valck and Malte Hagener (eds), Amsterdam: Amsterdam University Press, pp. 153–68.

Gormley, Paul (2005), *The New Brutality Film: Race and Affect in Contemporary Hollywood Cinema*, Bristol: Intellect.

Gross, Jason (2002), 'The Ghost World Soundtrack', *Film Comment* 38.2, p. 16.

Gunning, Tom (1986), 'The Cinema of Attraction: Early Cinema, its Spectator and the Avant Garde', *Wide Angle* 8.3–4, pp. 63–70.

—(1989), 'An Aesthetic of Astonishment: Early Film and the (In)Credulous Spectator', *Art and Text* 34, pp. 31–45.

Hainge, Greg (2004), 'Is Pop Music?' in Buchanan and Swiboda (eds), pp. 36–53.

Hampton, Howard (1997), 'Scorpio Descending: In Search of Rock Cinema', *Film Comment* 33.2, pp. 36–42.

—(2003), 'The Flannel-Swaddled Insomniac', *The Believer* (August), http://www.believermag.com/issues/200308/?read=article_hampton (last accessed 12 December 2006).

—(2006), 'Sweet and Lowdown: The misanthropic yet tender comic universe of Terry Zwigoff', *Film Comment* 42:2, pp. 30–2.

Hanson, Peter (2002), *The Cinema of Generation X*, Jefferson: McFarland and Co., Inc.

Harris, Steven and Deborah Berke (eds) (1997), *Architecture of the Everyday*, New York: Princeton Architectural Press.

Hartley, Hal (1994), 'In Images We Trust: Hal Hartley Interviews Jean-Luc Godard', *Filmmaker* 3.1, pp. 14, 16–18, 55–6.

Hayden, Dolores (2003), *Building Suburbia: Green Fields and Urban Growth, 1820–2000*, New York: Pantheon Books.

Henrie, Mark C. (2000), 'Film, comedy and Christian humanism: A first look at Whit Stillman', *Intercollegiate Review* 35.2, pp. 3–5.

Heung, Marina (1983), 'The New Family in American Cinema', *Journal of Popular Film and Television* 11.2, pp. 79–85.
Hillier, Jim (1993), *The New Hollywood*, London: Studio Vista.
—(ed.) (2001), *American Independent Cinema: A Sight and Sound Reader*, London: British Film Institute.
Hoberman, J. (1985), 'Ten Years that Shook the World', *American Film* 10, pp. 34–59.
—(2001), 'Look Homeward, Angel', *Village Voice* (11 December), http://www.villagevoice.com/2001-12-11/film/look-homeward-angel (last accessed 10 May 2008).
—(2004), 'Our Town', *Sight and Sound* 14.2, pp. 24–7.
Holland, Eugene (2006), 'The Utopian Dimension of Thought in Deleuze and Guattari' in Milner et al., pp. 217–42.
Holmlund, Chris and Justin Wyatt (2005), *Contemporary American Independent Film: From the Margins to the Mainstream*, London: Routledge.
Horton, Andrew and Stuart Y. McDougal (eds) (1998), *Play It Again, Sam: Retakes on Remakes*, Berkeley: University of California Press.
Horwath, Alexander (2004), 'The Impure Cinema: New Hollywood 1967–1976' in Elsaesser et al., pp. 9–18.
Hsu, Hsuan L. (2006), 'Racial Privacy, the L.A. Ensemble Film, and Paul Haggis's *Crash*', *Film Criticism* 31.1, pp. 132–56.
Hugo, Chris (1980/81), 'The Incoherent Text: Narrative in the '70s', *Movie* 27/28, pp. 24–49.
Hutcheon, Linda (1988), *A Poetics of Postmodernism*, London: Routledge.
—(1989), *The Politics of Postmodernism*, London: Routledge.
—(1995), *Irony's Edge: The Theory and Politics of Irony*, London: Routledge.
James, David E. (1989), *Allegories of Cinema: American Film in the Sixties*, Princeton: Princeton University Press.
Jameson, Fredric (1988), 'Of Islands and Trenches: Neutralization and the Production of Utopian Discourse' in *The Ideologies of Theory: Essays 1971–1986*, Minneapolis: University of Minnesota Press, pp. 75–101.
—(2005), *Archaeologies of the Future: The Desire Called Utopia and Other Science Fictions*, London: Verso.
Jess-Cooke, Carolyn (2009), *Film Sequels: Theory and Practice from Hollywood to Bollywood*, Edinburgh: Edinburgh University Press.
Jess-Cooke, Carolyn and Constantine Verevis (eds) (2009), *Second Takes: Critical Approaches to the Film Sequel*, New York: SUNY Press.
Jones, Kent (1998), 'Body & Soul: The Cinema of Atom Egoyan', *Film Comment* 34.1, pp. 32–9.
—(2001), 'Family Romance', *Film Comment* 37.6, pp. 24–7.
—(2002), 'Hearts and Flowers', *Film Comment* 38.6, pp. 23–7.
Kalinak, Kathryn (1992), *Settling the Score: Music and the Classical Hollywood Film*, Madison: University of Wisconsin Press.
Kassabian, Anahid (2001), *Hearing Film: Tracking Identifications in Contemporary Hollywood Film Music*, New York: Routledge.
—(2003), 'The Sound of a New Film Form' in *Popular Music and Film*, Ian Inglis (ed.), London: Wallflower, pp. 91–101.
Kaufman, Eleanor and Kevin Jon Heller (eds) (1998), *Deleuze & Guattari: New Mappings in Politics, Philosophy, and Culture*, Minneapolis: University of Minnesota Press.
Kaveney, Roz (2006), *Teen Dreams: Reading Teen Film From Heathers to Veronica Mars*, London: I.B. Tauris.
Keathley, Christian (2004), 'Trapped in the Affection Image: Hollywood's Post-traumatic Cycle (1970–1976)' in Elassaser et al., pp. 293–308.

—(2006), *Cinephilia and History, or The Wind in the Trees*, Bloomington: Indiana University Press.

Keats, John (1957), *The Crack in the Picture Window*, Boston: Houghton Mifflin.

Kemp, Phillip (1998), 'U for Utopia', *Sight and Sound* 8.2, pp. 24–5.

King, Cubie (2005), '*Punch Drunk Love*: The Budding of an Auteur', *Senses of Cinema* 35, http://www.sensesofcinema.com/contents/05/35/pt_anderson.html (last accessed 8 October 2007).

King, Geoff (2005), *American Independent Cinema*, London: I.B. Tauris.

—(2006), 'Following in the Footsteps: Gus Van Sant's *Gerry* and *Elephant* in the American independent field of cultural production', *New Review of Film and Television Studies* 4.2, pp. 75–92.

—(2009), *Indiewood: USA*, London: I.B. Tauris.

King, Noel (2004), '"The Last Good Time We Ever Had": Remembering the New Hollywood Cinema' in Elsaesser et al., pp. 19–36.

Kissin, Eva (1994), Review of *Barcelona*, *Films in Review* 45.11/12, pp. 59–60.

Kleinhans, Chuck (1998), 'Independent Features: Hopes and Dreams' in Lewis (ed.), pp. 307–27.

Kolker, Robert (1980), *A Cinema of Loneliness: Penn, Kubrick, Coppola, Scorsese, Altman*, New York: Oxford University Press.

Kumar, Krishan and Stephen Bann (eds) (1993), *Utopias and the Millennium*, London: Reaktion Books.

LaBute, Neil (2003), Director's Commentary, *Your Friends and Neighbors* (1998), DVD, Universal.

Lannin, Steve and Matthew Caley (eds) (2005), *Pop Fiction: The Song in Cinema*, Bristol: Intellect.

Lasch, Christopher (1979), *The Culture of Narcissism: American Life in an Age of Diminishing Expectations*, New York: Warner Books.

Le Doeuff, Michèle (1982), 'Utopias: Scholarly', *Social Research* 49.2, pp. 441–66.

Leitch, Thomas (1990), 'Twice-told tales: the rhetoric of the remake', *Film/Literature Quarterly* 18.3, pp. 138–49.Levy, Emmanuel (1999), *Cinema of Outsiders: The Rise of American Independent Film*, New York: New York University Press.

Lewis, Jon (ed.) (1998), *New American Cinema*, Durham, NC: Duke University Press.

Longworth, Karina (2005), Review of *The Squid and the Whale* (10 October), http://www.cinematical.com/2005/10/06/review-the-squid-and-the-whale (last accessed 20 September 2006).

Lopate, Phillip (2006), 'A Conversation with Noah Baumbach', *The Squid and the Whale* (2005), DVD, Sony Classics Home.

Macnab, Geoffrey (1997), Review of *Flirt*, *Sight and Sound* 7.3, pp. 47–8.

Maes, Hans (2005), 'A Celestial Taxonomy of Remakes?', *Cinemascope* 2, http://www.madadayo.it/Cinemascope_archive/cinema-scope.net/index_n2_def.html (last accessed 3 January 2007).

Malcolm, Paul (2005), 'Family Matters', *LA Weekly* (13 October), http://www.laweekly.com/2005–10–13/film-tv/family-matters/ (last accessed 28 August 2006).

Martin, Adrian (1994), *Phantasms*, Melbourne: McPhee-Gribble.

—(1997), 'Ultimatum: an introduction to the work of Nicole Brenez', *Screening the Past* 2, http://www.latrobe.edu.au/screeningthepast/reruns/brenezintro.html (last accessed 10 May 2008).

—(2000), 'The body has no head: corporeal figuration in Aldrich', *Screening the Past* 10, http://www.latrobe.edu.au/screeningthepast/firstrelease/fr0600/amfr10b.htm (last accessed 10 May 2008).

—(2004a), 'Grim Fascination: *Fingers*, James Toback and the 1970s American Cinema' in Elsaesser et al., pp. 293–308.

—(2004b), 'Possessory Credit', *Framework* 45.1, pp. 95–9.

Martin-Jones, David (2006), *Deleuze, Cinema and National Identity*, Edinburgh: Edinburgh University Press.

Matheou, Demetrios (2002), 'The Last Laugh', *Sight and Sound* 15.2, p. 29.

—(2005), 'The Sunshine Kids', *Sight and Sound* 17.5, p. 28.

Matthews, Peter (1995), 'Blunted Whit', *The Modern Review* 1.19, p. 16.

—(1998), 'The Big Freeze', *Sight and Sound* 8.2, pp. 12–14.

Mayshark, Jesse Fox (2007), *Post-Pop Cinema: The Search for Meaning in New American Film*, Westport: Praeger.

McCabe, Janet and Kim Akass (2007), *Quality TV: Contemporary American Television and Beyond*, London: I.B. Tauris.

McCarthy, Todd (2007), Review of *The Savages*, *Variety* 405.11, pp. 14–15.

McPartland, John (1957), *No Down Payment*, New York: Pocket Books.

Mendik, Xavier, and Steven Jay Schneider (2002), *Underground USA: Filmmaking Beyond the Hollywood Canon*, London: Wallflower Press.

Merritt, Greg (1999), *Celluloid Mavericks: The History of Independent Film*, New York: Thunder's Mouth Press.

Miller, Toby (2005), *Global Hollywood 2*, London: British Film Institute.

Milner, Andrew (2004), 'Darker Cities: Urban Dystopia and Science Fiction Cinema', *International Journal of Cultural Studies* 7.2, pp. 259–79.

Milner, Andrew, Matthew Ryan and Robert Savage (eds) (2006), *Imagining the Future: Utopia and Dystopia*, Victoria: Arena Publications Association.

Modleski, Tania (1989), *The Women Who Knew Too Much: Hitchcock and Feminist Theory*, New York: Routledge.

More, Thomas [1516] (1966), *Utopia*, Leeds: Scolar Press.

Morkowitz, Siegfried (2006), 'Sofia Coppola's *Marie Antoinette* rocks Cannes festival', *Monsters and Critics* (24 May), http://www.monstersandcritics.com/movies/features/article_1166446.php (last accessed 19 June 2008).

Morris, William [1891] (1970), *News from Nowhere; or an epoch of rest: being some chapters from a utopian romance*, James Redmond (ed.), London: Routledge.

Moskowitz, Eva S. (2001), *In Therapy We Trust: America's Obsession with Self Fulfillment*, Baltimore: The Johns Hopkins University Press.

Mottram, James (2006), *The Sundance Kids: How the Mavericks Took Back Hollywood*, London: Faber.

Moylan, Tom (1986), *Demand the Impossible: Science Fiction and the Utopian Imagination*, New York: Methuen.

Mulvey, Laura (1987), 'Notes on Sirk and Melodrama' in Gledhill (ed.), pp. 75–9.

Murray, Noel (2006), 'Interview with Whit Stillman', *The A.V Club* (28 February), http://www.avclub.com/content/node/45817 (last accessed 3 January 2007).

Naremore, James (ed.) (2000), *Film Adaptation*, London: Athlone.

Neale, Steve (2000), *Genre and Hollywood*, London: Routledge.

—(2006), '"The Last Good Time We Ever Had?" Revising the Hollywood Renaissance' in Williams and Hammond (eds), pp. 90–108.

Neale, Steve and Murray Smith (eds) (1998), *Contemporary Hollywood Cinema*, London: Routledge.

Newman, Kim (2006), Review of *X-Men: The Last Stand*, *Sight and Sound* 16.7, p. 84.

Nichols, Mary P. (2000), 'Whit Stillman's Comic Art', *Intercollegiate Review* 35.2, pp. 5–10.

Nordstrum, David (2006), 'The Life Fascistic: Fascist Aesthetics in the Films of Wes Anderson', *The High Hat*, http://thehighhat.com/Nitrate/006/Life_Nordstrom.html (last accessed 20 April 2007).

Norris, Chris (2002), 'Charlie Kaufman and Michael Gondry's Head Trip', *Film Comment* 40.2, pp. 20–1.
—(2008), Review of *Synecdoche, New York*, *Film Comment* 44.6, p. 71.
Nowell-Smith, Geoffrey (1987), 'Minelli and Melodrama' in Gledhill (ed.), pp. 70–9.
Oake, Jonathon (2004), '*Reality Bites* and Generation X as Spectator', *The Velvet Light Trap* 53, pp. 83–97.
Oates, Joyce Carol (1988), 'Adventures in Abandonment', *The New York Times* (28 August), http://www.nytimes.com/1988/08/28/books/adventures-in-abandonment. html (last accessed 15 February 2011).
Olsen, Mark (1999), 'If I Can Dream: The Everlasting Boyhoods of Wes Anderson', *Film Comment* 35.1, pp. 12–17.
—(2001), 'Long live the losers', *Film Comment* 37.3, pp. 30–2.
Orgeron, Devin (2007), 'La Camera-Crayola: Authorship Comes of Age in the Cinema of Wes Anderson', *Cinema Journal* 46.2, pp. 40–65.
Orlean, Susan (2002), 'Foreword' to *Adaptation: The Shooting Script*, by Charlie Kaufman, New York: Newmarket Press, pp. vii–ix.
Palmer, R. Barton (1988), '*Blood Simple*: Defining the Commercial/Independent Text', *Persistence of Vision* 6, pp. 5–19.
—(2004), *Joel and Ethan Coen*, Urbana: University of Illinois Press.
Patton, Paul (2007), 'Utopian Political Philosophy: Deleuze and Rawls', *Deleuze Studies* 1:1, pp. 41–59.
Peranson, Mark (2007), 'Cannes 2007: Hell is Not Other People', *Cinema Scope* 31, http://www.cinemascope.com/cs31/spot_peranson_paranoid.html (last accessed 11 June 2008).
Piechota, Carole Lyn (2006), 'Give Me A Second Grace: Music as Absolution in *The Royal Tenenbaums*', *Senses of Cinema* 38, http://www.sensesofcinema.com/ contents/06/38/music_tenenbaums.html (last accessed 20 April 2006).
Pierson, John (1995), *Spike, Mike, Slackers and Dykes: A Guided Tour Across a Decade of American Independent Cinema*, New York: Miramax Books.
Pincus, Adam (1998), 'At Whit's End', *Filmmaker* (Spring), http://www.filmmaker-magazine.com/issues/spring1998/ (last accessed 10 February 2007).
Pisters, Patricia (2001), *Micropolitics of Media Culture: Reading the Rhizomes of Deleuze and Guattari*, Amsterdam: Amsterdam University Press.
Polan, Dana (2001), 'Auteur Desire', *Screening the Past* 12, http://www.latrobe.edu.au/ www/screeningthepast/firstrelease/fr0301/dpfr12a.htm (last accessed 19 May 2007).
Pomeranc, Murray (ed.) (2008) *A Family Affair: Cinema Calls Home*, London: Wallflower.
Porton, Richard (1993), 'American Dreams, Suburban Nightmares', *Cinéaste* 20.1, pp. 12–15.
—(1997), 'Family Romances: An Interview with Atom Egoyan', *Cinéaste* 23.2, pp. 8–16.
Posin, Arie (2006), Director's Commentary, *The Chumscrubber* (2005), DVD, Dreamworks Video.
Potter, Susan (2004), 'Dangerous Spaces: Safe', *Camera Obscura* 57, pp. 125–57.
Powers, Stephen, David J. Rothman and Stanley Rothman (1996), *Hollywood's America: Social and Political Themes in Motion Pictures*, Boulder: Westview Press.
Quart, Leonard (2005), 'Divorce Brooklyn style: an interview with Noah Baumbach', *Cinéaste* 31.1, pp. 27–30.
Rancière, Jacques (2006), *Film Fables*, Emiliano Battista (trans.), Oxford: Berg.
Rappe, Elizabeth (2008), '*Donnie Darko* Sequel Coming – Unfortunately', *Cinematical* (9 May), http://www.cinematical.com/2008/05/09/donnie-darko-sequel-coming-unfortunately/ (last accessed 19 June 2008).

Rayns, Tony (2005), Review of *Palindromes, Sight and Sound* 17.5, pp. 72–4.

Reay, Pauline (2004), *Music in Film: Soundtracks and Synergy*, London: Wallflower Press.

Riesman, David (1950), *The Lonely Crowd: A Study of the Changing American Character*, New Haven: Yale University Press.

Ritter, Kelly (2000), 'Spectacle at the Disco: Boogie Nights, Soundtrack, and the New American Musical', *Journal of Popular Film and Television* 28.4, pp. 166–75.

Roddick, Nick (2005), Review of *Trilogy: The Weeping Meadow, Sight and Sound* 15.1, p. 70.

Rohdie, Sam (1990), *Antonioni*, London: BFI Publishing.

Rombes, Nicholas (ed.) (2005a), *New Punk Cinema*, Edinburgh: Edinburgh University Press.

Rombes, Nicholas (2005b), 'Sincerity and Irony' in Rombes (ed.), pp. 72–88.

Romney, Jonathan (2002), 'Family Album', *Sight and Sound* 12.3, pp. 12–15.

—(2004), 'A Silky Sadness', *Sight and Sound* 14.6, pp. 20–3.

—(2006), 'Natural Selection', *Sight and Sound* 16.3, pp. 34–6.

Rosenbaum, Jonathan and Adrian Martin (eds) (2003), *Movie Mutations: The Changing Face of World Cinephilia*, London: British Film Institute.

Routt, William D. (2000a), 'For criticism, part one', *Screening the Past* 9, http://www.latrobe.edu.au/screeningthepast/shorts/reviews/rev0300/wr1br9a.htm (last accessed 10 May 2008).

—(2000b), 'For criticism, part two', *Screening the Past* 9, http://www.latrobe.edu.au/screeningthepast/shorts/reviews/rev0300/wr2br9a.htm (last accessed 10 May 2008).

Ruppert, Peter (1986), *Reader in a Strange Land: The Activity of Reading Literary Utopias*, Athens: University of Georgia Press.

—(1989), '*Blade Runner*: The Utopian Dialectics of Science Fiction Films', *Cinéaste* 17.2, pp. 8–13.

Salinger, J.D. (1953), *Nine Stories*, Boston: Little, Brown.

—(1961), *Franny and Zooey*, Boston: Little, Brown.

—(1963), *Raise High the Roof Beam, Carpenters; and Seymour: An Introduction*, London: Heinemann.

Sarris, Andrew (1968), *The American Cinema: Directors and Directions 1929–1968*, New York: E.P. Dutton.

—(1978), 'After *The Graduate*', *American Film* 3.9, pp. 32–50.

Schamus, James (2001), 'A Rant' in *The End of Cinema as We Know It: American Film in the Nineties*, Jon Lewis (ed.), New York: New York University Press, pp. 253–60.

Schatz, Thomas (1981), *Hollywood Genres: Formulas, Filmmaking and the Hollywood System*, Philadelphia: Temple University Press.

—(1993), 'The New Hollywood' in Collins et al., pp. 8–36.

Schivelbusch, Wolfgang (1986), *The Railway Journey: the Industrialization of Time and Space in the 19th Century*, Berkeley: University of California Press.

Schneider, Steve (2005), 'Shot in the Darko', rev. of *The Chumscrubber, Orlando Weekly* (4 August), http://www.orlandoweekly.com/film/review.asp?rid=7450 (last accessed 28 August 2006).

Sconce, Jeffrey (1995), 'Trashing the Academy: Taste, Excess and an Emerging Politics of Cinematic Style', *Screen* 36.4, pp. 371–93.

—(2002), 'Irony, nihilism and the new American "smart" film', *Screen* 43.4, pp. 349–69.

—(2006), 'Smart Cinema' in Williams and Hammond (eds), pp. 429–39.

—(ed.) (2007), *Sleaze Artists: Cinema at the Margins of Taste, Style, and Politics*, Durham, NC: Duke University Press.

Scott, A.O. (2005), 'Growing Up Bohemian and Absurd in Brooklyn', *New York Times*

(5 October), http://query.nytimes.com/gst/fullpage.html?res=9E00E2DB1130F936A 35753C1A9639C8B63&fta=y (last accessed 20 September 2006).
Scott, Sophroma (1990), 'Proceeding with Caution', *Time* 136.3, pp. 56–62.
Shary, Timothy (2005), *Teen movies: American Youth on Screen*, London: Wallflower Press.
Sheil, Mark and Tony Fitzmaurice (eds) (2001), *Cinema and the City: Film and Urban Societies in a Global Context*, Oxford: Blackwell Publishers.
—(2003), *Screening the City*, London: Verso.
Silverman, Kaja (1995), *Threshold of the Visible World*, New York: Routledge.
Sjöman, Vilgot (1978), *L136: Diary with Ingmar Bergman*, Alan Blair (trans.), Ann Arbor: Karoma Publishers.
Skvirsky, Salomé Aguilera (2008), 'The Price of Heaven: Remaking Politics in *All that Heaven Allows, Ali: Fear Eats the Soul*, and *Far From Heaven*', *Cinema Journal* 47:3, pp. 90–121.
Smith, Gavin (2001), 'At Home with the Royal Family: Wes Anderson Interviewed', *Film Comment* 37.6, pp. 28–9.
Smith, Jeff (1998), *The Sounds of Commerce: Marketing Popular Film Music*, New York: Columbia University Press.
Smith, Murray (2006), 'The Sound of Sentiment: Popular Music, Film, and Emotion', *16:9* 4.19, http://www.16–9.dk/2006–11/side11_inenglish.htm (last accessed 19 December 2006).
Sobchack, Vivian (1987), *Screening Space: The American Science Fiction Film*, New York: Ungar.
Sorfa, David (2006), 'Reanimating the Auteur', *Film-Philosophy* 10.1, http://www.film-philosophy.com/2006v10n1/introduction.pdf (last accessed 20 April 2007).
Spigel, Lynn (1992), *Make Room for TV: Television and the Family Ideal in Postwar America*, Chicago: University of Chicago Press.
—(2001), *Welcome to the Dreamhouse: Popular Media and Postwar Suburbs*, Durham, NC: Duke University Press.
Stables, Kate (2008), Review of *The Savages, Sight and Sound*, pp. 83–4.
Stern, Lesley (1995), *The Scorsese Connection*, London: British Film Institute.
—(2000), 'Emma in Los Angeles: Remaking the Book and the City' in Naremore (ed.), pp. 221–38.
Suvin, Darko (1979), *Metamorphoses of Science Fiction: On the Poetics and History of a Literary Genre*, New Haven: Yale University Press.
Taubin, Amy (2005), 'Blurred Exit', *Sight and Sound* 15.9, pp. 16–19.
—(2007), 'Femmes Rule', *Film Comment* 43.4, pp. 54–6.
Taylor, Charles (1999), 'Welcome to the Nerdhouse', *Sight and Sound* 9.3, pp. 8–10.
Taylor, Ella (2007), 'Savage Love', *Village Voice* (20 November), http://www.villagevoice.com/2007–11–20/film/savage-love (last accessed 5 September 2008).
Taylor, Rumsey (2004), 'Wes Anderson's Tragic Comedy', *Not coming to a theater near you* (17 July), http://notcoming.com/features/tragiccomedy/ (last accessed 19 June 2008).
Thompson, Kristin (1986), 'The Concept of Cinematic Excess' in *Narrative, Apparatus, Ideology: A Film Theory Reader*, Philip Rosen (ed.), New York: Columbia University Press, pp. 130–42.
Thompson, Robert J. (1996), *Television's Second Golden Age*, New York: Continuum.
Turan, Kenneth (1998), 'Fade to pitch black', *Los Angeles Times* (22 November), http://articles.latimes.com/1998/nov/22/entertainment/ca-46482 (last accessed 5 July 2005).
Updike, John (1960), *Rabbit Run*, New York: Knopf.
—(1971), *Rabbit Redux*, New York: Knopf.

—(1981), *Rabbit is Rich*, New York: Knopf.
—(1990), *Rabbit at Rest*, New York: Knopf.
Urpeth, James (2004), 'Animal Becomings' in *Animal Philosophy: Essential Readings in Continental Thought*, Matthew Calarco and Peter Atterton (eds), London: Continuum, pp. 101–10.
Verevis, Constantine (1997), 'A Cinema of Seeing', *Antithesis* 8.2, pp. 101–11.
—(2006), *Film Remakes*, Edinburgh: Edinburgh University Press.
Waxman, Sharon (2006), *Rebels on the Backlot: Six Maverick Directors and How they Conquered the Hollywood Studio System*, New York: Harper Perennial.
Westwood, Sallie and John Williams (eds) (1997), *Imagining Cities: Scripts, Signs, Memory*, London: Routledge.
Whyte, William H. (1957), *The Organization Man*, New York: Doubleday.
Williams, Linda (1998), 'Melodrama Revised' in *Refiguring American Film Genres*, Nick Browne (ed.), Berkeley: University of California Press, pp. 42–88.
—(2006), Review of *Basic Instinct 2*, *Sight and Sound* 16.5, pp. 42–3.
Williams, Linda Ruth and Michael Hammond (eds) (2006), *Contemporary American Cinema*, Maidenhead: Open UP/McGraw-Hill Education.
Willemen, Paul (1991a), 'Distanciation and Douglas Sirk' in Fischer (ed.), pp. 268–72.
—(1991b), 'Towards an Analysis of the Sirkian System' in Fischer (ed.), pp. 273–8.
—(1994), *Looks and Frictions: Essays in Cultural Studies and Film Theory*, Bloomington: Indiana University Press.
—(1995), 'Regimes of Subjectivity and Looking', *The UTS Review* 1.2, pp. 101–29.
Williams, Raymond (1973), *The Country and the City*, London: Chatto and Windus.
—(1980), 'Utopia and Science Fiction' in *Problems in Materialism and Culture*, London: New Left Books, pp. 196–212.
Willis, Sharon (2003), 'The Politics of Disappointment: Todd Haynes Rewrites Douglas Sirk', *Camera Obscura* 18:3, pp. 130–75.
Winter, Jessica (2005), 'Arrested Development', *Village Voice* (20 September), http://www.villagevoice.com/2005–09–20/film/arrested-development/ (last accessed 28 August 2006).
Wood, Robin (1969), *Ingmar Bergman*, New York: Praeger.
—(1975), 'Smart-ass & Cutie-pie', *Movie* 21, pp. 1–17.
Wyatt, Justin (1994), *High Concept: Movies and Marketing in Hollywood*, Austin: University of Texas Press.
—(1998a), 'The formation of the "major independent" – Miramax, New Line and the New Hollywood', *Contemporary Hollywood Cinema*, Steve Neale and Murray Smith (eds), London: Routledge, pp. 74–90.
—(1998b), 'The Particularity and Peculiarity of Hal Hartley: An Interview', *Film Quarterly* 52.1, pp. 2–6.

<h1 style="text-align:center">INDEX</h1>